exciting world of
MICROWAVE COOKING
from LITTON

Contents

Pictured on cover: Tossed Salad, Hot Dinner Rolls, One Dish Macaroni Beef, page 31, Pineapple Upside Down Cake, page 31.

The photographs in this book illustrate the recipes as prepared using the microwave oven.

LITTON
Microwave Cooking

Pictured right: Fresh Apple Pie (using both microwave and conventional cooking), page 33, Simple Scalloped Potatoes, page 33, Broccoli, page 33, and Ham Slice in Orange Sauce, page 33.

Greetings from Litton---

This cookbook is your key to enjoying the benefits of microwave cooking. Microwaves cook food without creating heat and provide both time and energy savings.

Your microwave oven is a unique appliance which has the ability to defrost, cook and reheat food. Families, children – even today's bachelor – can enjoy quick defrosting, freshly heated leftovers, smooth sauces, hot sandwiches, easy casseroles and tender-crisp vegetables.

Home economists created this cookbook for use with microwave ovens having various settings or wattage levels. The settings used in this book are: HIGH (600-625 watts), MEDIUM (450-475 watts), DEFROST (300-325 watts), and WARM (90-100 watts). While all microwave ovens may not include all these features, this book can be used very successfully with ovens having only two or three of these settings.

The "Grey Box" at the beginning of each chapter serves as a guide when adapting your own recipes to microwave cooking. We have also included many quick reference charts for defrosting, roasting meats and poultry, convenience foods, food expectations and utensils. Some charts include cooking times for varying amounts of food, since you must increase cooking times as you increase volume.

The Litton Microwave Cooking Center works on new recipes and techniques to help people enjoy the many benefits of microwave cooking. We welcome your suggestions and ideas. Simply write: Litton Microwave Cooking Center, 1405 Xenium Lane North, Minneapolis, Minnesota 55441.

We wish you many delightful experiences with microwave cooking.

Verna Ludvigson
Director Consumer Affairs

INTRODUCING YOU TO **Microwave Cooking**

Welcome to the World of Microwave Cooking!

A totally new cooking concept needs careful explanation – even when it's as simple as microwave cooking. So this is not an ordinary introduction. Instead, these first pages are designed to help you understand microwaves and how they cook; the cooking techniques you need to know; and the utensils you need to use. You should also refer to your Use and Care Manual that deals with your particular oven.

Chapters are divided into food categories with "grey box" keys outlining microwave cooking techniques used in the recipes. The carefully selected recipes were developed and tested by home economists to make your oven usable every meal of the day, between meals and when company's coming. Flexibility and quality were recipe selection criteria. There are also examples in every microwave technique category that will let you adapt your own recipes.

You'll find you can use your oven for three basic functions: for defrosting foods; for primary cooking (using the great variety of recipes in this book); and for reheating foods. All in incredibly short times and achieving a fresh taste in foods.

Now...read on! As you turn the pages you'll join a new generation of modern cooks who know how to serve up old-fashioned goodness at every meal – in minutes.

Microwaves first cook the outside section of food. Arrange food in a ring and denser food toward the outside of a dish.

How Microwaves Cook

All food products are cooked by the addition of energy which causes an increase in molecular activity. The energy required must come from some source such as a gas flame, burning charcoal or electricity. When electricity is used for cooking, it must be converted into heat energy.

When you turn on a light bulb, you are seeing electrical energy being converted to light energy. When you turn on your microwave oven, electrical energy is being converted to electromagnetic energy by means of an electron tube, called a magnetron, that is contained inside the oven. When microwaves enter food, they simply cause the liquid or moisture molecules in the food to vibrate at a fantastic rate . . . friction created by this vibration produces heat energy and this heat is conducted throughout the food. If you rapidly rub the palms of your hands together you will feel another example of heat that is created by friction. Microwaves are electromagnetic waves that are classified as being of a "non-ionizing" frequency which means they do *not* cause a chemical change (as do "ionizing" rays such as x-rays).

Microwaves allow food to cook *itself* rather than being surrounded by an outside source of high heat such as 400°F. inside your conventional oven.

Because the energy necessary to heat food is so direct in your microwave oven, the food is cooked faster and more efficiently than conventional cooking.

How You Will Cook with Microwaves

There are two familiar questions to ask yourself in order to become a microwave oven expert.

First: What's to be done with the food you want to microwave — defrost it, heat it or cook it?

Second: What is the food like — volume, or how much; density, or compactness; temperature, before it goes in the microwave, and are any of the ingredients "critical" or sensitive to microwaves?

Answers to these two questions determine cooking time, cooking technique (including things like oven settings, covering, stirring or turning) and utensils used.

The following paragraphs help answer these questions, define necessary microwave cooking techniques and list cooking utensils usable in a microwave oven.

OVEN SETTINGS: This book is designed to show you how to cook with a microwave oven. Settings are HIGH and DEFROST. Other models also have a MEDIUM and WARM setting. Cooking time is expressed in minutes and seconds. Check all controls on your oven before beginning to cook. See your Use and Care Manual to make certain that all controls are in the correct position.

DEFROSTING: Defrosting gradually heats frozen foods to change ice molecules into water without beginning the cooking process. The process must be slow. The DEFROST setting automatically reduces the power for even thawing.

HEATING: Heating occurs when microwaves start food molecules vibrating. Porous food like bread quickly heats. Dense food, like meat, should be sliced to heat through without overcooking edges.

COOKING: Cooking is prolonged heating that changes food texture from a raw to a cooked state. Since microwaves are attracted to liquid, fat and sugar, different power provides energy levels that assure even, quality cooking.

HIGH ALTITUDE COOKING: The usual high altitude adjustments are not necessary in microwave cooking. The only change may be a slight increase in cooking time.

BROWNING: Sear steaks and chops on a microwave browning grill. Large meat items will brown in a microwave oven because the fat attracts microwaves and reaches a high temperature during cooking. Cakes and breads, however, will not brown in the oven. Recipes in this book suggest ingredients to enhance color.

VOLUME: As the volume of food put in the oven increases, the concentration of microwaves in a given food item decreases — so cooking time goes up slightly. For example, to make a single serving of instant coffee, heat one cup of water for about 2½ minutes, or until hot. Then add desired amount of instant coffee and stir. For two cups of coffee, heat two cups of water for 3½ minutes. You have increased the cooking time about 1 minute to allow for the second cup of water.

STARTING TEMPERATURE: Cold food takes longer to cook than room temperature or warm food. Lukewarm tap water heats faster than cold. You may want to try the following experiment: fill one cup with cool tap water and another with warm tap water. Heat both cups of water for 1 minute and then remove from oven. Notice the cup that had warm water in it is hot already but the other one will need 30-45 seconds more to reach the same stage.

DENSITY: Denser, more compact foods take longer to heat than porous foods. This is because microwaves penetrate deeper into porous items creating instant heat throughout. Microwaves first penetrate the outer portion of dense food and the center must be heated by conduction from the hot, outer edges. A slice of meat, for example, heats in 2 to 3 minutes while a slice of bread the same size takes 30 seconds.

This fact of cooking from outside toward the center (similar to conventional cooking) is the reason behind several of the techniques of cooking with microwaves. It affects your defrosting and stirring of food, your allowing a standing time for food before serving and your arranging food in the oven.

ARRANGEMENT OF FOOD: Think of the shape of a ring when arranging food in the oven. Because microwaves first cook the outer section of food, the center takes the longest to cook. The hole in a ring creates more outside edges and does away with the more difficult to cook center. If you place several items, such as baking potatoes, in the oven, it is best to leave spaces between each of them so there are more separate outside edges. If they are all grouped together, you create a dense center that would be difficult to cook.

When arranging food on a plate or cooking dish, place the larger and thicker part of the food toward the outside edge of the dish and the thinner and smaller part of the food toward the center so it will not overcook.

STIRRING: Because the outside edges of food tend to cook first, stir some food mixtures during the cooking period. This stirring of mixtures such as scrambled eggs or pudding keeps the cooking even by bringing the outside cooked portion toward the center and bringing the less cooked center portion toward the outside.

TURNING FOOD OVER: Turn over meat and other dense pieces of food to make certain it cooks more evenly.

COVERING: Glass covers, plastic wrap, wax paper, glass plates and saucers trap steam and hasten cooking. Remove covers carefully to avoid steam burns. Small pieces of aluminum foil may be used to prevent overcooked spots on large pieces of meat.

CRITICAL INGREDIENTS: This term is used throughout the book and refers to food items that microwave very quickly and can overcook, curdle or "pop". These foods are cheese, eggs, cream, sour cream, condensed milk, mayonnaise, snails, scallops, oysters, kidney beans and mushrooms.

STANDING TIME: Cooking continues after food comes from a microwave oven. It is often advisable to undercook or underthaw food slightly and let the process finish during the standing time as designated in recipes.

This standing time allows heat to be conducted toward the center. It varies depending on the volume and density of the food. The time is most often as short a period as it takes to put the food on the table, but larger and more dense foods take more time. The recipes note the standing time when it is necessary. The temperature of the food rises during the standing time because of the continued heat transfer, so food is removed from the oven before it reaches a serving temperature. For example, microwave a medium size baking potato for about 4 minutes. Notice that the potato is still quite firm to the touch when you remove it from the oven, but after it stands for a few minutes it will be ready to eat.

ADAPTING RECIPES: Favorite family recipes can be adapted to microwave cooking. Select a similar recipe in this book as a model. Check its **"grey box" key** for techniques and tips. Always take "critical" ingredients into consideration. A general conversion chart for adapting recipes is not possible — experiment.

Stirring food by bringing the outside cooked portion toward the center and bringing the less cooked center portion toward the outside.

Microwave Oven Power Settings

Four energy setting words are used in these recipes: WARM, DEFROST, MEDIUM and HIGH (or Cook). These denote major cooking techniques for which a particular microwave speed is used. All recipes can be done either on HIGH and DEFROST settings. However, we have given additional directions to use MEDIUM and WARM settings when using these settings would benefit the recipes.

HIGH setting radiates the most power and should be used to cook foods with high moisture content or foods that require fast, quick cooking to retain natural goodness, flavor and texture. Do not use this setting for "delicate" cooking.

- Cook fish and seafood dishes.
- Quickly heat tender beef roasts; finish cooking on DEFROST.
- Cook vegetables.
- Cook poultry such as tender young cut-up chicken or small whole birds weighing 3 pounds or under.
- Quickly heat many less tender beef cuts before final cooking on a lower setting.
- Heat beverage liquids until bubbling to dissolve instant mixes or to reheat previously cooked beverages.
- Boil water before cooking rice or pasta.
- Finish cooking cakes and quick breads on this setting to set batter or dough after it raises.
- Cook fresh fruit and fresh fruit desserts.
- Cook savory or dessert sauces made with flour or cornstarch.
- Cook fillings made with flour or cornstarch.
- Preheat microwave browning grill.

DEFROST setting is used to defrost frozen foods that require a low energy setting and to cook some delicate foods.

- Cook rice or pasta — after water boils on HIGH.
- Cook baked custards and desserts with baked custard bases which cannot be stirred.
- Thaw meat, poultry and fish.
- Bake yeast breads.
- Raise cakes and quick bread mixes — batter sets using higher energy on HIGH.
- Cook soft custards and custard-base desserts with eggs.
- Cook less tender beef — during major part of cooking time.
- Total cooking of small veal cuts and final cooking period of large veal cuts.
- Bake bars and cookies.

If your microwave oven has the additional MEDIUM and WARM settings, you should enjoy them with the following dishes:

MEDIUM setting has many functions because it uses medium energy. It cooks many meats and mixtures with critical ingredients especially well.

- Cook critical ingredient recipes — those containing mushrooms, cheese, sour cream, cream, mayonnaise, eggs, kidney beans, clams or scallops.
- Finish cooking tender beef roasts.
- Cook most pork and lamb.
- Cook large, whole chicken or turkey, plus geese, ducks and pheasants.
- Sauté finely-cut vegetables in butter.
- Cook frostings with lots of butter.
- Cook candy.
- Cook egg and cheese dishes.
- Bake pie shells.

WARM setting is the gentlest of the gentle in the variable power spectrum.

- Raise yeast breads.
- Keep a main dish warm for about an hour if a meal must wait.
- Soften cream cheese and butter.

USER INSTRUCTIONS

PRECAUTIONS TO AVOID POSSIBLE EXPOSURE TO EXCESSIVE MICROWAVE ENERGY

(a) Do not attempt to operate this oven with the door open since open-door operation can result in harmful exposure to microwave energy. It is important not to defeat or tamper with the safety interlocks.

(b) Do not place any object between the oven front face and the door to allow soil or cleaner residue to accumulate on sealing surfaces.

(c) Do not operate the oven if it is damaged. It is particularly important that the oven door close properly and that there is no damage to the: (1) Door (bent), (2) hinges and latches (broken or loosened), (3) door seals and sealing surfaces.

(d) The oven should not be adjusted or repaired by anyone except properly qualified service personnel.

Glass cooking dishes, straw and paper supplies used in microwave cooking.

Microwave Oven Cooking Utensils

GLASS UTENSILS: Ovenproof glass or glass ceramic oven-baking dishes are the most-used microwave cooking utensils. These dishes allow microwaves to pass through directly to food. Dishes will remain cool unless cooking is prolonged causing hot food to heat the dish.

Glass, sturdy china and pottery serving dishes can also be used. These should not have silver, gold, platinum or other metal trim which will be damaged by the microwaves.

Fine china is not ovenproof. Do not use it at all if it has a metal signature on the bottom or any other metal trim. Fine china without metal trim may be used to heat precooked foods for short periods of time.

Some paints or glazes used on glass dishes do contain metallic substances and should not be used in a microwave oven.

If in doubt about any glass, pottery or china utensil, place it in the oven on HIGH for 15 to 20 seconds. If the container feels warm when taken from the oven, do not cook or heat in it.

PLASTICS: Dishwasher-safe plastics, usually quite rigid material, can be used for cooking or heating.

Hard plastic trays, picnic ware, thermal cups, mugs and bowls (including the sturdy bowls in which a number of dairy toppings and other products are packaged) may be used in the oven. Melamine ware has a tendency to absorb energy, so you should give it a 15 to 20 second test on HIGH to be certain your particular brand is safe. (See Glass Utensils.)

Plastic foam cups and dishes can be used for heating. Cover loosely to avoid dish distortion.

Plastic baby bottles are safe for heating milk or formulas.

Spatulas and spoons designed for non-stick pans can be left in the oven for short-time periods.

Heat rolls quickly in straw basket. Metal skewers can be used in the microwave oven provided the proportion of food is greater than the metal.

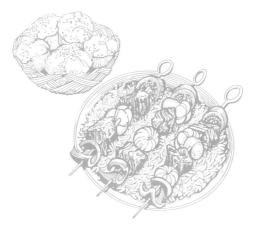

Plastic wrap can be used as a tight covering, but it should be pierced before being removed to prevent steam burns on hands or arms.

Plastic cooking pouches can also be used to heat and/or cook contents, but should be slit before cooking so excess steam can escape.

Cooking bags can be used according to manufacturer's directions. These bags are designed to withstand boiling, freezing and oven heat (not bags designed only for storage).

PAPER: Paper cups, plates, towels, wax paper and paper cartons can be used for heating. Prolonged time in the oven can cause paper to burn. Wax paper can be used as a covering during cooking.

STRAW: Baskets can be used in the oven for the very short time it takes to heat rolls.

METAL: Metal dishes and foil reflect microwaves and inhibit cooking. Gaps in the metal particles of an object can also cause arcing. The walls of a microwave oven are made of smooth, continuous metal with no particle gaps.

Metal objects can be used in the oven under certain conditions although care must be taken that metal does not touch oven surfaces and arc.

Small pieces of aluminum foil can be used to cover spots on large pieces of meat which appear to be overcooking.

Foil TV-type trays can be used if no more than ¾ inch deep because microwaves reflect off the foil and must heat from the top food surface.

Metal skewers and clamps are usable when the proportion of food is much greater than the metal. Chunks of food filling shish kabob skewer microwave well without arcing. Metal clamps and clips on turkeys may be left on during cooking.

Do not use metal twister, it will arc. The sparks may ignite paper and plastic.

WOOD: Moisture in wooden utensils evaporates during microwave cooking and will cause wood to crack. Small items such as a wooden spoon or wood-handled rubber spatula can be left in the oven for short periods of time.

MEAT AND CANDY THERMOMETERS: Only microwave meat thermometers may be used during microwave cooking. Conventional meat and candy thermometers may be inserted to test temperature after food is taken out of the oven. The reason? Mercury in conventional thermometers reflects microwaves and makes them inaccurate.

MICROWAVE ROASTING RACK: This accessory may be purchased from the oven manufacturer. It is used to hold meat above pan drippings during open pan cooking. Inverted glass or pottery saucers (without metal trim) can be used to simulate a rack.

MICROWAVE BROWNING GRILL: The browning grill is an accessory which may be purchased from the oven manufacturer. The unit is preheated in the microwave oven; then food is added to sear and/or brown.

If a dish tends to become warm during cooking, it will take longer to cook the food since the dish is absorbing some microwaves. If used for extended periods of time, the dish may become so hot that scorching or cracking of the dish may occur.

EFFECT OF THE MICROWAVE OVEN ON CONTAINERS AND WRAPS.

China plates and cups. Generally, no effect.

China plates and cups with metal trim (not recommended). Arcing (sparking) which will tarnish the trim permanently. Will not necessarily damage oven.

Paper plates, cups and napkins. Suitable for microwave. Absorbs moisture from baked goods.

Melamine dishes (not recommended). Will become hot, often too hot to handle. Food will take longer to cook.

Soft plastics such as dessert topping cartons and Tupperware®. Will withstand most lower temperatures reached in reheating. Will distort or melt if used for cooking or reheating foods with high fat or sugar content.

Pottery mugs, plates and bowls. Generally, suitable for microwave. If pottery is unglazed, it may absorb moisture. Moisture may cause it to heat up.

Earthenware (ironstone) mugs, plates and bowls. Generally, suitable for microwave. Thickness has no effect on ability for microwaves to penetrate. If dish is refrigerated, may take longer to heat food, since it will absorb heat from food.

Special plastic roasting racks. Suitable for microwave. Allows juices to drain away from meat. Juice can be used for gravy later.

Cooking pouches. Suitable for microwave. Slit pouch so steam can escape. Seal on bag is made to withstand low pressure — will not explode if bag is not slit.

Wax paper. Microwaves have no effect on wax. However, hot food temperature may cause some melting. Will not adhere to hot food. (Remember, chocolates that you eat are often part paraffin.)

Plastic Wrap. Suitable for microwave. Always puncture to allow steam to escape. Otherwise, could cause steam burn.

Oven film and cooking bags. Material is suitable. Do not use metal twister (use rubber band); it will spark (arc) and melt bag. Bag itself will not cause tenderizing. Do not use film with foil edges.

Deep metal pots and pans (not recommended). Depth of metal would cause microwaves to penetrate through top opening only. No time advantage when cooking does not occur from all sides.

T.V. dinner trays (metal). Shallow metal, ¾″ is suitable. However, microwaves still penetrate from the top only, and food will receive heat from the top surface.

Metal spoons (not silver). If there is a quantity of food, there is no arcing. Handle may become warm to the touch. Do not leave in oven with small amounts of food.

Wooden spoons. Material can withstand microwaves for short periods of cooking.

Wooden cutting boards and wooden bowls. Microwaves will cause natural moisture in wood to evaporate, causing drying and cracking.

Corningware® casseroles. Suitable for microwave. This material can be used on surface units, oven and broiler as well, with no breakage.

Pyrex® casseroles. Suitable for microwave. Do not use dishes with metal trim, or arcing will occur.

Centura® dinnerware (not recommended). This absorbs microwaves and can become too hot to handle. Eventually can break or crack.

Corelle® Livingware dinnerware. Suitable for microwave. Closed-handle cups should not be used.

Micro-Browner™ grills and skillets. These special dishes absorb microwaves and preheat to high temperatures. A special coating on the bottom makes this dish unique.

Coverings used with microwave cooking: glass lid, plastic wrap and wax paper.

BEGINNING TO COOK **Breakfast**

Now that you've read the introductory section about microwaves and how they act, you're ready to start your discovery of carefree cooking. It may take a little time to get used to this way of cooking so we've organized a section of beginning recipes for BREAKFAST, LUNCH and DINNER to introduce you to microwave cooking as easily and thoroughly as possible. We've given the reasons why a recipe calls for certain ingredients or cooking techniques to help you completely understand what you're doing. We've also tried to explain as many varying conditions under which you might prepare a recipe and what adjustments you can expect to make with those conditions. Following recipe directions will assure you of cooking success.

Water Temperature Know-How

● Starting temperature of water for coffee will affect the heating time.

● The cooking time necessary to heat the water will increase with the size of the cup and the number of cups.

● Stirring after heating (when coffee is added) distributes the heat.

● We have added the coffee after the water is hot. If it were added before heating and boiled, it would taste bitter, similar to conventionally boiled coffee.

INSTANT COFFEE OR TEA

Setting: HIGH

Fill coffee cups or mugs with cold tap water. MICROWAVE, until steam appears:

        1 cup   — 2¼ to 2½ MINUTES
        2 cups — 3¼ to 3½ MINUTES
        3 cups — 4¼ to 4½ MINUTES
        4 cups — 5½ to 5¾ MINUTES
        5 cups — 6¾ to 7 MINUTES
        6 cups — 8¼ to 8½ MINUTES

Add desired amount of instant coffee or tea and stir or add tea bag and steep as directed on package.

TIPS Perked coffee that has cooled can be reheated using the heating chart for beverages, page 42. Some oven owners perk the coffee, unplug it, let it cool and then reheat cups as needed.

● Any type of paper, foam, mug or coffee cup can be used.

Heating Milk Know-How

● Hot cocoa can be made in the microwave oven using chocolate flavored milk, instant cocoa mix or combining cocoa, sugar and milk. All the same techniques apply since you are basically heating milk. These techniques are very similar to heating water for instant coffee except that the milk will boil over if it gets too hot.

Marshmallow Know-How

● A marshmallow can be added during the last seconds of heating. Because of the difference in volume as compared with the milk and because of the high sugar concentration, it would overcook before the milk was hot if added for the full time.

● By adding it during the last 10 to 15 seconds, the marshmallow has time to puff up and soften.

● When the oven shuts off, the puffed marshmallow slowly collapses.

HOT COCOA

Setting: HIGH

CHOCOLATE MILK: Fill cups or mugs with chocolate flavored milk. Microwave as directed below.

HOT COCOA MIX: Fill cups or mugs with milk. Microwave as directed below. Stir in amount of cocoa mix as directed on package.

UNSWEETENED COCOA: In each cup or mug combine 1 tablespoon unsweetened cocoa, 2 tablespoons sugar and pinch of salt. Add enough milk to form a paste; mix until smooth. Stir in milk to fill cups. Microwave as directed below.

COOKING TIMES: MICROWAVE, until steam appears;

        1 cup   — 2 to 3 MINUTES
        2 cups — 3 to 4 MINUTES
        3 cups — 4 to 5 MINUTES
        4 cups — 5 to 8 MINUTES
        5 cups — 6 to 9 MINUTES
        6 cups — 8 to 12 MINUTES

Stir before serving to distribute heat.

TIP For larger quantities of cocoa, prepare and heat cocoa in a glass pitcher or tea pot. The times may be slightly longer than for the same volume heated in individual cups.

HOT INSTANT BREAKFAST

Empty envelope of instant breakfast in coffee mug. Stir in milk to fill cup. Microwave, using times for hot cocoa as guide.

Pictured: Hot Cocoa, this page, topped with Marshmallow, Baked Apple, page 16, Hot Cereal (oatmeal), page 15, topped with fresh peaches, Warm Doughnut (see Warm Sweet Roll), page 12, Pancakes (reheated in microwave oven), page 13, Bacon, page 15, Scrambled Eggs, page 14.

- A bagel is one of the most ideal shapes to heat with microwaves. The lack of a center in a bagel or doughnut makes heating very even and quick because the center of food is the most difficult area to heat.

- If serving with coffee, heat coffee first since it will hold heat while bagel is heated.

BAGELS

Setting: HIGH

1. Place 1 bagel on paper plate or napkin.

2. MICROWAVE for 10 to 15 SECONDS or until surface is warm. For 2 bagels, microwave for 15 to 20 SECONDS.

TIPS For heating other quantities and heating frozen bagels, see Bread Chapter.
- Bagels can be split and topped with cream cheese before heating. During heating, the cream cheese will soften and can be spread easily on the warm bagel.

- A whole frozen coffee cake can be thawed and heated or individual pieces can be removed to be heated and the remainder left frozen.

- Frozen coffee cake is removed from the metal container to allow it to thaw and heat from all sides. Microwaves bounce off metal so it would only heat from the top side if left in the foil container.

- The coffee cake reheats best if placed on paper or cloth that absorbs moisture. When placed directly on a plate, the moisture condenses on the cool surface and makes the bottom of the coffee cake soggy. A plate can be used if first lined with a paper or cloth napkin.

- A resting time is necessary to allow heat to reach the center of the cake and thaw it without overcooking the edges. When heating 1 serving, the resting time is not necessary because it is easy to reach the center of a smaller piece.

HEATING FROZEN COFFEE CAKE

Setting: HIGH

1. Remove a frozen coffee cake (about 11 oz.) from foil container and place on paper plate or towel.

2. MICROWAVE for 2 to 2½ MINUTES or until surface is warm. Let stand a few seconds to distribute heat.

1 Coffee Cake

TIP To reheat 1 piece of frozen coffee cake, cut 1/6 of coffee cake and remove to a paper plate or napkin (return remainder to freezer). MICROWAVE for 20 SECONDS or until surface is warm.

- Bread items reheat best if placed on a paper or cloth surface that absorbs moisture.

- When placed directly on a glass plate, the moisture condenses and makes the bottom of the roll soggy.

- The inside of the sweet roll is at serving temperature when the bread surface feels warm to the touch.

- For reheating, we used room temperature rolls that weighed about 2 ounces, sweet rolls that were about 5 inches in diameter and cinnamon rolls that were about 2½ inches in diameter. Other sizes take a few seconds more or less to heat.

- Because microwaves are attracted to sugar, a sugar filling or topping heats very quickly and can become very hot.

WARM SWEET ROLLS

Setting: HIGH

1. Place sweet rolls on napkins or paper plates.

2. MICROWAVE 1 roll for 15 to 20 SECONDS or until surface is warm.

3. MICROWAVE 2 rolls 20 to 25 SECONDS. Let stand a few seconds to distribute heat.

TIPS For complete reheating chart for rolls, see Bread chapter, page 127.
- Since microwaves cook sugar very quickly, be careful not to overcook sweet rolls because frosting or jelly can become very hot and the roll might toughen.

- When softening butter to be served at the table, you want to retain its shape so you allow standing times after cooking periods.

- If you are softening butter to be used in cooking, the shape is not important so you can cook without any standing time.

SOFTENING BUTTER

Setting: DEFROST

1. Place stick of cold butter on serving plate.

2. MICROWAVE for 15 SECONDS, let stand 15 seconds.

3. MICROWAVE for 15 SECONDS; let stand 15 seconds. If necessary, MICROWAVE 5 more SECONDS.

TIP MICROWAVE on WARM 1½ to 2½ MINUTES.

Pancakes, Waffles and French Toast Know-How

• Although pancakes, waffles and French toast need to be cooked conventionally, they are ideal for cooking ahead or cooking extras to be kept in the refrigerator or freezer for reheating in the microwave oven.

Moisture Know-How

• Unlike most bread products, pancakes, waffles and French toast can be heated directly on a serving plate rather than a paper napkin; excess moisture is not a problem because normally they will be served with syrup.

PANCAKES

Setting: HIGH

1. To reheat refrigerated pancakes, stack on serving plate.

2. MICROWAVE until center of bottom pancake is hot:

AMOUNT	REFRIGERATED	FROZEN
1 plate with 1 pancake	20 to 35 seconds	45 to 50 seconds
1 plate with 2 pancakes	35 to 40 seconds	1 to 1½ seconds
1 plate with 3 pancakes	50 to 55 seconds	1½ to 2 minutes
2 plates with 2 pancakes each	1 to 1½ minutes	2 to 2½ minutes

FRENCH TOAST

Setting: HIGH

1. To reheat refrigerated or frozen French toast, place on serving plate in single layer.

2. MICROWAVE, until center of slice is hot:

AMOUNT	REFRIGERATED	FROZEN
1 small plate with 1 slice toast	30 to 35 seconds	1 to 1½ minutes
1 large or 2 small plates with 2 slices toast	45 to 50 seconds	2 to 2½ minutes
1 large plate with 3 slices toast	1 to 1½ minutes	3 to 3½ minutes
1 large plate with 4 slices toast	1½ to 2 minutes	4 to 4½ minutes

WAFFLES

Setting: HIGH

1. Prepare and cook favorite waffles. Let cool in single layer on cooling rack. Wrap tightly and refrigerate or freeze.

2. To reheat, MICROWAVE on serving plate until center feels warm.

AMOUNT	REFRIGERATED	FROZEN
1 section	15 to 20 seconds	20 to 30 seconds
2 sections	25 to 30 seconds	35 to 40 seconds
3 sections	35 to 40 seconds	45 to 50 seconds
4 sections (2 plates)	45 to 50 seconds	1 to 1½ minutes

Syrup Know-How

• Any metal such as a cap on the syrup container is removed so it can heat from all sides.

• Our syrup was at room temperature. If syrup is at refrigerator temperature, the times will be a little longer.

• This same technique of heating syrup can be used to heat and remove the last few drops of syrup from a bottle. The time is about 10 or 15 seconds, depending on the amount of syrup.

• Because the sugar concentration is high in syrup, you will notice it heats more quickly than the same amount of water.

HEATING SYRUP

Setting: HIGH

1. Remove metal cap from bottle of syrup.

2. MICROWAVE for 30 to 45 SECONDS for a 12 oz. bottle or until bubbles begin to appear. If serving from a pitcher, syrup can be heated in pitcher if it contains no metal trim.

● Custard, rich with eggs and milk, is good at any meal. We have included it with breakfast because it is easy to mix together the night before and leave in refrigerator. Then individuals can cook or simply reheat their own custards when ready to eat breakfast.

● It is interesting to watch custard cook because you can see it start to firm around sides and then puff in the center.

● You will have an idea of the cooking pattern within your oven and which areas of the oven may tend to cook a little faster or slower than others.

● You may find it desirable to remove some custards from the oven before others are cooked.

BAKED CUSTARD

1¾ **cups milk**
¼ **cup sugar**
3 **eggs**
¼ **teaspoon salt**
½ **teaspoon vanilla**
Nutmeg

Setting: DEFROST

1. Combine all ingredients, except nutmeg, in 4-cup measure. Beat well with rotary beater. Pour into four 6-ounce glass custard cups, filling each ¾ full. Sprinkle with nutmeg.

2. MICROWAVE for 10 to 15 MINUTES or until knife inserted near center comes out clean. Let stand 5 minutes before serving.

4 Custards

TIPS Custards may cook at slightly different rates because amount of custard in each cup tends to vary. Remove custards from oven as they finish cooking.
● To cook 1 custard, MICROWAVE for 2 to 3 MINUTES. To cook 2 custards, MICROWAVE for 4 to 5 MINUTES.
● To bring a cooked custard that has been refrigerated to room temperature, MICROWAVE about 1 MINUTE on DEFROST and then let stand 1 minute to distribute heat.
● To microwave custard in 1-quart casserole, mix together ingredients in casserole; cover. MICROWAVE on DEFROST for 10 to 15 MINUTES, or until knife inserted near center comes out clean.

● Scrambled eggs are the easiest way to cook eggs because the yolks and whites, (which cook at different rates with microwaves are mixed together and thus cook evenly.

● Butter is added mainly for flavor so it can be melted before adding the eggs or stirred in with the eggs without melting.

● Stirring is not necessary until the eggs begin to set and coagulate. This will begin about ⅔ of the way through the cooking time.

● Because eggs cook so quickly, they should still be moist at end of cooking time; during standing they will finish cooking and setting.

● During this standing time you may want to heat coffee and a roll.

● A tight fitting cover is used with the eggs to hold in the heat and help with the cooking.

● It is easy to reheat leftover scrambled eggs. If you are cooking them primarily for reheating, undercook them just a little.

INDIVIDUAL SCRAMBLED EGGS

Setting: HIGH

1. In soup bowl or 20-oz. glass casserole, MICROWAVE 2 teaspoons butter or margarine for 25 to 30 SECONDS. Add 2 eggs and 2 tablespoons milk. Mix with fork until well scrambled together; cover.

2. MICROWAVE for 1 MINUTE. Stir with fork; recover.

3. MICROWAVE for ½ to 1 MINUTE (eggs should still be moist). Stir again. Let stand, covered, 1 to 2 minutes to finish cooking. Season to taste.

1 Serving

TIPS If making the eggs ahead to reheat, undercook, cool and refrigerate. Reheat by placing on glass serving plate and covering with small bowl. MICROWAVE for 45 SECONDS for 2 eggs. Let stand about a minute to distribute heat.
● For 2 servings (4 eggs) use 1-quart glass casserole or mixing bowl, 4 teaspoons butter, 4 eggs, 4 tablespoons milk. MICROWAVE for 2 MINUTES, stir and then MICROWAVE for ½ to 1 MINUTE.
● As with any dish used to cook eggs, they are difficult to clean unless soaked immediately after emptying. You may find it convenient to use a vegetable spray-on coating on the dish before cooking to make clean-up easier.
● MICROWAVE on MEDIUM for 1½ MINUTES in step 2 and 1 MINUTE in step 3.

- Timing for bacon will depend on thickness.
- If you vary brands of bacon, you may notice a slight difference in cooking times as the sugar, salt, and fat content will affect the cooking time.
- Bacon can be stacked in layers if paper towels are used between, remembering that the layers should be even thickness for even cooking.
- The paper towels absorb the fat as bacon cooks. You can also cook bacon without the towel in a shallow baking dish with sides such as a pie plate or 12 x 7 baking dish and then drain before eating.
- Cook larger quantities of bacon without paper if desired.
- You may wish to cover with a towel to prevent spattering.
- If using a paper plate under the towel, it is best if the plate is not plastic coated because the coating would not absorb any excess fat.
- We do not suggest cooking more than ½ lb. of bacon at a time because of the accumulation of grease and little time advantage.

BACON

Setting: HIGH

1. Place 1 or 2 layers of paper towel in shallow glass baking dish. Lay strips of bacon on towel.

2. If additional space is needed, top with 1 or 2 more layers of towel and then another layer of bacon. Top with a layer of paper towel to prevent spattering.

3. MICROWAVE to desired crispness:
  1 slice — 1 to 1½ MINUTES
  2 slices — 2 to 2½ MINUTES
  3 slices — 3 to 3½ MINUTES
  4 slices — 4 to 4½ MINUTES
  5 slices — 4½ to 5 MINUTES
  6 slices — 5 to 6 MINUTES
  8 slices — 8 to 9 MINUTES

TIP If bacon is hard to separate into slices, place the slices you are planning to cook in oven and MICROWAVE about 30 SECONDS. Loosen and separate, reducing additional cooking time by about 30 seconds.

- Both Canadian bacon and cooked ham are precooked, and need only be heated to serving temperature.
- When heating several pieces at one time, the pieces should all be of similar size and shape; otherwise it may be necessary to remove some before the others are heated to avoid overcooking.
- If serving with eggs, cook eggs first and leave covered to stay hot while heating meat. Heat rolls or bread just before serving.

CANADIAN BACON

Setting: HIGH

1. Place ½-inch slices of Canadian bacon on individual glass plates or on platter; cover.

2. MICROWAVE until the edges of meat begin to sizzle.
  1 slice — 1½ to 2 MINUTES
  2 slices — 2 to 2½ MINUTES
  3 slices — 3 to 3½ MINUTES
  4 slices — 4 to 4½ MINUTES

Let stand a few minutes to distribute heat.

TIPS For ham, use same guide as for Canadian bacon, but cut cooked ham into slices about ¼ inch thick and 4 to 5 inches in diameter.
- MICROWAVE on MEDIUM for 1 MINUTE longer than suggested.

- Cereal is especially easy to cook in the microwave oven because it can be cooked in a serving dish.
- If other types of cereal are desired, you can go by the proportions on the package.
- We found the oven was most convenient for the quick-cooking cereals.
- If the cereal is not quick-cooking, it should be covered and will need to cook after boiling for about as long as is directed on the package.
- The instant cereals need only to be mixed with water and then heated in the microwave oven for the time suggested on the package.

HOT CEREAL

  ¾ cup water
  ⅓ cup quick-cooking rolled oats
  Dash salt

Setting: HIGH

1. In glass cereal bowl, combine all ingredients.

2. MICROWAVE for 1½ to 2 MINUTES, or until mixture boils, stirring once. Let stand 1 TO 2 minutes before serving.

1 Serving

TIPS For additional servings, prepare in individual cereal bowls as directed. For 2 servings, MICROWAVE for 2½ to 3 MINUTES; for 3 servings, MICROWAVE for 3½ to 4 MINUTES; for 4 servings, MICROWAVE for 4½ to 5 MINUTES.
- When preparing more than one serving, the cereal can be prepared in a casserole dish and then served in individual dishes.
- Combining the cereal with cold water gives a creamy textured cereal. If you prefer more texture, first heat the water to boiling and then stir in cereal. MICROWAVE covered, 1 to 1½ MINUTES. Stir and let stand.
- When cooking cream of wheat, use 2 tablespoons quick-cooking cream of wheat for rolled oats in recipe above and proceed as directed. Milk can be used for water, if desired.
- MICROWAVE on MEDIUM for same times.

Grapefruit Know-How

• Grapefruit can be heated easily in the sauce dish used for serving. Some type of dish or container is necessary to collect any juice that may run over edge of fruit during heating.

• The grapefruit are left uncovered during cooking because they will not dry out with microwave cooking, there is little chance of spattering and the time would not be reduced by covering.

GLAZED GRAPEFRUIT

    2 grapefruit
    4 teaspoons packed brown sugar
    2 teaspoons butter or margarine

Setting: HIGH

1. Cut grapefruit in half, removing core and seeds. Place in sauce dishes. If desired, cut around each section to loosen.

2. Sprinkle each half with 1 teaspoon brown sugar. Place ½ teaspoon butter in center of each half.

3. MICROWAVE for 3½ to 4 MINUTES, or until heated through. Let stand 1 minute to distribute heat.

4 Servings

TIP For 2 halves, MICROWAVE 2½ to 3 MINUTES. For 1 half, MICROWAVE 1½ to 2 MINUTES.

Dehydrated Fruit Know-How

• Timing is not critical when cooking prunes because you are only heating the water to about the boiling point in order to speed the rehydrating of the dried fruit.

• By starting with hot tap water, the cooking time is shorter than if you begin with cold water.

• We suggest covering with the casserole lid but a plate or other tight fitting cover would hold in the heat just as well.

SPICY BREAKFAST PRUNES

    1½ cups dried prunes
     2 cups hot water
     ¼ cup packed brown sugar
     1 stick cinnamon or 1 teaspoon ground
        cinnamon
    10 whole allspice or ¼ teaspoon ground
        allspice

Setting: HIGH

1. In 1 or 1½-quart glass casserole, combine all ingredients; cover.

2. MICROWAVE for 4 to 5 MINUTES or until mixture starts to boil.

3. Allow to cool at room temperature 4 hours or overnight. Remove cinnamon stick and whole allspice before serving. Store leftovers in refrigerator.

6 Servings

Apples Know-How

• Apples are easy to cook when learning how to operate your oven and they make a quick breakfast or snack fruit.

• The apples we used in testing the recipe were at refrigerator temperature. Room temperature apples may take slightly less cooking time.

• Cooking times will vary with the size and shape of the apple.

• When additional ingredients such as raisins and nuts are added to the apples the time is increased because there is more food volume to heat and cook.

• The apples have been left uncovered during cooking because they are not easy to cover and the time is not shortened appreciably by covering.

• There may be a little spattering which can be easily wiped up after cooking. If you prefer to prevent this spattering, place a piece of wax paper over apples during cooking.

BAKED APPLES

    4 medium cooking apples, washed and
       cored
    ¼ cup packed brown sugar
    2 tablespoons butter or margarine
       Cinnamon
       Sweet or sour cream

Setting: HIGH

1. Place apples in 2-quart (8 x 8) glass baking dish. Place 1 tablespoon brown sugar and 1 tablespoon butter in center of each apple. Sprinkle with cinnamon.

2. MICROWAVE for 8 to 9 MINUTES or until apples are tender. Serve warm with sweet or sour cream.

4 Servings

TIPS For 1 apple, use individual custard cup and MICROWAVE 2 to 2½ MINUTES. For 2 apples, use individual custard cups and MICROWAVE 3 to 3½ MINUTES. For 6 apples, use 2-quart (8 x 8 or 12 x 7) baking dish and MICROWAVE 10 to 11 MINUTES.

• If desired, add ½ tablespoon raisins, chopped nuts or mincemeat to filling in center of each apple, adding about 1 additional minute cooking time for 4 apples.

Metal Tray Know-How

• The frozen breakfasts are packaged in a foil (metal) tray with a foil covering. Therefore, the foil covering must be removed before cooking and be replaced with wax paper; or you may place the uncovered tray back into its paper carton which holds in heat.

• The breakfast can be cooked in the foil tray because it is very shallow.

• Cooking times can be decreased 15 seconds by transferring the contents of the tray to a glass or paper plate because it can then be cooked from all sides rather than only the top surface.

T.V. BREAKFASTS

Setting: HIGH

1. Remove foil cover from 4½-oz. frozen T.V. breakfast. Return to outer carton or cover with wax paper.

2. MICROWAVE until meat is hot:
French toast and sausage patties —
2½ to 3 MINUTES

Pancakes and sausage patties —
2½ to 3 MINUTES,

Scrambled eggs, sausage patty, country style fried potatoes — 3 to 3½ MINUTES

TIP When cooking 2 breakfasts in foil trays, double above cooking times. Be certain that foil trays do not touch oven walls. Reduce cooking times by 30 seconds when 2 breakfasts are transferred to glass or paper plates.

Frozen Fruit Juice Know-How

• When thawing fruit juice, you first want to loosen the concentrate from the can and then soften it enough to easily mix it with water.

• Since the can is often surrounded by metal with metal ends and foil-lined paper wrapper, it is necessary to remove one end so the microwave energy can reach the food. This process is slow because the energy can penetrate from only one side of the container.

• To speed the thawing, remove the concentrate from the metal can as soon as it has thawed enough to loosen.

• On some types of packaging there may be a tendency for a few thin pieces of foil paper to protrude from the can after the lid is removed. If these are not trimmed, the microwave energy may cause sparks (arcing).

• In thawing there is usually a rest period to allow the heat at the outside to penetrate toward the center. With fruit juice, the resting takes place while you transfer the juice from the can to the pitcher.

DEFROSTING FRUIT JUICE CONCENTRATE

Setting: DEFROST

1. Remove top from a 6-oz. can frozen juice concentrate, being sure there are no stray pieces of foil paper sticking up around edge.

2. MICROWAVE for 3 to 3½ MINUTES. Let stand 2 to 3 minutes.

3. Empty concentrate into glass or plastic pitcher. Add water as directed on pacakge and mix together.

TIP For 12-oz. can MICROWAVE for 5 to 6 MINUTES.

Defrosting Frozen Fruits Know-How

• In thawing frozen fruits, it is best to still have a few ice crystals in the fruit so it retains its shape and texture.

• If you find the fruit is not thawed as much as you like, just cook a few more seconds, allowing it to stand a minute to distribute the heat.

Plastic Pouch Know-How, for Defrosting Fruit

• Fruits packaged in plastic pouches are easy to thaw in the oven without transferring to the serving dish during the thawing process.

• When cooking frozen vegetables in pouches, steam builds up inside the pouch so it is necessary to make a small slit in the top of the pouch to allow the steam to escape. However, when thawing fruit, it should not get hot so there is no steam and this step is not necessary.

THAWING FRUIT IN POUCHES

Setting: DEFROST

1. Place a 10-oz. pouch of frozen fruit in the oven.

2. MICROWAVE for 1½ to 2 MINUTES to distribute heat before opening pouch and serving.

Paper Container Know-How, for Defrosting Fruit

• Fruits packaged in paper containers have a thicker shape than those packaged in pouches so it is necessary to stir and break up the fruit during the thawing process.

• Since stirring is not possible in the container, the fruit is transferred to a serving dish after partial thawing. Otherwise, the fruit near the outside of the package may be partially cooked and the fruit in the center still frozen solid.

• Packaging for fruit does vary and if the package has metal on some sides, the thawing times may be slightly longer because the microwaves cannot pass through the metal.

• A resting time is necessary in thawing fruits to allow the heat to penetrate toward the center without cooking the outside. The resting time with these directions takes place during the transfer of the fruit from the freezing container to the serving dish.

• Since the fruit will not become hot, a plastic container can be used.

THAWING FRUIT IN PAPER PACKAGING

Setting: DEFROST

1. If ends of a 10-oz. carton of frozen fruit are metal, remove one end; otherwise package can be placed in oven unopened.

2. MICROWAVE for 1 MINUTE to loosen fruit from carton. Empty into glass or plastic serving dish breaking up fruit with fork.

3. MICROWAVE for 1 to 1½ MINUTES and stir. Let stand 1 minute to distribute the heat before serving.

BEGINNING TO COOK **Lunch**

Ground Beef Patty Know-How

• Meats that cook as quickly as ground beef patties do not have much chance to brown. We found we could achieve an attractive brown color and good flavor by first coating the meat with gravy mix. By cooking the meat and gravy mix together for a short period, the gravy mix combines with the meat juices to give a brown color and flavor.

• You may find it handy to keep gravy mix on hand in an extra salt shaker.

• There are other types of brown and season sprinkle ons that are available in some markets that have a similar browning effect with the meat.

• If you prefer conventionally browned hamburgers, it can be browned first and then placed in the oven for a minute or two to finish the cooking.

• The oven also works well for reheating leftover beef patties that have been broiled, fried or grilled. One patty takes about 45 seconds to reheat. Some oven owners tell us they cook additional patties for this purpose when barbecuing.

HAMBURGERS

Setting: HIGH

1. Season 1 lb. ground beef with salt and pepper. Shape into 4 patties (¼ lb. each). Arrange in 2-quart (8 x 8) glass baking dish; cover.

2. MICROWAVE for 4 to 5 MINUTES or until done. Let stand 2 minutes to finish cooking.

3. Place cooked patties in split buns and wrap each one loosely in paper napkin or paper towel.

4. MICROWAVE until heated through:
     1 hamburger — 15 to 20 SECONDS
     2 hamburgers — 25 to 30 SECONDS
     4 hamburgers — 45 to 50 SECONDS
     6 hamburgers — 1 to 1½ MINUTES

TIP For ground beef patties cooked on microwave browning grill, see page 80.

Soup Know-How

• For ease in adding the right amount of water, use a measuring cup or other guide to add equal amounts of soup and water.

• A 10½-oz. can of condensed soup usually contains about 1¼ cups so you can divide these amounts for the number of servings you desire.

• A cover is used on the soup to hold in the heat and speed the heating process.

• A saucer makes an easy cover or use the plate on which you will set the soup bowl for serving.

• Soup stays hot for several minutes if left covered so heat it first while assembling a sandwich. Then heat the sandwich while soup stands.

CANNED SOUP

Setting: HIGH

1. Divide contents of 10½-oz. can of condensed soup between 2 or 3 glass soup bowls. Add equal amounts of water to each. Cover with small plate.

2. MICROWAVE for 5 to 6 MINUTES or until steaming hot. Let stand 1 minute to distribute heat.

TIP For 4 to 6 servings using 2 cans of soup, MICROWAVE for 8 to 9 MINUTES.

Pictured: Hamburger, this page, and Hot Dog, page 19.

Hot Dogs Know-How

- Wieners need only heating so the wiener and bun for a hot dog sandwich can be heated together, making these especially easy.

- We suggest wrapping the sandwich loosely in a paper napkin. This wrapping holds the wiener inside the bun and helps hold in some of the heat while allowing the steam to be absorbed by the paper napkin.

- To avoid cooling the hot wiener when adding relishes, add the mustard, catsup, pickles or relish before heating.

- These timings are based on room temperature buns and refrigerator temperature wieners; the wieners are the size that come from 1 lb. package with 10 wieners.

- Larger wieners will take longer and in some cases may need to be heated separately since the bread could overheat and toughen before the larger wiener is hot.

- If the buns are frozen, they can be used with the refrigerated wieners, using the same times, since the filling, not the bread, is the main factor in sandwich timing.

HOT DOGS

Setting: HIGH

1. Place wieners in split hot dog buns and wrap each one loosely in paper napkin or paper towel in oven.

2. MICROWAVE until heated through:
    1 hot dog — 30 to 35 SECONDS
    2 hot dogs — 45 to 50 SECONDS
    4 hot dogs — 1 to 1½ MINUTES
    6 hot dogs — 2 to 2½ MINUTES

TIPS Heat wieners without buns on glass plate. MICROWAVE until warm: 1 wiener 25 to 30 SECONDS; 2 wieners 35 to 40 SECONDS; 4 wieners 50 to 55 SECONDS; 6 wieners 1 to 1¼ MINUTES.
- MICROWAVE on MEDIUM for a little longer.

Leftover Scrambled Egg Know-How

- It is easy to make extra scrambled eggs for breakfast and then reheat leftovers for lunchtime sandwiches.

- Toast the bread first to give more body to the sandwich. If using a bun which has a crust, the toasting step is optional.

- Our times are based on leftover cold scrambled eggs. For warmer eggs, times are reduced slightly, depending on temperature.

- If eggs have cooled completely, the sandwiches can be assembled early, loosely wrapped and stored in refrigerator.

SCRAMBLED EGG SANDWICH

Setting: HIGH

1. For each sandwich, toast 2 slices of bread. If desired, butter and spread with catsup or mustard.

2. Top one slice of toast with cool scrambled eggs (about 2 eggs per sandwich). Cover with other slice of toast. Place on paper napkin or plate.

3. MICROWAVE for 1 to 1½ MINUTES or until egg steams when bread is lifted. Let stand 1 minute to distribute the heat.

1 Sandwich

TIPS For Cheese 'n Egg sandwich, use only 1 scrambled egg per sandwich and top with slice of Cheddar or Swiss cheese. Reduce cooking time to about 45 seconds or until cheese is melted.
- Chopped ham and green pepper can be added to egg before scrambling for a Denver flavored egg sandwich.

Arrangement of Food Know-How

- Wieners normally require a longer time to cook than any of the fillings.

- By placing the wieners in an outside circle, they will be heated first.

- The quicker cooking filling is placed in the center of the dish; since this center is the more difficult to heat spot, the filling will not be overcooked before the wieners are done.

- However, the filling should not be mounded too high in the center.

- The temperature and density of the filling will affect heating times. These times are based on room temperature fillings.

- These can be prepared and left covered on plates ready for quick, fix-yourself heating. If stored in refrigerator, add about 30 seconds to the cooking time for each plate.

WIENERS IN THE ROUND

Setting: HIGH

1. For each serving, take 2 wieners, slice almost through at ½-inch intervals on outside edge.

2. On serving plate with slit sides of wieners to the outside, bring the 2 wieners together to form a circle.

3. Fasten ends together with toothpicks.

4. Fill center with pork and beans, baked beans, canned spaghetti, macaroni and cheese, sauerkraut, German potato salad or mashed potatoes. Brush wiener with catsup or barbecue sauce.

5. MICROWAVE one plate at a time, for 1½ to 2 MINUTES, or until hot. Remove toothpicks and serve. If desired, garnish with crushed potato chips or French fried onion rings.

Bread Know-How

• Bread that is first toasted has more body and supports the filling better after heating; untoasted bread tends to become very limp when heated.

• For sandwich making, the firmer textured breads make the best sandwiches. Very light, airy bread can be used, but it is easier to overcook, causing the bread to become tough and chewy.

• During heating of bread items, the moisture in the bread becomes hot and turns to steam.

• If breads are covered, this steam will make the bread and crust soggy; if left uncovered, this steam escapes into the oven.

• As with the bread items for breakfast, sandwiches are best heated on a paper or cloth surface that absorbs the moisture from the roll.

Sandwich Know-How, for Creamy Fillings

• We find the differences in melting times of cheese very slight so you can use any cheese of your choice in almost any recipe. We especially like Cheddar, American or Swiss with the tuna flavor.

• Mushroom soup adds a mild, creamy flavor to tuna and cheese in this easy to heat open-faced sandwich.

TUNA 'N CHEESE SANDWICHES

> 1 can (6½ oz.) turn fish, drained
> Half of 10½-oz. can condensed cream of
>   mushroom soup
> 4 slices bread, toasted
> Onion or garlic powder
> 4 slices cheese

Setting: HIGH

1. In small mixing bowl, combine tuna and soup, breaking tuna into small pieces.

2. Place toasted bread on paper napkin covered plate or tray. Spread with tuna mixture. Sprinkle with onion powder; top with cheese slices.

3. MICROWAVE for 2 to 2½ MINUTES or until cheese is bubbly.

4 Sandwiches

TIPS Since the tuna, soup and cheese contain salt, the sandwiches will be too salty if onion salt is used for powder.

• If desired, omit onion powder and top hot sandwiches with a few French-fried onion rings. The heat from the sandwich will warm the onions while keeping their crispness.

Pictured above: Tomato Cheese Sandwich, this page, and Canned Tomato Bisque Soup, page 18.

Pictured next page: Tacos, page 21, and Wieners in the Round, page 19.

Open Face Sandwich Know-How

• The cheese is placed over the tomato in an open face sandwich because you only want to warm the tomato, rather than cook it.

• Times are similar for both open-faced and regular sandwiches with 2 pieces of bread. The filling is usually the important factor in deciding cooking times because bread heats quickly and easily.

TOMATO CHEESE SANDWICH

> 1 slice of bread, toasted
> Mayonnaise or salad dressing
> 2 slices tomato, ½ inch thick
> 1 slice process American cheese,
>   ¼ inch thick

Setting: HIGH

1. Spread toasted bread slice with mayonnaise. Top with tomato slices, then cheese. Arrange sandwich on napkin or towel in oven.

2. MICROWAVE for 35 to 45 SECONDS or until cheese bubbles and is melted.

1 Sandwich

TIPS If natural cheese is used, cook a few seconds longer.

• MICROWAVE on MEDIUM for 45 to 60 SECONDS.

• If desired, use crumbled bacon as garnish.

Ground Beef Know-How

• For chunks of ground beef in a recipe, first crumble it into the cooking dish and cook for about 5 minutes. This sets the meat which can then be stirred to break the meat into the size pieces desired.

• After you drain off the fat juices, add the seasonings so that you do not lose the seasoning when you drain the juices.

• If you use lean ground beef, there is very little excess fat and no need to drain.

• The filling for tacos is easily cooked in the microwave oven; the meat filled shells can be heated to serve piping hot if necessary.

• This mixture should thicken during cooking, so leave uncovered to allow the steam to evaporate.

• To eliminate spatters in the oven, place a paper towel over the casserole dish; this is porous enough to allow some moisture to pass through or be absorbed.

SLOPPY JOE SANDWICHES

    1 **lb. ground beef**
  ½ **cup chopped onion**
  ½ **cup chopped green pepper**
    1 **tablespoon packed brown sugar**
    1 **teaspoon salt**
  ½ **teaspoon paprika**
  ¼ **teaspoon pepper**
    1 **cup (8 oz.) tomato sauce**
    6 **hamburger buns**

Setting: HIGH

1. Crumble ground beef into 2-quart glass casserole. Stir in onion and green papper. Cover with glass lid or plastic wrap.

2. MICROWAVE for 5 MINUTES; drain. Stir in remaining ingredients, except buns; recover, and MICROWAVE for 12 to 14 MINUTES or until hot. Let stand, covered, 5 minutes before serving. Spoon into warm hamburger buns.

About 6 Servings

TIP Warm 6 buns 25 to 30 seconds.

TACOS

    1 **lb. ground beef**
1½ **teaspoons chili powder**
  ½ **teaspoon salt**
  ½ **teaspoon garlic powder**
  ¼ **teaspoon pepper**
  ⅛ **teaspoon cayenne pepper**
  ¼ **cup water**
      Taco shells
      Cheddar cheese, shredded
      Lettuce, shredded
      Onion, finely chopped
      Tomato, chopped

Setting: HIGH

1. Crumble ground beef in 1-quart glass casserole.

2. MICROWAVE for 6 MINUTES; drain. Stir in seasonings and water.

3. MICROWAVE for 3 to 4 MINUTES or until meat is well done.

4. Fill each taco shell with about 2 heaping tablespoons of meat filling. Top with remaining ingredients.

10 to 12 Tacos

TIP Taco shells can be heated for about 30 seconds.

CARAMEL APPLES

    1 **package (14 oz.) caramels**
    2 **tablespoons hot water**
    6 **medium apples**
    6 **wooden sticks**

Setting: HIGH

1. Place unwrapped caramels in buttered deep medium-size glass bowl. Add water. Cover with plastic wrap.

2. MICROWAVE for 2 to 3 MINUTES. Stir and MICROWAVE for about 2½ MINUTES or until melted.

3. Skewer each apple with wooden sticks. Dip each apple in melted caramel mixture; turn to coat evenly. Place dipped apples on buttered cookie sheet or buttered wax paper.

6 Apples

TIPS If caramel mixture thickens while dipping apples, return to oven and re-soften, covered, on ROAST

• Buttering cookie sheet or wax paper keeps caramel from sticking to cooling surface and pulling off apple.

• MICROWAVE on MEDIUM for about 5 MINUTES.

Refreshing Baked Goods Know-How

- The oven can be used to quickly heat purchased or homemade baked goods to give them a freshly baked taste.
- They should be heated just until they feel warm and are a temperature that can be eaten immediately.
- They can be warmed on either a paper or glass plate.

WARM CAKE SQUARES

Setting: HIGH

1. Place squares of UNFROSTED cake on paper napkin, plate or glass serving plate.

2. MICROWAVE just until cake feels warm:
     1 piece — 15 to 20 SECONDS
     2 pieces — 25 to 30 SECONDS
     3 pieces — 35 to 40 SECONDS
     4 pieces — 50 to 55 SECONDS

TIP Do not use frosted cake because the frosting might melt in the time it takes for a room temperature cake to become warm.

WARM COOKIES

Setting: HIGH

1. Place cookies on paper napkin or plate.

2. MICROWAVE uncovered, just until cookie feels warm:
     1 cookie — 10 to 15 SECONDS
     2 cookies — 15 to 20 SECONDS
     3 cookies — 20 to 25 SECONDS
     4 cookies — 25 to 30 SECONDS

TIP If you were to overcook a cookie, it would become dry and might cause raisins or dates, which attract energy because of their high sugar content, to be too hot or even burned.

Sauce Know-How

- This thick fudgy sauce used the convenience of frosting mix. Keep on hand for quick reheating.

Chocolate Know-How

- Melt chocolate on HIGH setting.

LICKETY THICK FUDGE SAUCE

    ⅔ cup (5-oz. can) evaporated milk
    1 package (15.4 oz.) fudge frosting mix
    ½ cup butter or margarine

Setting: HIGH

1. In 4-cup glass measure, measure milk; stir in frosting mix until moistened. Add butter.

2. MICROWAVE for 4 to 5 MINUTES, stirring occasionally and watching carefully at the last minute to avoid boiling over. Serve warm or cool over cake, ice cream or pudding.

3 Cups Sauce

TIP MICROWAVE on MEDIUM for 6 to 7 MINUTES.

Cobbler Know-How

- A roll or cookie on top of prepared pie filling, canned fruit or prepared pudding makes a quick and tasty dessert that can be prepared and heated in a serving dish.
- The dessert should be heated just until it reaches serving temperature.
- Although a roll is usually larger than a cookie, they will heat in similar times because the roll is more porous than a cookie.

QUICK COBBLER DESSERT

Setting: HIGH

1. For each serving, spoon ½ cup prepared pie filling, canned fruit and syrup or prepared pudding into glass serving dish. Top with a sweet roll or a soft cookie.

3. MICROWAVE until warm:
     1 serving — 35 to 40 SECONDS
     2 servings — 1 to 1½ MINUTES
     3 servings — 1½ to 1¾ MINUTES
     4 servings — 1¾ to 2 MINUTES

S'mores Know-How

- The marshmallow heats far faster than the chocolate so they need to stand a minute after cooking to allow the heat from the marshmallow to melt the chocolate.
- The S'mores are wrapped in a napkin to hold in the heat and melt the chocolate.
- The marshmallow puffs about 3 times its size when it heats and the napkin helps control this puffing so the marshmallow will not push the top cracker off and then roll off the bottom cracker.

S'MORES

Setting: HIGH

1. For each S'more, place 2 squares of milk chocolate candy bar on a graham cracker square.

2. Top with 1 large marshmallow and then another graham cracker square. Wrap in a napkin. MICROWAVE until marshmallow melts:
     1 S'more — 15 to 20 SECONDS
     2 S'mores — 25 to 30 SECONDS
     3 S'mores — 35 to 40 SECONDS
     4 S'mores — 45 to 50 SECONDS

Let stand 1 minute to melt chocolate.

TIPS Graham crackers can be spread with peanut butter before topping with chocolate. Use same cooking times.
- When using miniature marshmallows, use 9 marshmallows for each S'more.
- If you were to overcook a marshmallow, it would scorch. It will turn dark and scorch first in the center before any dark spot shows on the outside.

Pictured: Caramel Apples, page 21, S'mores, page 22, and Pudding, this page.

Tapioca Know-How

● This interesting fruit tapioca has the consistency of sauce when warm and is set up like pudding when cold. It makes an easy and good addition to fresh fruits in season.

● As with pudding, stirring is necessary to distribute the heat and to distribute the tapioca that will tend to settle toward the bottom.

● Stirring is most important during the second half of cooking when the tapioca begins to thicken.

● The container is covered with a tight fitting lid to hold in the heat and speed the cooking process because you are cooking fruits as well as thickening tapioca.

● This tapioca has a water base rather than milk base so it will not boil over easily.

FRUIT TAPIOCA

   3 **medium apples, sliced**
   2 **tablespoons butter or margarine**
   ½ **teaspoon salt**
   ¼ **teaspoon cinnamon or nutmeg**
   1 **tablespoon lemon juice**
   ⅓ **cup quick-cooking tapioca**
   1 **cup packed light brown sugar**
   2¼ **cups water**

Setting: HIGH

1. In 2-quart glass casserole, combine all ingredients; cover.

2. MICROWAVE for 10 to 12 MINUTES or until apples are tender, stirring occasionally. Serve warm or cold.

6 Servings

TIP Try with 3 cups cut-up rhubarb, or 3 cups (1½ pts.) blueberries. For best color, use white sugar with these fruits.

Pudding Know-How

● Puddings and sauces cook easily in the oven because the heat comes from all sides, eliminating the possibility of scorching.

● Stirring occasionally is necessary to distribute the heat and to mix in the thickening ingredients that tend to settle toward the bottom.

● The stirring is only necessary during the last half of the cooking time and then only about once every minute.

● Pudding can easily be put in the oven to cook while you start to prepare foods for lunch or dinner. It is then slightly warm for serving after meals.

● Garnish pudding with toasted coconut, fresh fruits, crushed cookie crumbs or baked pastry leftovers.

Cooking Container Know-How

● In selecting a cooking container, it is best to use one that holds twice the milk measurement because when the mixture starts to boil it will rise in the container.

● A 4-cup measure is very convenient because the milk can be measured and then the pudding added. A 1-quart (4 cup) mixing bowl can also be used if you prefer.

Utensils Know-How

● A wooden spoon or rubber scraper that is being used for stirring can be left in the pudding for short cooking periods.

● The wood may become a little warm, but will not affect the cooking times or the stirring utensil.

PUDDING

Setting: HIGH

1. Select favorite flavor of 4-serving size pudding and pie filling mix.

2. In 4-cup glass measure, measure milk as directed on package. Stir in pudding mix, stirring until dissolved.

3. MICROWAVE for 5 to 6 MINUTES or until mixture starts to boil, stirring occasionally during last half of cooking time. Pour into 3 or 4 serving dishes and cool.

3 to 4 Servings

TIPS For 6-serving package of pudding, use 1½-quart glass mixing bowl or pitcher and MICROWAVE for 8 to 9 MINUTES.

● Not stirring the pudding will cause it to be lumpy. If this happens, just beat until smooth with an egg beater or wire whip.

● Leftover refrigerated pudding can be heated in the oven to a freshly cooked temperature by heating one serving, about 30 seconds or until warm. Let stand 1 minute to distribute the heat.

BEGINNING TO COOK **Dinner**

The dinner menus provide timing helps to organize your meal preparation so all will go smoothly. The menus are only guides to give you an idea of what can be done with your oven and how foods are prepared one at a time, in sequence. If you feel like preparing only one or two of the recipes in a particular menu, by all means go ahead. The information in this section is here to acquaint you with your oven, how it cooks and some suggestions about what it can do for you.

Becoming familiar with the speed of microwave cooking may be easier if you make a practice of checking foods shortly before they should be done. In other words, tend to undercook rather than overcook when you first begin with your oven. You can always cook the food a little longer if necessary.

MENU

Fillet of Sole in Almond Butter, 26
Parslied Rice, 133
Tomatoes with Mayonnaise Topping, 26
Relishes
Grand Marnier Sauce with Cake or Fruit, 26

This menu has quick-cooking last minute foods, which means table setting and relish or salad preparation should be done before the main dishes are begun. If expecting company, you may want to do as much preparation as possible before your guests arrive so that you can spend more time with them.

In this menu we suggest YOU DO WELL IN ADVANCE: THE RELISHES, ASSEMBLING THE TOMATOES, AND PREPARING THE SAUCE AND FRUITS OR CAKE SQUARES. Although the Grand Marnier Sauce will be served warm, it is easier to cook first and then reheat while clearing main course dishes just before serving dessert. Wait to add the liqueur until after reheating for the strongest liqueur flavor.

With these quick-cooking, last minute foods, rice may be easiest to prepare conventionally and then, if necessary, reheat in the serving dish just before placing on the table. If preparing in the oven, COOK RICE BEFORE THE FISH AND TOMATOES as it needs to stand about 10 minutes after cooking. You may want to add a little parsley to the rice just before serving.

THE FIRST PART OF FISH RECIPE CAN BE DONE AHEAD: the almonds can be toasted and other sauce ingredients added and then left to stand at room temperature. ADD THE FISH about 10 minutes before serving, and continue with the cooking.

In arranging fish in the baking dish, place larger ends and pieces toward the outside and small, thin pieces toward the center.

Fish is usually cooked covered to speed the cooking process by holding in heat and steam. The covering can be either plastic wrap, since it will not be touching the food, or wax paper across the top of the dish.

Since fish cooks so quickly, standing time is necessary to distribute the heat to the center. When testing doneness, test toward the outside. If this flakes, the center should flake after the fish has been standing several minutes.

Pictured clockwise: Grand Marnier Sauce with cake, page 26, Parslied Rice, page 33, Fillet of Sole in Almond Butter, page 26, Tomatoes with Mayonnaise Topping, page 26.

COOK THE TOMATOES AFTER THE FISH IS COOKED. The tomatoes can be sliced and topped with the mayonnaise mixture up to an hour before time to heat; keep stored in the refrigerator.

The tomatoes can be heated right on the serving plate or dish if can be used in the oven.

A cover is not used on this recipe because it would stick to the topping and the tomatoes heat so quickly that a cover is unnecessary.

If the rice needs reheating, put it in the oven as you place other foods on the table.

While clearing the table, REHEAT THE GRAND MARNIER SAUCE.

Sauces are easy to cook ahead and then reheat before serving. When adding a liqueur as in this recipe, it is best added just before serving. Each time the sauce is boiled or heated a little of the flavor evaporates.

Reheat perked coffee or heat water for instant coffee while placing sauce and fruit or cake on the table.

FILLET OF SOLE IN ALMOND BUTTER

- ⅓ **cup slivered or sliced almonds**
- ⅓ **cup butter or margarine**
- 2 **tablespoons lemon juice**
- 2 **tablespoons white wine or sherry**
- ½ **teaspoon dill weed or seed**
- ½ **teaspoon salt**
- 1 **lb. fresh or frozen sole, halibut or perch fillets, thawed**

Setting: HIGH

1. In 2-quart (8 x 8) glass baking dish, combine almonds and butter.

2. MICROWAVE for 5 to 6 MINUTES or until butter and almonds are golden brown. Stir in lemon juice, wine, dill and salt. Arrange fillets in butter mixture spooning sauce over fillets; cover.

3. MICROWAVE for 5 to 6 MINUTES or until fish flakes easily. Let stand, covered, 2 minutes before serving. If desired, garnish with lemon slices or dill pickle slices.

4 Servings

TIP If desired, omit wine.

TOMATOES WITH MAYONNAISE TOPPING

- 4 **tomatoes**
- **Salt**
- **Pepper**
- ¼ **cup mayonnaise or salad dressing**
- 2 **teaspoons instant minced onion**
- 2 **tablespoons prepared mustard**
- **Paprika**

Setting: HIGH

1. Cut tomatoes in half crosswise; place on glass serving platter or baking dish and sprinkle with salt and pepper.

2. Combine mayonnaise, mustard and onion. Spread on tomato halves. Sprinkle with paprika.

3. MICROWAVE for 3 to 4 MINUTES or until topping begins to bubble. Let stand a few seconds to distribute heat.

TIPS Tomatoes and topping can be assembled up to an hour before heating. Store in refrigerator.

● For 2 tomatoes, use half of the ingredient amounts and MICROWAVE for about 1½ MINUTES.

GRAND MARNIER SAUCE

- ¼ **cup sugar**
- 1 **tablespoon cornstarch**
- ¾ **cup orange juice**
- 2 **to 4 tablespoons Grand Marnier or other orange liqueur**

Setting: HIGH

1. In 2-cup glass measure combine sugar and cornstarch; stir in orange juice.

2. MICROWAVE for 2 to 2½ MINUTES or until mixture boils and thickens slightly, stirring occasionally during last half of cooking time. Stir in liqueur. Serve warm or cold.

1 Cup Sauce

TIP To use as a fondue dip, reduce cornstarch to ½ tablespoon. Serve with fresh fruits, cake squares, ice cream, steamed pudding or a dessert soufflé.

MENU

Chicken Atop Rice, 28
Buttered Carrots, 27
Creamy Wilted Lettuce, 28
Ice Cream with
Warm Topping

This dinner can be prepared in less than an hour. You can assemble most of the other foods in this menu during the half hour it takes to cook the chicken.

COOK BACON for Creamy Wilted Lettuce first because it is easier to cook before starting the other parts of the meal than at the last minute. If the salad were the only food being prepared in the oven, the bacon could be cooked just before completing the salad. While the bacon is cooking, begin preparing the chicken dish.

Arrange chicken on the rice with larger, thicker ends toward the outside of the dish.

If you want to cook the giblets with the chicken, tuck them under other pieces of chicken toward the center of the dish so they will not overcook.

Paprika is sprinkled on the chicken to accent the browning that will take place in the microwave oven. If you prefer more browning or a crisper skin, place the chicken under the broiler while cooking other food in the microwave oven. The chicken will brown and stay hot at the same time.

Chicken cooks with a piece of wax paper placed loosely over the top. The wax paper holds in enough heat to speed the cooking and yet the chicken pieces have a chance to brown.

WHILE THE CHICKEN COOKS, prepare the buttered carrots and the salad dressing for cooking. Wash and tear the lettuce into pieces, slice the onions and return to the refrigerator; set the table.

COOK CARROTS after chicken is cooked, covered and set aside.

Most fresh vegetables are best cooked with a small amount of water and then seasoned before serving. Salt added during the cooking would draw moisture out of the carrots.

Vegetables are cooked covered and with a small amount of liquid. This provides steam in the cooking dish so that they will not become dry. Stirring helps vegetables cook evenly and keeps them moist from the liquid in the bottom of the dish. When not stirred or if overcooked, the top carrots may become slightly withered.

THE SALAD DRESSING COOKS when the carrots are done. As it is cooking, place the chicken and carrots on the table, leaving them covered to hold in the heat. When the dressing is cooked, mix with lettuce and onions and bring to the table.

The bacon and warm dressing can be cooked in the same salad dish used for serving. If you are planning to use a wooden salad bowl, cook bacon and dressing in a glass bowl and then assemble the salad in the wooden bowl because the wooden bowl would dry out and might crack with repeated use in the oven.

When clearing the table, pour a jar of prepared ice cream topping into a serving glass pitcher or bowl and HEAT TOPPING in the oven about 45 seconds or until bubbles begin to appear. Stir to distribute heat and spoon over ice cream. If you are heating about a half jar of topping, it can be left in its original container. However, a completely full jar of topping boils over very easily and can be difficult to pick up without a handle.

BUTTERED CARROTS

   4 to 5 medium carrots, sliced
   2 tablespoons water
   2 tablespoons butter or margarine
   ¼ teaspoon salt
   ¼ teaspoon dill weed, if desired

Setting: HIGH

1. In 1-quart glass casserole combine carrots and water; cover.

2. MICROWAVE for 6 to 7 MINUTES or until carrots are just about tender, stirring occasionally. Add butter, salt and dill weed.

3. MICROWAVE for 1 to 1½ MINUTES, stirring once after butter melts to glaze carrots. Let stand, covered, several minutes to finish cooking.

5 to 6 Servings

CHICKEN ATOP RICE

1½ cups quick-cooking rice, uncooked
½ cup (4 oz. can) drained mushroom
    stems and pieces
1 stalk (½ cup) celery, chopped
1 can (10½ oz.) condensed cream of
    chicken soup
1 soup can milk (1⅓ cups)
2½ to 3-lb. frying chicken, cut up
1 teaspoon salt
Paprika
Poultry seasoning

Setting: HIGH

1. In 2-quart (12 x 7) glass baking dish, combine rice, mushrooms, celery, soup and milk; mix well.

2. Cut larger pieces of chicken in half for uniform size. Arrange on top of rice, skin-side up. Sprinkle with salt, paprika and poultry seasoning. Cover with wax paper.

3. MICROWAVE for 28 to 30 MINUTES or until chicken is done.

5 to 6 Servings

TIPS Other flavors of cream soup can be used; try celery and omit chopped celery, try mushroom and omit mushrooms or try asparagus soup.
• MICROWAVE on MEDIUM for 30 to 35 MINUTES.

CREAMY WILTED LETTUCE

6 slices bacon
½ cup sour cream
1 egg, slightly beaten
¼ cup vinegar
2 tablespoons sugar
Dash salt
1 head (6 cups) lettuce, torn
3 to 4 medium green onions, sliced

Setting: HIGH

1. In large glass mixing bowl or serving bowl, MICROWAVE bacon between pieces of paper towel 3 to 4 MINUTES, or until crisp.

2. Remove paper and bacon, leaving about 3 tablespoons drippings in dish. Stir in sour cream, egg, vinegar, sugar and salt.

3. MICROWAVE for 3 to 4 MINUTES or until thickened, stirring occasionally during last half of cooking. Add lettuce, onions and crumbled bacon, tossing until well coated. Serve immediately.

6 Servings

TIPS When fresh spinach is available, use half spinach and half lettuce.
• Extra dressing can be refrigerated for reheating. It is delicious served over sliced fresh tomatoes. Use crumbled bacon as a garnish.

MENU

Ranch Meat Loaf, 29
German Potato Salad, 29
French-cut Green Beans
Easy Rice Pudding, 29

You should allow at least an hour to prepare this dinner when you are first learning to use your new oven. It is better to have too much time because any of the foods can be returned to the oven for quick reheating.

PREPARE RICE PUDDING FIRST because it needs to cool and other foods need to be prepared near serving time.

By using a pudding mix, you can make rice pudding that has the flavor of the old-fashioned baked type and the preparation ease of a pudding mix. The cooking times and directions for preparing plain custard mix are similar to the pudding directions.

THE GERMAN POTATO SALAD IS NEXT because it has more preparation steps and takes longer than the meat loaf. The potatoes take about 10 minutes to cook and during this time you can combine the meat loaf mixture and leave it in the refrigerator. By keeping it refrigerated, the recipe cooking times still apply. If it stood at room temperature long enough to start to warm, the times may be less than the directions state. You may also want to set the table during this time.

German Potato Salad takes a while to make, but we have found it convenient in the oven because the potatoes, bacon and dressing can be quickly cooked. Also, it need not be a last minute preparation since it can easily be reheated.

Potatoes should still feel a little firm when they are removed from the oven. They continue to cook before they are peeled and sliced and cook a little more when added to the hot dressing.

When the bacon drippings add flavor to a recipe, cook the bacon in the same dish used to prepare the remainder of the recipe.

COOK THE MEAT LOAF after the potato salad is cooked and has been set aside, covered, to hold the heat. While it cooks, finish setting the table and put the canned green beans into a serving dish that can also be used in the oven. Cover the beans with a plate to hold in the heat.

When the meat loaf comes out and is standing, HEAT THE BEANS by cooking about 3 minutes or until steaming hot. Return the potato salad to the oven for about 1 minute to heat through.

EASY RICE PUDDING

> 1 package (4-serving size) vanilla pudding and pie filling mix
> 2½ cups milk
> ½ cup raisins
> ½ cup quick-cooking rice

Setting: HIGH

1. In 4-cup glass measure or casserole combine all ingredients.

2. MICROWAVE for 6 to 7 MINUTES or until mixture boils, stirring occasionally during last half of cooking time. Serve warm or cool.

4 to 6 Servings

TIP A 3-oz. package custard mix can be used for pudding mix, preparing and cooking as directed. The custard mix needs to cool before it will set.

RANCH MEAT LOAF

> 1½ lbs. ground beef
> 2 cups soft bread cubes
> ½ cup finely chopped celery
> ½ cup catsup
> ¼ cup finely chopped green pepper
> 1½ teaspoons salt
> 1 egg, beaten

Setting: DEFROST

1. Combine all ingredients in medium mixing bowl; mix well. Pat into (8 x 4) glass loaf dish.

2. MICROWAVE for 35 to 40 MINUTES or until well done in center. Let stand, covered, 5 minutes before serving.

5 to 6 Servings

TIPS Drizzle with catsup and garnish with parsley.
• Meat loaf can be prepared several hours ahead and stored in the refrigerator. Microwave longer.
• MICROWAVE on MEDIUM for 25 to 30 MINUTES.

GERMAN POTATO SALAD

> 4 medium potatoes
> 4 slices bacon
> ½ cup (1 med.) chopped onion or 6 green onions, sliced
> 2 tablespoons sugar
> 1 tablespoon all-purpose flour
> 1 teaspoon or cube beef bouillon
> 1 teaspoon salt
> ¼ teaspoon ground allspice, if desired
> Dash pepper
> ¼ cup vinegar
> ½ cup water

Setting: HIGH

1. Cook potatoes as directed on page 117; set aside. In glass mixing bowl (can be bowl in which you will serve the salad), cut bacon into pieces so that it will lie in a single layer in bowl.

2. MICROWAVE for 3 to 3½ MINUTES, or until crisp. Remove bacon leaving drippings in bowl. Add onion to drippings.

3. MICROWAVE for 1 MINUTE. Stir in sugar, flour, bouillon, salt, allspice and pepper. Blend in vinegar and water.

4. MICROWAVE for 3 to 4 MINUTES or until mixture boils and thickens, stirring twice. While mixture cooks, peel potatoes. Slice potatoes into hot mixture and toss lightly to coat potatoes. Crumble bacon over top and serve warm.

4 to 5 Servings

TIPS Salad can be prepared several hours ahead and then heated, covered, in oven about 1 minute.
• For 2 to 3 servings, use half of ingredients, MICROWAVE bacon 1½ to 2 MINUTES, and dressing mixture 2 MINUTES.

MENU
One Dish Macaroni Beef, 31
Tossed Salad
Hot Dinner Rolls
Pineapple Upside Down Cake, 31

This meal can be prepared, including dessert, in less than 45 minutes.

FIRST COOK UPSIDE DOWN CAKE so it can cool while the rest of the meal is being cooked. When time for dessert, the cake should still be slightly warm.

Many cake mixes can be cooked in the oven, but we would suggest starting with upside down cake since the timing is less critical. Upside down cake has an exceptionally moist, delicate texture. When a sweet pineapple or other fruit layer is added to the bottom of the cake, part of the energy is attracted to the sweet fruit layer, allowing the cake to cook more slowly and evenly.

Most cakes and baked type products are cooked uncovered. The top has more of a crust-like appearance when moisture can escape.

While the cake is cooking, PREPARE THE MACARONI AND BEEF CASSEROLE. When the cake comes from the oven, begin cooking the casserole. Use a tight fitting lid to hold in the heat and moisture.

WHILE CASSEROLE COOKS, prepare the salad, set the table and arrange rolls in basket for heating.

PLACE ROLLS IN OVEN 30 seconds to heat when casserole is cooked and other foods are on the table.

Pictured clockwise: Pineapple Upside Down Cake, this page, One Dish Macaroni Beef, this page, Hot Dinner Rolls and Tossed Salad.

PINEAPPLE UPSIDE DOWN CAKE

   ¼ **cup butter or margarine**
   ½ **cup packed brown sugar**
   6 **slices canned pineapple, drained**
   6 **maraschino cherries**
   1 **package (9 oz.) yellow cake mix**

Settings: HIGH/DEFROST

1. Place butter in 9-inch round glass baking dish.

2. MICROWAVE on HIGH for about 2 MINUTES or until melted. Stir in brown sugar. Arrange pineapple on top. Place a cherry in center of each pineapple slice. Prepare cake mix as directed on package. Pour over pineapple.

3. MICROWAVE on DEFROST for 7 MINUTES.

4. MICROWAVE on HIGH for 3 to 4 MINUTES or until toothpick inserted near center comes out clean. Let stand 1 minute. Turn out onto platter and serve warm or cool.

                          4 to 6 Servings

TIPS About 1 cup (half of 21-oz. can) of prepared pie filling can be used for the brown sugar and pineapple.
● The Pineapple Upside Down Cake Mix can be prepared as directed on pacakge and cooked, using above times.

ONE DISH MACARONI BEEF

   ½ **lb. ground beef**
   1 **small onion, finely chopped**
   1 **cup uncooked macaroni**
   1 **can (8 oz.) tomato sauce**
 1½ **cups water**
   ⅓ **cup catsup**
   1 **can (7 oz.) whole kernel corn, undrained**
   1 **tablespoon packed brown sugar**
   ½ **teaspoon salt**
   ¼ **teaspoon pepper**
   ¼ **teaspoon chili powder**

Settings: HIGH/DEFROST

1. Crumble ground beef in 2-quart glass casserole. Stir in onion. Cover with glass lid.

2. MICROWAVE on HIGH for 3 MINUTES. Drain and stir in remaining ingredients; recover.

3. MICROWAVE on DEFROST for 35 to 40 MINUTES or until macaroni is tender. Let stand, covered, 5 minutes, and stir before serving.

                          4 to 6 Servings

MENU

Ham Slice in Orange Sauce, 33
Simple Scalloped Potatoes, 33
Fresh or Frozen Broccoli, 33
Salad
Apple Pie, 33

Microwave an "all American" dinner – ham, scalloped potatoes and fruit pie. This menu calls for four dishes cooked in the microwave oven. Before starting, think through the entire menu. And, while you're cooking, check oven setting and timing device before putting the next dish in the oven.

The easy three-recipe cooking sequence for beginning cooks is adaptable to this meal if the pie is baked earlier in the day. If you elect to make a tossed salad, mix greens ahead of time, refrigerate and toss with dressing just before dinner.

COOK POTATOES BEFORE HAM AND BROC-COLI because potatoes cook the longest of the main meal foods and hold the heat while they are standing covered. They can be peeled and mixed with other ingredients while the pie is in the microwave oven. Then they will be ready to cook when the pie comes out.

In this easy recipe for scalloped potatoes, the ingredients for a white sauce cook and thicken as the potatoes cook.

The casserole called for may seem a little large, but the extra space is necessary to allow the milk to boil. With a smaller casserole, part of the milk may boil over, making it necessary to add more milk toward the end of the cooking time.

The potatoes are occasionally stirred to mix those at the outside that cook first with those in the center that cook more slowly. The stirring also helps mix the white sauce as it cooks. In a recipe such as this, you may want to stir 3 or 4 times during the cooking process. While the potatoes cook, prepare the ham slice and set the table.

COOK THE HAM SLICE when the potatoes are finished cooking. The ham is cooked now because it holds the heat better than the vegetable.

A specially purchased ham slice can be used for this or buy a ready-to-eat boned ham and cut a slice of about the same thickness. If you can use the remaining ham, this is probably a better buy than the ham slice.

The cooking time allows the sauce to boil and thicken and the ham to heat through. If the slices are thinner than in this recipe, the time needed to heat will be less.

Since ham shapes and sizes vary, you can use any shallow dish that will hold the ham slice easily. If you are using smaller individual slices of ham, use a 1½-quart (10 x 6 or 8-inch round) glass baking dish. While the ham slice cooks, prepare the broccoli and fix a salad of your choice.

MAKE THE APPLE PIE AHEAD because it is easy to reheat after cutting and placing on serving plates. A two-crust pie cooked only in the microwave oven will not brown and will not be crisp. A pastry shell of a one crust pie can become crisp because the filling is cooked separately. When there is moisture from a filling as in a two crust pie, some conventional cooking is needed to dry and crisp the crust.

Since the filling cooks very quickly in the microwave oven, the crust will be more crispy and flaky than when cooked just conventionally. The crust is evenly hot when it goes into the conventional oven which provides even browning.

For a golden brown color, use the pie crust stick or mix that has a yellow color to the dough, or add 7 to 8 drops yellow food color to the water for your home recipe pastry. While it is in the microwave oven, you can begin preparing other foods to go into the oven.

COOK THE BROCCOLI after the ham is cooked and covered with a tight fitting cover or foil to hold in heat.

Frozen and fresh vegetables cook quickly in the oven and retain a fresh flavor and bright color.

The vegetables are covered to hold in the heat and steam and to prevent dehydration. By placing frozen vegetables in the container, icy side up, the moisture runs over the vegetables as they cook.

With frozen broccoli, additional water is not necessary during the cooking process. With fresh, a little extra moisture is needed to keep the vegetables from dehydrating. This water addition varies with each vegetable.

Salt tends to draw moisture out of foods, so we suggest adding it after cooking. If it is more convenient to put on before cooking, place it in the bottom of the dish before adding the vegetable.

Where it is possible to arrange the spears in the cooking dish, as with a fresh vegetable, the part that takes the longest to cook (stalk) is placed toward the outside of the dish.

If foods are still piping hot, place them on table, removing covers just before sitting down to eat. If they have cooled, return to oven for about 1 minute to heat before placing on table along with broccoli.

When it is time for dessert, HEAT COFFEE BEFORE THE PIE because the coffee will take longer to heat and will hold the heat better than the pie.

FRESH APPLE PIE

Setting: HIGH

1. Prepare favorite recipe for two crust fresh apple pie in 9-inch glass pie plate. Preheat conventional oven to 450°F. while preheating.

2. MICROWAVE pie, for 7 to 8 MINUTES or until apples are just about tender or juice begins to bubble through slits in the crust. Transfer to preheated oven.

3. Bake for 10 to 15 minutes or until light golden brown.

9-inch Pie

TIPS To cook other fruit pies or unbaked frozen fruit pies, see Pie Chapter.
• To reheat slices of pie, MICROWAVE 1 slice for about 15 SECONDS; MICROWAVE 2 slices for about 25 SECONDS.

SIMPLE SCALLOPED POTATOES

    5 **cups (4 medium) peeled and sliced potatoes**
    1 **tablespoon all-purpose flour**
    1 **teaspoon salt**
    ¼ **cup chopped onion**
    1½ **cup milk**
    1 **tablespoon butter or margarine**

Setting: HIGH

1. In 2½ or 3-quart glass casserole, arrange sliced potatoes. Add flour, salt, and onion; toss lightly. Stir in milk and dot with butter; cover.

2. MICROWAVE for 15 to 18 MINUTES or until potatoes are desired doneness, stirring occasionally. If desired, sprinkle with paprika or parsley.

3. Let stand, covered, 5 minutes to finish cooking.

4 to 5 Servings

TIPS For 2 to 3 servings, use half the ingredients in 1½ or 2-quart casserole and MICROWAVE about 10 MINUTES.
• MICROWAVE on MEDIUM for 20 to 22 MINUTES.

HAM SLICE IN ORANGE SAUCE

    ½ **cup packed brown sugar**
    1 **tablespoon cornstarch**
    ⅛ **teaspoon ground ginger**
    1 **cup orange juice**
    8 to 10 **whole cloves**
    1 **ham slice, cut 1-inch thick**

Setting: DEFROST

1. In shallow glass baking dish (a size that ham slice will fit), combine brown sugar, cornstarch and ginger. Stir in orange juice. Add ham slice, turning to coat both sides. Sprinkle with cloves.

2. MICROWAVE for 12 to 15 MINUTES or until hot and bubbly, ocassionally spooning sauce over ham. Let stand, covered, 2 minutes to finish cooking.

4 to 5 Servings

TIP For ½-inch thick ham slice, use half the orange sauce and MICROWAVE for 8 to 9 MINUTES — serves 3 to 4.

BROCCOLI

Setting: HIGH

1. Place frozen broccoli spears from a 10-oz. package in 1-quart glass casserole, icy side up; cover.

2. MICROWAVE for 6 to 7 MINUTES or until just about tender, rearranging once. Let stand, covered, 1 to 2 minutes to finish cooking. Drain and season as desired.

4 Servings

TIP For 2 packages of broccoli spears, use 1½-quart glass casserole and cover. MICROWAVE for 9 to 10 MINUTES.

MICROWAVE TIME SAVERS **Adapting Recipes**

Here are some tips on microwave cooking various food items, and what you should expect when you cook such foods in your microwave. Keep them handy while you are learning to use your microwave!

FOODS	WHAT TO EXPECT
Fruits & Vegetables	Tender-crisp end results. Penetration of microwaves uses natural moisture in fruits and vegetables to cook. They do not depend on thermal transfer of heat from water. Very little additional water needed. Microwaves cook fruits and vegetables and steam conducts heat for even cooking. No scorching.
Fish & Seafood	Fish will be more moist because of lack of dry heat. Excellent results because it is a tender high-moisture product, often cooked in sauces, which create excellent results.
Poultry & Game Birds	Microwaves increase surface temperatures because of attraction to fat. Good tender poultry. Skin will be soft except for more fatty birds, such as duckling. Golden brown rather than crispy brown.
Meats Roasting tender cuts such as rib, leg of lamb, pork loin	Microwaves increase surface temperatures because of attraction to fat, causing browning. Meat will brown somewhat but not as much as with conventional cooking. Standing time is important, as some cooking occurs after removing from the oven. This happens by conduction of heat, occurring from the outside toward the center. Use meat thermometer for doneness.
Braising less tender cuts such as chuck, heel or round roast	Not as much browning as conventional cooking. Defrost button, lower cooking setting, allows for tenderizing of meat fibers; the longer the cooking, the more tender the results. Complementary cooking by pre-browning on top of conventional range will enhance results.
Stewing less tender cuts such as stew beef	Some ingredients tend to cook at different rates. Acceptable results in minimum time. The longer the cooking, the more tender the results. Use less liquid for stew than in conventional cooking, as no evaporation occurs. Use Defrost.
Frying tender cuts of meats such as bacon, steak or chops	Bacon will brown because of high fat content. No searing occurs on steak and chops without browning grill. Breaded products will not be as crisp because of the steam rising to the surface of foods, resulting in a moist surface.
Baking tender cuts such as meatloaf and ham	Good results. Not as much crisping on outside as with conventional cooking. Cured meat must be watched carefully, as overcooking may happen easily because microwaves concentrate in spots with food containing sugar.
Appetizers & Sandwiches	Toasted bread gives better results. Do not assemble canapés until ready to microwave, or crackers and toast will be soggy because moisture has no dry heat source to drive it off. Appetizers with crust do not microwave well; pastry because of lack of dry heat. Heated dips in microwave are smooth and free from scorching since cooking occurs from all sides of the dish.

FOODS	WHAT TO EXPECT
Eggs, custard & cheese	The high fat content of the yolk will cook faster than the white. Do not do eggs in the shell because the egg will explode. Scrambled eggs are light and tender. Fried eggs can be done on microwave browning grill. Soufflés and puffy omelets cannot be done because of moist condition in microwave oven. There is no heat to hold and dry structure. Custard requires low power setting to avoid curdling. Cheese must be melted or cooked in recipes at a low power level. Stirring helps in cheese sauce and fondue. Process cheese has better melting properties. Use Defrost setting for best results.
Rice & Pastas	Rehydration must be done through time. Minimal time-saving items. Add 1 tablespoon cooking oil to boiling water to prevent boilovers. Use large dish, or rub oil around edge of dish.
Sauces & Fillings (thickened by starch)	Blend thickening agent well at beginning. Exceptional results. Stir half-way through cooking to prevent lumpiness. Scorching is no problem because cooking occurs from all sides at once. Use slightly less liquid than conventional recipes because evaporation does not occur.
Frostings & Candies	Use buttered large bowl. Requires very little stirring. Check temperature with candy thermometer after cooking periods. Microwaves are attracted to sugar mixtures and cook fast. Excellent results. Since this food reaches high temperatures, use a heat proof dish.
Cakes, Quick Breads, Yeast Breads & Cookies	Lack of dry heat source develops these products in a unique way. Since they are not restricted by a crust, they are fluffier. Top of cakes will be moist and wet-looking after cooking, as steam rises to surface. Do not overcook to remove this moist appearance from these baked goods, as they will toughen. When adapting a conventional recipe, use about half the amount of baking powder and soda. Baked products will be pale (except chocolate) and not crusty. Low power setting may help prevent irregular shaped top. Will not bake angel food and chiffon cakes. Select cookies such as bars that need no browning and are soft.
Pies	Flaky crust but does not brown. Acceptable. Cook crust first before adding wet filling to be cooked to prevent sogginess. Complementary cooking gives excellent results by starting in the microwave and finishing conventionally.
Frozen Foods	Reheat well in microwave. More moisture than with conventional cooking. Better results on lower settings. Important to use dish that conforms to shape of frozen food to prevent overcooking of melted food. Breaded foods do not get crisp.
Combining Foods	Several foods cooked at same time in a microwave will cook at a different speed. Cooking time will at least double from the fastest cooking item. Remove food as it gets done.

MICROWAVE TIME SAVERS **Tips**

BUY AND STORE FOR EASY MICROWAVE MEAL PREPARATION

● Live alone? Buy a beef round steak when the "price is right." Divide and freeze in pieces, strips and cubes for future microwave meals. Use more tender top round for steak pieces; less tender bottom round for strips and cubes. At least 4 "singles" meals can be cut from a 2½ to 3-pound beef round steak.

● Ask the meat man to saw a large package of frozen fish into individual servings. Keep frozen at home; use one at a time.

● Order a larger piece than needed when buying a standing rib roast, boneless sirloin tip roast, pork loin roast or ham for company. Have the meat man slice off 1 to 3 individual steaks or chops for future use.

● Season a pound of ground beef, then shape and freeze individual patties — microwave as needed.

● Freeze individual portions of meat in flat single layers. When ready to use thaw quickly on DEFROST.

● Freeze left-overs in single-serving-portions for a few days on a paper plate placed in a plastic bag. Heat on uncovered plate on HIGH.

● Make party appetizer mixtures or dips ahead. Refrigerate or freeze until party time. Put toppings on crackers just before heating so crackers stay crisp. See Appetizers and Beverages chapter for ideas.

COOKING KNOW-HOW

● "Mix well" means just that. Blend liquids completely to avoid separation during cooking.

● Stir food thoroughly and/or turn it over, when specified, to assure rearrangement of mixtures in cooking containers. Microwaves cook first at the edges of a dish.

● Avoid possible steam burns. Split or pierce plastic wrap covers before removing from hot dishes.

● Cover dishes and casseroles with a glass plate or saucer (without metal trim) if no glass lid, plastic wrap or wax paper are available.

● Evaporation is minimal in microwave cooking. When adapting favorite recipes, find a model recipe in this book because less butter and liquid will probably be needed.

● Trim excess fat from all meat to prevent fatty meat juices and oven spatters.

● Small cubes and thin strips of meat cook and tenderize fastest.

● Cut pot roasts in half or quarters. Rearranging is easier and even cooking is assured.

● Bone and fat cause variations in meat roast cooking time. Use the meat roasting chart on page 73 as a guide. A meat thermometer, however, is the only accurate test for doneness. Only a microwave meat thermometer can be used in the oven during cooking.

● Do not try to cook eggs in the shell in a microwave oven. Pressure builds up inside shell and can cause egg to burst.

● Make a big pot of coffee for breakfast. Remove grounds and let coffee cool. Microwave cup-by-cup as needed, thus avoiding bitter flavors that often develop when coffee is kept hot over long periods of time.

● When heating several cups of beverage at once, place them on a glass tray or in a shallow glass dish to move them easily in and out of the oven.

● Marshmallows melt beautifully when added to a cup of cocoa during the last 15 seconds of heating. Let the kids each add their own and watch the process.

● Heat a snifter of brandy or a glass of wine — enjoy superb aroma and flavor.

● Barbecuing for a crowd? Grill meat out of doors ahead of time. Finish cooking and heating in the microwave oven when guests arrive — or reverse the procedure.

● Poach eggs in individual dishes so every person has his done "exactly right."

● Toast bread for hot sandwiches in a conventional toaster. Bread has more body and doesn't get soggy during heating.

● Cooked meat heats most evenly if thinly sliced and layered in sandwiches.

● Reheat individual servings of meat or main dishes quickly on a dinner plate.

● Warm leftover custards and pour over unfrosted cake for a dessert change.

● Freshen or heat a piece of leftover pie right on a glass serving plate.

● Defrost or freshen cookies in a wink on a paper napkin or paper-doilie-lined glass serving plate (without metal trim).

FIRST COURSE **Appetizers**

APPETIZER KEY: "Non-critical" appetizers and dips microwave nicely on HIGH in a few minutes because the ingredients cook easily without precise timing or watching. Many appetizers are very convenient because they can be made ahead and then heated right on a plastic tray, paper plate or in a serving bowl or dish. You can heat or reheat just the amount that you need at a time. The fillings for canapés can be made ahead and the base toasted but they should be assembled just before heating and serving to prevent any sogginess. Refresh any limp potato chips or crackers by heating a plateful about 1 minute; let stand another minute to crisp. Microwave on lower setting any appetizer food or mixture which contains a "critical" ingredient — cheese that may burn; shellfish that may toughen; mushrooms that may "pop"; meat mixtures that should blend and tender-cook gently.

Microwave appetizers in glass casserole or baking dish. Use a fitted glass cover, plastic wrap or wax paper.

Bowl-shaped natural shells are also safe attractive microwave cooking containers for appetizer mixtures.

WIENERS IN MUSTARD SAUCE

    1 lb. wieners, cut into ½-inch slices
    1 can (10½ oz.) condensed cream
      of celery soup
    1 cup (½ pt. or 8 oz.) sour cream
    ¼ cup prepared mustard
    1 teaspoon prepared horseradish

Setting: HIGH

1. In 1½-quart glass casserole, combine wieners, soup, sour cream, mustard and horseradish; mix well and cover.

2. MICROWAVE for 5 to 6 MINUTES or until sauce begins to bubble around edge of dish, stirring occasionally. Serve with toothpicks.

6 to 8 Servings

TIPS For half a recipe, use 1-quart glass casserole and MICROWAVE on HIGH for 3 to 4 MINUTES.
• MICROWAVE on MEDIUM for 7 to 8 MINUTES.

SWEET-SOUR TIDBITS

    1 can (13¼ oz.) pineapple chunks,
      undrained
    ½ cup packed brown sugar
    ½ teaspoon salt
    4 teaspoons cornstarch
    ¼ cup vinegar
    ½ cup water
    2 cans (5 oz. each) Vienna sausages,
      drain and cut into 1-inch chunks
    ½ green pepper, cut into ¾-inch squares

Setting: HIGH

1. Drain pineapple, reserving ½ cup syrup. In 1½-quart glass casserole, combine brown sugar, salt and cornstarch. Stir in pineapple syrup, vinegar and water.

2. MICROWAVE for 2 to 3 MINUTES or until mixture boils, stirring occasionally. Add pineapple, sausages and green pepper; cover.

3. MICROWAVE for 3 to 4 MINUTES or until hot, stirring occasionally. Serve with toothpicks.

6 to 8 Servings

TIP This recipe can be made ahead through adding pineapple and sausages; refrigerate. At serving time, MICROWAVE 4 to 5 MINUTES.

This bacon-cheese mixture can be put on toast rounds ahead of time because there is no liquid to make the toast soggy.

HOT BACON APPETIZERS

    ½ lb. bacon (about 12 slices)
    ¾ cup (3 oz.) shredded American or
      Cheddar cheese
    2 teaspoons caraway seed
    30 melba toast rounds

Setting: HIGH

1. In 2-quart (12 x 7) glass baking dish, layer bacon between layers of paper towels.

2. MICROWAVE for 8 to 10 MINUTES or until crisp. Crumble bacon into small bowl. Mix in cheese and caraway seed. Arrange toast rounds on glass tray or plates. Top each with a heaping teaspoonful of cheese mixture, spreading to edges.

3. MICROWAVE for 1 to 1½ MINUTES or until cheese is melted.

30 Appetizers

TIP If cooking a plate at a time (about 10 appetizers), MICROWAVE, 15 to 30 SECONDS, or until cheese is melted.

TANGY WIENER PICK UPS

  1 package (⅝ oz.) homestyle or brown
    gravy mix
½ cup cold water
½ cup apple or currant jelly
  2 tablespoons catsup
  1 lb. wieners or smokie links, cut into
    ½-inch slices

Setting: HIGH

1. In 1½-quart glass casserole, combine gravy mix and water; mix well. Stir in remaining ingredients.

2. MICROWAVE for 7 to 8 MINUTES or until sauce thickens and wieners are heated through, stirring occasionally. Serve with toothpicks.

8 to 10 servings

TIP MICROWAVE on MEDIUM for 10 to 11 MINUTES.

This popular Mexican snack can be heated, a plate at a time, in just seconds.

NACHOS

Setting: HIGH

Place a single layer of taco or corn chips on a paper plate or plastic tray. Cut ¼-inch thick slices of cheese into 1-inch squares. Place a square of cheese on each corn chip. MICROWAVE 45 SECONDS to 1 MINUTE or until cheese is melted. Serve. Prepare additional nachos as needed.

TIP MICROWAVE on MEDIUM for 1 to 1½ MINUTES.

TERIYAKI WRAP UPS

  1 tablespoon sugar
  1 tablespoon chopped onion or
    1 teaspoon instant minced onion
  1 clove garlic, minced, or ⅛ teaspoon
    instant minced garlic
¼ teaspoon ginger
¼ cup soy sauce
½ lb. sirloin steak, cut into thin strips
  1 can (5 oz.) water chestnuts, drained

Setting: HIGH

1. In small bowl, combine sugar, onion, garlic, ginger and soy sauce; mix well. Add steak strips, tossing to coat with soy mixture. Let stand 15 to 30 minutes, stirring occasionally.

2. Drain steak strips and wrap each around water chestnut (cut larger water chestnuts in half), fastening with toothpicks. Place on glass plate or shallow baking dish.

3. MICROWAVE for 3 to 4 MINUTES or until steak is desired doneness.

About 16 Snacks

TIPS To make ahead, marinate the steak strips and wrap around water chestnuts. Refrigerate until ready to cook. Increase cooking time by 30 seconds.
● If desired, use ⅓ cup bottled prepared teriyaki sauce for the sugar, onion, garlic, ginger and soy sauce.

(A) Tangy Wiener Pick ups, this page, (B) Escargot, page 41, (C) Teriyaki Wrap Ups, this page, (D) Coquilles St. Jacques, page 53

Chicken livers with broth are cooked in the oven before chopping to make the topping for these hot canapés. Use DEFROST to prevent "popping".

HOT LIVER CANAPES

> 8 oz. chicken livers
> ½ cup water
> 1 cube or teaspoon chicken bouillon
> 1 tablespoon chopped onion
> 2 tablespoons cream or chicken broth
> 2 tablespoons butter or margarine, softened
> ¼ teaspoon salt
> 4 slices bread or 16 crackers

Setting: DEFROST

1. In 1-quart glass casserole, combine chicken livers, water and bouillon; cover.

2. MICROWAVE for 8 to 10 MINUTES, stirring once. Let stand 5 minutes to finish cooking. Remove livers from broth. Chop fine or process in blender until fine.

3. Add remaining ingredients except bread, mixing well. Toast bread and cut each slice into 4 squares. Place squares on napkin-lined glass plate or tray. Top each square with teaspoon of liver mixture. Garnish if desired (see Tip).

4. MICROWAVE for 2 to 3 MINUTES or until hot.

16 Canapés

TIP For garnish, use sliced stuffed green olives, pickled onions, pickle slices, chopped almonds, pimento strips, sliced water chestnuts or add parsley sprigs after heating.

HOT CRABMEAT CANAPES

> 1 cup (7¾-oz. can) crabmeat
> ½ cup mayonnaise or salad dressing
> ½ teaspoon prepared mustard
> ½ teaspoon Worcestershire sauce
> 1 teaspoon prepared horseradish
> ½ cup grated Parmesan cheese
> 6 slices bread, toasted, or 24 crackers

Setting: HIGH

1. In small mixing bowl, flake crabmeat. Add mayonnaise, mustard, Worcestershire sauce and horseradish; mix well.

2. Cut each slice bread into 4 squares. Arrange on 2 napkin-lined glass plates or trays. Top each with about 1 teaspoon crab mixture; sprinkle with Parmesan cheese.

3. MICROWAVE 1 plate at a time, for 1 to 1½ MINUTES or until edges of filling begin to bubble.

24 Canapés

TIP To make ahead, toast bread and combine crab mixture. Assemble and heat just before serving.

PEPPERONI CHIPS

Setting: HIGH

Arrange thin slices of pepperoni or hard salami on paper plate. Cover with paper towel. MICROWAVE about 1 MINUTE for each 10 to 15 slices or until meat is crisp. Serve warm or cold with dips.

TIP Regular salami will not become crisp so be sure to use the hard salami.

(E) Cheese Shrimp Puffs, page 41, (F) Hot Liver Canapés, this page, (G) Nachos, page 38, (H) Hot Clam Dip, page 40.

MIXED SPICED NUTS

- ¾ **cup packed brown sugar**
- ¾ **teaspoon salt**
- 1 **teaspoon cinnamon**
- ½ **teaspoon ground cloves**
- ¼ **teaspoon ground allspice**
- ¼ **teaspoon nutmeg**
- 2½ **tablespoons water**
- 1 **cup walnut halves**
- 1 **cup pecan halves**
- 1 **cup Brazil nut halves**

Setting: HIGH

1. In 1-quart glass casserole, combine brown sugar, salt, spices and water.

2. MICROWAVE for 1½ to 2 MINUTES, stirring once. Add about ½ cup nuts at a time to syrup mixture. Stir with fork until coated. Lift out cup of nuts, draining off excess syrup and place in single layer in oblong glass utility dish.

3. MICROWAVE, 1 cup of nuts at a time, for 4 to 5 MINUTES or until syrup begins to harden slightly (nuts will be somewhat soft yet). Transfer nuts to wax paper to cool until crisp. Continue until all nuts have been cooked.

3 Cups Nuts

STUFFED MUSHROOMS

- 2 **cups (16 oz. or 1 pt.) whole fresh mushrooms**
- 2 **tablespoons butter or margarine**
- ¼ **cup chopped almonds**
- 2 **tablespoons chopped onion or 1½ teaspoons instant minced onion**
- ½ **teaspoon salt**
- 1 **teaspoon lemon juice**
- ½ **cup (1 slice) crumbled bread crumbs**
- 1 **tablespoon sherry or water**

Setting: HIGH

1. Wash mushrooms and remove stems (save and use in sauces, soups or with vegetables). Arrange mushroom caps, hollow side up in pie plate or shallow baking dish. In small glass mixing bowl, combine butter and almonds.

2. MICROWAVE for 3 to 4 MINUTES or until golden brown. Add remaining ingredients except mushroom caps; mix well. Spoon into mushrooms. Cover with wax paper.

3. MICROWAVE for 2 to 3 MINUTES or until hot.

6 to 8 Servings

TIPS To make ahead, stuff mushrooms and refrigerate. When ready to serve, cook as directed, increasing time 30 seconds when mushrooms are completely cold.
- MICROWAVE on MEDIUM for 3 to 4 MINUTES in step 3.

HOT CHEDDAR DIP

- 1 **can (10¾ oz.) condensed Cheddar cheese soup**
- 2 **tablespoons catsup**
- ⅛ **teaspoon leaf oregano**
- ½ **small clove garlic, minced, or 1/16 teaspoon garlic powder**

Setting: HIGH

1. In small glass bowl, blend all ingredients.

2. MICROWAVE for 3 to 4 MINUTES or until hot, stirring occasionally.

1½ Cups Dip

HOT TACO DIP

- 1 **cup (8 oz. or ½ pt.) sour cream**
- 1 **can (10½ oz.) condensed bean and bacon soup**
- ½ **cup (2 oz.) shredded Cheddar or American cheese**
- 2 **tablespoons dry taco seasoning mix**
- ½ **teaspoon instant minced onion**

Setting: HIGH

1. In 1½-quart glass mixing bowl or serving dish, combine all ingredients; mix well.

2. MICROWAVE for 3 to 4 MINUTES or until heated through, stirring occasionally. Serve warm with corn or taco chips.

About 3 Cups Dip

TIPS For a hotter flavored dip, use 3 tablespoons (1 pkg.) dry taco seasoning mix.
- Dry taco dip mix can be used for taco seasoning mix.
- MICROWAVE on MEDIUM for 6 to 7 MINUTES.

HOT CLAM DIP

- 1 **package (8 oz.) cream cheese**
- 1 **can (8 oz.) minced clams, drained**
- 2 **tablespoons chopped almonds**
- 1 **tablespoon instant minced onion**
- 1 **tablespoon prepared horseradish**
- ¼ **teaspoon garlic salt**
- ¼ **teaspoon salt**
- **Dash pepper**
- 3 **tablespoons milk**

Setting: DEFROST

1. In 1½-quart glass mixing bowl or serving dish, soften cream cheese (2 min.). Stir in remaining ingredients.

2. MICROWAVE for 4 to 6 MINUTES or until hot, stirring occasionally. If desired, garnish with paprika or parsley.

About 2½ Cups Dip

TIP To make ahead, mix ingredients together and refrigerate. Heat when ready to serve.

Shrimp are tucked between toast squares and a buttery cheese topping.

CHEESE SHRIMP PUFFS

    8 slices bread or 32 crackers
    ¼ cup butter or margarine
    2 cups (8 oz.) shredded Cheddar cheese
    1 egg, separated
    1 can (4½ oz.) small cooked shrimp

Setting: HIGH

1. Toast bread and cut each slice into 4 squares. Arrange on 2 napkin-lined plates or trays. In glass mixing bowl, soften butter (10 sec.). Cream together butter and cheese. Mix in egg yolk, placing white in small mixing bowl.

2. Beat egg whites until soft mounds form. Fold into cheese mixture. Drain shrimp well and divide among toast squares. Top each, with spoonful of cheese mixture so there is space for spreading during heating.

3. MICROWAVE 1 plate at a time, for 1 to 1½ MINUTES or until hot.

                                            32 Snacks

TIPS Large shrimp can be used, but they are usually more expensive. If using the large shrimp, cut into pieces to divide among the pieces of bread.
• These can be assembled up to two hours ahead and left at room temperature until ready to heat.
• MICROWAVE on MEDIUM for 1½ to 2 MINUTES.

PARTY SNAX

    2 cups bite-size shredded corn cereal
    2 cups oat puffs cereal
    2 cups bite-size shredded wheat cereal
    4 oz. thin pretzel sticks
    1½ cups (½ lb.) Spanish peanuts
    ½ cup butter or margarine
    2 tablespoons Worcestershire sauce
    1 teaspoon each, celery, onion and
       garlic salt

Setting: HIGH

1. In 3-quart glass casserole or mixing bowl, combine cereals, pretzel sticks and peanuts. In 1-cup glass measure or bowl, combine butter, Worcestershire sauce and salts.

2. MICROWAVE for about 1 MINUTE or until melted. Drizzle in fine stream over cereal mixture, stirring to coat evenly.

3. MICROWAVE for 8 to 10 MINUTES or until warm, stirring occasionally. Serve warm or cold.

                                          About 8 Cups

OYSTERS ROCKEFELLER

    1 package (10 oz.) frozen creamed spinach
   12 large oysters
       Tabasco sauce
       Salt
    2 tablespoons butter or margarine
    ¼ cup grated Parmesan cheese
    ¼ cup dry bread crumbs

Setting: HIGH

1. Make small slit in pouch of frozen spinach and place in oven.

2. MICROWAVE for 5 to 6 MINUTES. Place each oyster in individual shell or dish for appetizers; 3 oysters in each shell or small serving dish for main course. Sprinkle with Tabasco sauce and salt.

3. In small glass bowl, MICROWAVE butter 15 seconds. Stir in cheese and bread crumbs. Top oysters with cooked spinach. Sprinkle with crumb mixture. Cover with wax paper.

4. MICROWAVE for 5 to 6 MINUTES or until oysters are done.

            12 Appetizer or 4 Main Course Servings

TIPS If desired, 2 tablespoons slivered almonds can be toasted with butter for topping; MICROWAVE for 3 to 4 MINUTES, stirring occasionally.
• If you prefer Oysters Rockefeller without a cream sauce, use frozen chopped spinach for creamed spinach. Cook as directed, squeeze spinach in paper towels to drain and use it to top oysters.

DEFROST cooks snails and butter sauce in shells without spattering. Lower setting is used as butter has tendency to overflow. The pottery escargot dishes can be used in the oven.

ESCARGOT

    ½ cup butter or margarine
    ½ to 1 teaspoon garlic powder or
       instant minced garlic
    1 teaspoon dried parsley flakes
       Dash nutmeg
    1 can (4½ oz.) snails (about 24)

Setting: DEFROST

1. In 1-cup glass measure or small bowl, combine butter, garlic, parsley and nutmeg.

2. MICROWAVE for 2 to 2½ MINUTES or until butter bubbles. Place snails in the compartments of four special 6-hole dishes or in four sauce dishes. Half fill compartments with seasoned butter, or in sauce dishes pour ¼ of sauce into each dish. Cover loosely with wax paper.

3. MICROWAVE for 1 to 1½ MINUTES or until butter begins to bubble.

                                            4 Servings

TIP When using snails in shells, follow above times.

FIRST COURSE Beverages

HOW TO MAKE HOT BEVERAGES

- Microwave on HIGH.
- Microwave hot drinks in glass or pottery cups and serving pitchers without silver or other metal trim.
- Heat ½ pints of milk in the carton. OPEN carton to prevent bulging. DO NOT OVERHEAT or waxed paper will dissolve.

- Heat liquids almost to a boil for best taste.
- WATCH MILK carefully so it does not boil over.
- Add a marshmallow to hot chocolate drinks during the last 10 to 15 seconds of heating.

BEVERAGE	6-OZ. SERVING	MINUTES	8-OZ. SERVING	MINUTES
WATER OR MILK to make regular tea, instant beverages or instant breakfasts	1 cup 2 cups 4 cups 6 cups	2 to 2½ 3 to 3½ 5 to 6½ 8 to 9	1 mug 2 mugs 4 mugs 6 mugs	3 to 3½ 4 to 5½ 8 to 9 12 to 14
REHEATING COFFEE OR COCOA made with water or milk	1 cup 2 cups 4 cups 6 cups	1½ to 2 2 to 2½ 4 to 5 5 to 6	1 mug 2 mugs 4 mugs 6 mugs	2 to 2½ 3 to 3½ 6 to 7 7 to 8
MILK OR CHOCOLATE MILK in opened ½-pt. waxed carton			1 carton 2 cartons 4 cartons 6 cartons	2 to 2½ 3 to 3½ 5½ to 6 7½ to 8
MILK OR CHOCOLATE MILK	1-qt. glass pitcher	7 to 8		

HOT BEVERAGE KEY: Heat beverages quickly — use Microwave HIGH setting. Reheat cooled beverages at the same setting.

Use glass or pottery pitchers, 8-ounce mugs, juice jars, brandy snifters — and everyday 6-ounce coffee cups. Do not use dishes with gold, silver or other metal trim.

Paper "hot" cups, styrofoam cups and even small waxed milk cartons work in a microwave oven. DO OPEN the carton to prevent bulging. DO NOT OVERHEAT or wax surface will dissolve.

Why keep a coffee pot plugged in all day? Perk coffee, then reheat a cup or two at a time using the directions in the beverage chart next page.

Heat beverages, or water for beverages, almost to a boil for full flavor in the finished drink. Watch milk closely so it does not boil over.

Add instant coffee or tea after water is hot to avoid bitter taste.

The timings in the general heating chart are helpful when you are adapting a home recipe for a beverage with a similar amount. Recipes in this chapter include those for both alcoholic and non-alcoholic beverages and those with a fruit or a milk base. Don't forget, simply reheat any beverage that has cooled.

A temperature of 150°F. is generally a good heating temperature for beverages.

IMPORTANT: Before you begin, refer to the "Beginning to Cook" section for basic technique and these example recipes:

Energy-wise consumers brew coffee once, reheat by the cup using microwaves.

TOM AND JERRYS

> 2 **eggs, separated**
> 1 **cup powdered sugar**
> ½ **teaspoon vanilla**
> **Dash nutmeg**
> **Rum**
> **Brandy**

Setting: HIGH

1. For Tom and Jerry batter, beat egg whites with ½ cup powdered sugar until soft peaks form.

2. Beat egg yolks with remaining ½ cup powdered sugar until thickened, about 5 minutes. Blend in vanilla and nutmeg. Pour over egg whites and by hand, fold together until well blended. (Can be covered and stored in refrigerator for up to two weeks.)

3. To make Tom and Jerrys, fill mugs ¾ full with water and heat, uncovered, using chart on page 42. Add 1 heaping tablespoon of batter and 1½ tablespoons each rum and brandy to each cup; stir to combine. Sprinkle with nutmeg.

About 15 (1 cup) Servings

TIP The prepared batter that you buy can be used for this home recipe batter.

Red cinnamon candies give the peppy flavor to this cranberry punch. It is also good chilled and served over ice.

CRANBERRY SIPPER

> ½ **cup sugar**
> ½ **cup red cinnamon candies**
> 1 **quart (4 cups) cranberry juice**
> 1 **can (6 oz.) frozen pineapple or orange juice concentrate, undiluted**
> 1 **can (¾ cup) water**
> 1 **tablespoon lemon juice**

Setting: HIGH

1. In 1½-quart glass pitcher or bowl combine all ingredients.

2. MICROWAVE for 7 to 8 MINUTES or until hot, stirring occasionally. If desired, garnish with orange slices.

6 (1 cup) Servings

TIP For individual servings, place 4 teaspoons sugar, 4 teaspoons cinnamon candies, 2 tablespoons juice concentrate, 2 tablespoons water and ½ teaspoon lemon juice in each mug. Fill with cranberry juice. Heat, using chart on page 42.

This hot punch is good served plain or with the addition of rum.

MULLED APRICOT NECTAR

> 5 **cups (46-oz. can) apricot nectar**
> 1 **cup orange juice**
> 4 **cinnamon sticks**
> ⅛ **to ¼ teaspoon whole cloves**
> ¼ **teaspoon whole allspice**
> 1 **lemon, sliced, if desired**

Setting: HIGH

1. In 2-quart glass pitcher or bowl, combine all ingredients except sliced lemon.

2. MICROWAVE for 15 to 18 MINUTES or until hot. Stir and remove spices. Garnish with lemon slices.

7 (1 cup) Servings

TIPS Rum can be added to hot nectar. Fill cups ¾ full with mulled nectar; add rum, according to taste, mixing well.

● For individual servings, place ½ cinnamon stick, 2 whole cloves, 2 whole allspice and 1 tablespoon orange juice in each mug. Fill with apricot nectar. Heat, using chart on page 42. Garnish with lemon slice.

This hot punch is terrific for cold weather entertaining. Try it after skiing when warming up around the fireplace.

MULLED ROSE PUNCH

> 1 **tablespoon whole cloves**
> 1 **tablespoon whole allspice**
> 2 **cinnamon sticks**
> 1 **cup water**
> 1 **teaspoon instant tea**
> 1 **can (6 oz.) frozen orange juice concentrate, undiluted**
> 1 **can (6 oz.) frozen Hawaiian punch, undiluted**
> 3 **cups (4/5 quart) Rosé wine**
> **Lemon slices**

Setting: HIGH

1. In 2-quart glass pitcher or bowl, combine spices, water and tea.

2. MICROWAVE for 5 to 6 MINUTES. Remove spices. Stir in orange juice, punch and wine.

3. MICROWAVE for 8 to 9 MINUTES or until hot. Serve with lemon slices.

6 (1 cup) Servings

This beefy tomato juice cocktail makes a good pre-dinner drink or appetizer.

TOMATO NOGGINS

    1 can (46 oz.) tomato juice
    2 cans (10½ oz. each) beef broth
    1 lemon, sliced
    Vodka

Setting: HIGH

1. Fill mugs ⅔ full with tomato juice; finish filling with beef broth.

2. Heat, using chart on page 42. Add lemon slice and 2 tablespoons Vodka to each mug.

        9 (1 cup) Servings

TIP 3 cubes or teaspoons beef bouillon and 2½ cups water can be used for beef broth.

HOT BUTTERED RUM

In each mug, place 1 tablespoon brown sugar; fill mugs ¾ full with water or apple cider. Microwave, using chart on page 42. Add 1 jigger (1½ tablespoons) rum and top with 1 teaspoon butter or margarine.

BOUILLON SIPPER

    2 cans (10½ oz. each) condensed beef
      bouillon
    1⅓ cups (1 soup can) hot water
    2 to 3 tablespoons sherry

Setting: HIGH

1. In 1½ or 2-quart glass pitcher or bowl combine all ingredients.

2. MICROWAVE 6 to 7 MINUTES or until hot, stirring occasionally. If desired, garnish with lemon slices and parsley.

        4 (1 cup) Servings

TIP For individual servings, fill mugs ⅔ full with bouillon. Finish filling with water, adding about 1 tablespoon sherry to each. Heat, using chart on page 42.

HOT SPICED CIDER

    2 quarts (½ gallon) apple cider or juice
    4 cinnamon sticks
  16 whole allspice
  16 whole cloves
    2 tablespoons packed brown sugar
    2 lemons, sliced
    2 oranges, sliced

Setting: HIGH

1. In 3-quart glass pitcher or bowl, combine all ingredients.

2. MICROWAVE for 15 to 18 MINUTES or until hot. Stir and remove spices.

        8 (1 cup) Servings

TIP For making individual servings, place ½ cinnamon stick, 2 whole allspice, 2 whole cloves, scant teaspoon brown sugar, 1 lemon slice and 1 orange slice in each mug. Fill with cider. Heat, using chart on page 42.

A spicy apple cider that is easy to keep on hand for quick reheating. The clove studded orange makes a pretty garnish for the punch bowl or pitcher.

WASSAIL BOWL

    1 orange
    ½ teaspoon whole cloves
  1½ quarts apple cider or juice
    2 tablespoons lemon juice
    3 cinnamon sticks

Setting: HIGH

1. Insert cloves into peel of orange. Place in 2-quart glass pitcher or bowl.

2. MICROWAVE for 2 MINUTES. Add remaining ingredients.

3. MICROWAVE for 8 to 9 MINUTES or until hot.

        6 (1 cup) Servings

TIPS If desired, add 1 to 1½ cups vodka and ¼ cup brandy before serving. Or, pour a little Vodka and Brandy into each mug before filling with the hot punch.

● For individual servings, place 1 orange slice, 4 whole cloves, 1 teaspoon lemon juice and ½ cinnamon stick in each mug. Fill with apple cider and heat, using chart on page 42.

MAIN COURSES **Fish & Seafood**

HOW TO DEFROST FISH AND SEAFOOD

● Thaw fish and seafood in original closed package in a glass baking dish.

● Microwave on DEFROST setting. This thawing technique sends enough heat into food center to warm and defrost it without starting cooking process at outer edges.

● Let fish or seafood rest 5 minutes in package after removing from oven.

● Rinse whole fish or seafood under cold running water to finish thawing center before cooking.

● Carefully separate fish fillets under cold running water.

FISH/SEAFOOD	WEIGHT	DEFROSTING TIME
FROZEN FILLETS: Sole, Perch, Pike, Halibut, Whitefish, Snapper, Flounder	1-lb. pkg.	3 min.; turn over; 3 to 4 min.
WHOLE FISH	1½ to 1¾ lbs.	5 min.; turn over; 5 to 6 min.
SALMON STEAKS (3)	1 lb.	4 to 5 min.
SCALLOPS	12-oz. pkg. 1-lb. pkg.	3 to 4 min. 4 to 5 min.
SHRIMP	8-oz. pkg. 1-lb. pkg.	2 to 3 min. 4 to 5 min.
LOBSTER TAILS (2)	8-oz. pkg.	3 to 4 min.

HOW TO COOK FRESH FISH AND SEAFOOD

● Cook flaky-tender fresh or frozen fish and seafood (thawed) in a microwave oven.

● Thaw fish or seafood before cooking. Use defrosting chart above. Complete thawing under cold, running water.

● Cook fish or seafood in a glass baking dish or casserole. Glass or pottery serving platters may be used if they do not have gold, silver, platinum or other metal trim.

● Place steaks and fillets in baking dish with thicker edges and larger pieces toward outside of baking dish. Arrange small whole fish with tail ends toward center of baking dish.

● Cover cooking dish with a fitted glass lid or plastic wrap tucked tightly across the top. Pierce plastic wrap to slow steam to escape.

● Quick-cook on Microwave HIGH.

● Let fish stand, covered, for 5 minutes to complete cooking.

● Fish is done if it flakes when lifted gently with a fork near center.

FISH/SEAFOOD	WEIGHT	GLASS CONTAINER	MINUTES
FILLETS: Sole, Halibut, Perch, Pike, Whitefish, Flounder, Snapper	1 lb. 2 lbs.	2-qt. (12 x 7) baking dish	6 to 7 min. 8 to 9 min.
WHOLE FISH	1½ to 1¾-lb.	3-qt. (13 x 9) baking dish	10 to 12 min.
SHRIMP OR SCALLOPS	8-oz. pkg.	1-qt. casserole	6 to 7 min.

FISH AND SEAFOOD KEY: You have to taste fish and seafood prepared in a microwave oven to realize what a superior product it is. Delicate, flaky fish and tender seafood will highlight many of your menus.

Your meal planning will have to take into account the speed with which fish cooks. Because it is a fairly last minute food, the table should be set and other foods completely prepared or ready to go into the oven immediately after removing the fish or seafood. If you think that you will find it necessary to reheat fish, try to undercook it the first time.

Oven-cook fish and seafood on Microwave HIGH to retain juices and delicate flavors. DO NOT OVERCOOK!

Most fish and seafood need covering during cooking and standing time. Fish is cooked most often in shallow baking dishes that usually don't have covers so the recipes indicate using wax paper or plastic wrap as a cover. Seafood is most often cooked in a casserole that has an accompanying cover. The covering is especially important during standing time to hold in the heat to cook the center without drying the outside or fish.

Fish: The recipes use whole fish, fillets, steaks and canned fish. Steaks can be substituted for fillets with a slight increase in time, remembering with both to keep the larger end of the fish toward the outside of the cooking dish. The following are some fish that can be used interchangeably in the recipes: sole, perch, halibut, snapper, flounder and whitefish.

Seafood: The recipes include a variety of seafood such as lobster, crab, shrimp, scallops, oysters and clams. Many recipes mention frozen seafood because of its wide availability, but of course, fresh seafood can always be substituted. Seafood cooked in the shell has no different timing than seafood cooked without a shell. Also, serving dishes of natural shell can be used in the oven.

IMPORTANT: Before you begin refer to the "Beginning to Cook" section for basic technique and this example recipe:

Filet de Sole in Almond Butter 26

The hint of lemon in this creamy mushroom sauce goes well with the mild fish flavor.

MUSHROOM-LEMON FILLETS

- ¼ **cup butter or margarine**
- 2 **cups sliced fresh mushrooms**
- ¼ **cup sliced green onion**
- 2 **tablespoons all-purpose flour**
- 1 **teaspoon salt**
- 1 **teaspoon dried parsley flakes**
- 1 **teaspoon grated lemon peel**
- ⅛ **teaspoon pepper**
- 1 **cup milk**
- 2 **lbs. frozen fish fillets, thawed**

Setting: HIGH

1. Place butter, mushrooms and onion in 2-quart (12 x 7) glass baking dish.

2. MICROWAVE for 2 to 3 MINUTES or until onion is partly cooked. Blend in flour, salt, parsley flakes, lemon peel and pepper. Stir in milk; mix well and cover.

3. MICROWAVE for 4 to 5 MINUTES or until mixture bubbles. Stir well. Arrange fillets with thick edges toward outside of dish. Spoon sauce over fillets; cover.

4. MICROWAVE for 11 to 12 MINUTES or until fish flakes easily. Let stand, covered, 5 minutes before serving.

6 to 8 Servings

TIPS Substitute 1 can (4 oz.) mushroom stems and pieces, drained, for fresh mushrooms.
• For 3 to 4 servings, use 2-quart (8 x 8) baking dish and half the ingredients; reduce cooking times to 2 MINUTES for mushrooms, 3 MINUTES for sauce, and 5 MINUTES for fish.

RED SNAPPER AMANDINE

- 1 **lb. frozen red snapper, thawed**
- 1 **teaspoon lemon juice**
- **Salt**

Sauce
- ⅓ **cup slivered almonds**
- ⅓ **cup butter or margarine**

Setting: HIGH

1. Place red snapper in 1½-quart (10 x 6) glass baking dish. Rub lemon juice on top and salt lightly; cover.

2. MICROWAVE for 6 to 7 MINUTES or until fish flakes easily. Let stand, covered, while making sauce.

3. Sauce: Combine almonds and butter in 1-cup glass measure. MICROWAVE for about 2 MINUTES or until melted. Stir and MICROWAVE for 2 to 3 MINUTES or until lightly browned. Serve over fillets.

About 4 Servings

Bits of cucumber and fresh tomato in mushroom soup make an attractive and tasty sauce with fish.

FISH FILLETS IN CUCUMBER SAUCE

    1 medium cucumber, unpeeled and
      chopped
    ½ teaspoon dill weed
    2 tablespoons butter or margarine
    1 can (10¾ oz.) condensed cream of
      mushroom soup
    ⅓ cup sour cream
    1 medium tomato chopped
    2 tablespoons butter or margarine
    ½ teaspoon salt
    2 lbs. frozen fish fillets, thawed

Setting: HIGH

1. Combine cucumber, dill weed and 2 table-spoons butter in 4-cup glass measure.

2. MICROWAVE for 2 to 3 MINUTES or until butter is melted. Stir in soup, sour cream and tomato; set aside. Combine butter and salt in 2-quart (12 x 7) glass baking dish.

3. MICROWAVE for about 1 MINUTE or until melted. Arrange fish with thick edges toward outside of dish. Pour sauce over fish, cover.

4. MICROWAVE for 12 to 14 MINUTES or until fish flakes easily. Let stand, covered, 5 minutes before serving.

6 to 8 Servings

TIP Recipe can be cut in half, using half the ingredient amounts and 2-quart (8 x 8) baking dish. Decrease cooking time to 2 minutes for cucumber, 4 to 6 minutes for fish.

Serve with fruit and you can put a meal on the table in about 20 minutes.

FILLETS WITH LEMON RICE

    1½ cups quick-cooking rice
    ¼ cup chopped onion
    1 teaspoon salt
    1 teaspoon dried parsley flakes
    ½ teaspoon ground thyme
    2 tablespoons lemon juice
    1¼ cups water
    1 lb. frozen fish fillets, thawed
    2 tablespoons butter or margarine
    Dash paprika

Setting: HIGH

1. Combine rice, onion, salt, parsley, thyme, lemon juice and water in 2-quart glass casserole. Arrange fillets on top of rice mixture with thick edges toward outside of dish. Dot with butter; sprinkle with paprika; cover.

2. MICROWAVE for 10 to 12 MINUTES or until fish flakes easily. Let stand, covered, 5 minutes before serving.

About 4 Servings

SOLE IN LEMON PARSLEY BUTTER

    ½ cup butter or margarine
    2 tablespoons cornstarch
    3 tablespoons lemon juice
    1 teaspoon dried parsley flakes
    ⅛ teaspoon celery salt
    Dash pepper
    2 lbs. frozen sole fillets, thawed

Setting: HIGH

1. Place butter in 2-quart (12 x 7) glass baking dish.

2. MICROWAVE for about 2 MINUTES or until melted. Blend in cornstarch, lemon juice, parsley, celery salt and pepper. Dip each fillet in seasoned butter. Arrange fillets with thick edges toward outside of dish; cover.

3. MICROWAVE for 8 to 9 MINUTES or until fillets flake easily. Let stand, covered, 5 minutes before serving.

6 to 8 Servings

TIP For even cooking, place thickest ends of fish toward edges of dish.

Bay leaf adds a special flavor.

SAUCY SOLE IN WINE

    1 lb. frozen sole fillets, thawed
    2 teaspoons all-purpose flour
    ⅓ cup dry white wine or water
    ½ teaspoon salt
    2 green onions, sliced
    1 teaspoon dried parsley flakes
    ½ bay leaf
    2 tablespoons milk

Setting: HIGH

1. Arrange fillets in 1½-quart (10 x 6) glass baking dish with thick edges toward outside of dish. Combine flour and wine in small mixing bowl. Add salt, onions, parsley and bay leaf. Pour over fillets; cover.

2. MICROWAVE for 4 MINUTES. Spoon sauce over fish again; recover, and MICROWAVE for 3 to 4 MINUTES or until fillets flake easily. Let stand, covered, 5 minutes before serving.

About 4 Servings

STUFFED WALLEYED PIKE

 1½ **lbs. fresh whole walleyed pike**
 Salt
 2 **tablespoons butter or margarine**
 2 **tablespoons chopped green onion**
 ⅛ **teaspoon dried parsley flakes**
 ⅓ **cup dry white wine or water**
 1 **cup crushed herb seasoned stuffing mix**

Setting: HIGH

1. Cut off large fin on back of pike. Sprinkle inside of pike with salt; set aside. Combine butter, onion and parsley in medium glass mixing bowl.

2. MICROWAVE for 1 to 2 MINUTES or until onion is partly cooked; stir in wine and stuffing mix. Stuff and tie with string or fasten with toothpicks. Place fish in 2-quart (12 x 7) glass baking dish; cover.

3. MICROWAVE for 5 MINUTES; turn fish, and MICROWAVE for 5 to 6 MINUTES or until fish flakes easily. Let stand, covered, 5 minutes before serving.

About 4 Servings

TIP Place several towels in bottom of oven for absorption of moisture and easy removal of fish after cooking.

Frozen broccoli and fish are thawed in packages, then cooked together and topped with an easy and colorful sauce made from shrimp soup.

HALIBUT DIVAN

 1 **lb. frozen halibut fillets, thawed**
 1 **package (10 oz.) frozen broccoli spears, thawed**
 ½ **teaspoon tarragon**
 1 **can (10¾ oz.) condensed cream of shrimp soup**

Setting: HIGH

1. Arrange halibut in 2-quart (8 x 8) glass baking dish with thick edges toward outside of dish. Place broccoli, stalks toward outside of dish, on top of fillets. Sprinkle with tarragon; cover.

2. MICROWAVE for 12 to 14 MINUTES or until fish flakes easily and broccoli is tender-crisp. Let stand, covered, while making sauce.

3. Pour soup in 2-cup glass measure or glass serving bowl.

4. MICROWAVE for 3 to 4 MINUTES or until hot. Serve sauce over fillets and broccoli.

About 4 Servings

TIPS MICROWAVE frozen broccoli 2 MINUTES to thaw and separate.
● If broccoli is fresh, place in covered casserole with 1 tablespoon water and MICROWAVE for 3 MINUTES to start cooking.

This dish is actually 4 individual servings of fish and stuffing cooked in custard cups. They are cooked right side up but inverted for serving. Great for entertaining.

TURBAN OF SOLE

 2 **tablespoons butter or margarine**
 ½ **cup finely chopped celery**
 ¼ **cup finely chopped onion**
 1½ **teaspoons dried parsley flakes**
 ¼ **teaspoon leaf chervil, if desired**
 ⅛ **teaspoon ground thyme**
 ⅛ **teaspoon pepper**
 1 **teaspoon lemon juice**
 1½ **cups soft bread cubes**
 1 **lb. frozen sole fillets, thawed**

Sauce
 ½ **can (10¾ oz.) condensed cream of mushroom soup**
 1 **tablespoon chopped pimento**
 1 **tablespoon milk**

Setting: HIGH

1. Combine butter, celery, onion, seasonings and lemon juice in medium glass mixing bowl.

2. MICROWAVE for about 2 to 3 MINUTES or until vegetables are partly cooked. Stir in bread cubes; set aside. Butter four 6-oz. custard cups. Line sides and bottom with thin pieces of fish; reserve some pieces of fish for top. Evenly divide stuffing among the 4 custard cups. Top with reserved pieces of fish; cover.

3. MICROWAVE for 5 to 6 MINUTES or until fish flakes easily. Let stand, covered, while making sauce. Invert on serving platter before serving. Spoon Sauce over turban and serve.

4. Sauce: Combine all ingredients for sauce in 2-cup glass measure. MICROWAVE for 1½ to 2 MINUTES or until mixture is bubbly.

4 Servings

TIPS The stuffing can also be used to stuff four 8 to 10 oz. whole fish.
● You can use preseasoned bread cubes and eliminate seasonings in recipe.

Pictured, top to bottom: Stuffed Walleyed Pike, this page, Turban of Sole, above, Salmon Ring, page 50, topped with mushroom sauce, and Halibut Divan, this page.

Garlic in butter sauce gives this dish an added zest.

HALIBUT WITH PIQUANT SAUCE

- ¼ **cup butter or margarine**
- ½ **teaspoon dry mustard**
- 1½ **teaspoons dried parsley flakes**
- ⅛ **teaspoon garlic powder**
- 1½ **teaspoon lemon juice**
- 1 **lb. frozen halibut fillets, thawed**

Setting: HIGH

1. Place butter in 1½-quart (10 x 6) glass baking dish.

2. MICROWAVE for about 1 MINUTE or until melted. Add mustard, parsley flakes, garlic powder and lemon juice. Cut each fillet into 4 pieces. Dip in seasoned butter; arrange with thick edges toward outside of dish; cover.

3. MICROWAVE for 6 to 7 MINUTES or until fish flakes easily. Let stand, covered, 5 minutes before serving.

4 Servings

This recipe has a mild, pleasant salmon flavor with colorful bits of carrot, celery and onion. You need only add rice or noodles and a fruit salad to complete the meal.

TENDER-CRISP VEGETABLES WITH SALMON

- 4 **medium carrots, thinly sliced**
- 3 **stalks celery, sliced ¼ inch thick**
- 6 **small onions, cut in half**
- 1 **cup water**
- 1 **teaspoon salt**
- 3 **tablespoons all-purpose flour**
- 1 **cup milk**
- 1 **can (16 oz.) salmon, undrained and flaked**
- 1 **tablespoon Worcestershire sauce**
- **Dash pepper**
- ½ **cup shredded Cheddar cheese**

Setting: HIGH

1. Combine carrots, celery, onions, water and salt in 2-quart glass casserole; cover.

2. MICROWAVE for 10 to 12 MINUTES or until vegetables are partly cooked. Combine flour and milk in medium mixing bowl; mix well. Stir in flaked salmon, Worcestershire sauce and pepper. Mix into vegetables; recover.

3. MICROWAVE for 11 to 12 MINUTES or until vegetables are tender-crisp and sauce thickened. Stir in cheese. Let stand, covered, 5 minutes before serving.

4 to 6 Servings

SALMON WITH MUSHROOM STUFFING

- 4 **salmon steaks, cut ¾ inch thick**
- ¼ **teaspoon salt**
- ¼ **cup butter or margarine**
- ¼ **cup chopped onion**
- ½ **cup chopped celery**
- 3 **cups soft bread cubes**
- 2 **cups fresh sliced mushrooms**
- 2 **teaspoons dried parsley flakes**
- ¼ **teaspoon salt**
- ⅛ **teaspoon pepper**
- 1 **tablespoon lemon juice**
- ½ **cup milk**

Setting: HIGH

1. Arrange salmon steaks in 2-quart (12 x 7) glass baking dish with thick edges toward outside of dish. Sprinkle with salt; set aside. Combine butter, onion and celery in large glass mixing bowl.

2. MICROWAVE for 2 to 3 MINUTES or until vegetables are partly cooked. Stir in bread cubes, mushrooms, parsley, salt, pepper and lemon juice; mix well. Sprinkle on top of salmon steaks. Pour milk over all; cover.

3. MICROWAVE for 12 to 14 MINUTES or until salmon flakes easily. Let stand, covered, 5 minutes before serving. Garnish with lemon slices.

About 4 Servings

TIP If desired, add 2 tablespoons sherry to stuffing.

This salmon loaf gets its ring shape from a casserole dish with a glass in the center. Canned tuna may be used, also.

SALMON RING

- 3 **eggs, beaten**
- 2 **cups (1-lb. can) red salmon, drained and flaked**
- 1 **cup fine dry bread crumbs**
- ½ **cup (1 stalk) chopped celery**
- ¼ **cup chopped green pepper**
- 2 **tablespoons minced onion or**
  - 2 **teaspoons instant minced onion**
- 1 **tablespoon lemon juice**
- ¾ **cup milk**

Setting: HIGH

1. In 1½-quart glass casserole, combine all ingredients; mix well. Move mixture away from center and place glass in center to make the ring shape.

2. MICROWAVE for 12 to 14 MINUTES or until mixture around glass is set. Remove glass and invert onto serving plate.

6 Servings

TIPS Substitute 2 cans (7 oz. each) tuna for salmon.
- The center of the ring can be filled with creamed peas or other vegetables before serving.
- MICROWAVE on MEDIUM for 18 to 20 MINUTES.

SALMON STEAKS WITH LEMON DILL SAUCE

> 4 **salmon steaks, ¾ inch thick**
> 1 **medium onion, sliced**
> 1 **teaspoon instant chicken bouillon**
> 1 **tablespoon lemon juice**
> 1 **teaspoon dill weed**
> ½ **teaspoon salt**
> 1 **cup water**

Sauce
> 2 **tablespoons butter or margarine**
> 2 **tablespoons all-purpose flour**
> ½ **teaspoon salt**
> ½ **cup light cream**
> 2 **tablespoons lemon juice**

Setting: HIGH

1. Arrange salmon steaks in 2-quart (12 x 7) glass baking dish with thick edges toward outside of dish. Top with onion, instant bouillon, lemon juice, dill, salt and water; cover.

2. MICROWAVE for 10 to 12 MINUTES or until fish flakes easily. Let stand, covered, 5 minutes and serve with hot Sauce. Garnish with parsley.

3. Sauce: Place butter in 2-cup glass measure.

4. MICROWAVE for about 1 MINUTE or until melted. Blend in flour and salt. Stir in cream, lemon juice, fish liquid; mix until smooth.

5. MICROWAVE for 2 MINUTES. Stir and MICRO-WAVE for 1 to 2 MINUTES or until mixture bubbles.

About 4 Servings

TIP For 2 servings, use 1½-quart (8-inch round) baking dish, half the ingredients (can use 1 cube bouillon) and cooking times of about 6 MINUTES for fish and 2 MINUTES for Sauce.

Biscuits start out on the bottom of this casserole, but during cooking, they rise to the top with an attractive glaze from the cheese soup.

TUNA AND CHEESE CASSEROLE

> 1 **can (8 oz.) refrigerated biscuits**
> 1 **can (10¾ oz.) condensed Cheddar cheese soup**
> 2 **cans (6½ oz. each) tuna fish, drained**
> 1 **cup milk**
> 1 **teaspoon parsley flakes or 1 tablespoon minced parsley**

Setting: HIGH

1. In 1½-quart (10 x 6) glass baking dish, arrange biscuits in 2 rows along length of dish. Combine soup, fish, milk and parsley. Spoon over biscuits.

2. MICROWAVE for 12 to 14 MINUTES or until biscuits are no longer doughy, spooning sauce over biscuits once during last half of cooking.

6 Servings

TUNA NOODLE CASSEROLE

> 1 **cup water**
> 1½ **cups uncooked noodles**
> 1 **can (6½ oz.) flaked tuna, drained**
> 1 **can (10¾ oz.) condensed cream of mushroom soup**
> 1 **can (4 oz.) mushroom stems and pieces, drained**
> 1 **can (17 oz.) green beans, drained**
> ½ **cup coarsely crushed potato chips**

Settings: HIGH/DEFROST

1. Pour water into 2-quart glass casserole; cover.

2. MICROWAVE on HIGH for 3 to 5 MINUTES or until water comes to a boil. Stir in noodles. Recover and cook on DEFROST for 11 to 12 MINUTES or until noodles are tender. Drain and stir in remaining ingredients except potato chips; recover.

3. MICROWAVE on HIGH for 8 to 10 MINUTES or until hot. Let stand, covered, 5 minutes. Sprinkle potato chips on top and serve.

6 to 8 Servings

Shrimp adds special flavor to fish stuffing. This recipe can be used for flounder, white fish or catfish as well.

SHRIMP STUFFED TROUT

> 1 **green onion, chopped**
> ¼ **cup finely chopped celery**
> 1 **tablespoon finely chopped pimento**
> 2 **tablespoons butter or margarine**
> 1 **tablespoon lemon juice**
> ¼ **teaspoon leaf chervil**
> **Dash pepper**
> 1 **can (4½ oz.) broken shrimp**
> 1½ **cups coarsely crushed dry bread**
> 1 **egg, slightly beaten**
> 4 **(8 to 10 oz. each) trout**

Setting: HIGH

1. Combine green onion, celery, pimento, butter, lemon juice and seasonings in medium glass mixing bowl.

2. MICROWAVE for 2 to 3 MINUTES or until vegetables are partly cooked. Add shrimp, bread crumbs and egg; mix well. Stuff each trout with ⅓ to ½ cup dressing. Tie trout with string or secure with toothpicks. Place fish, tail ends toward center, in 3-quart (13 x 9) glass baking dish; cover.

3. MICROWAVE for 12 to 14 MINUTES or until trout flakes easily. Let stand, covered, 5 minutes before serving.

About 4 Servings

TIP When cooking less fish, use these cooking times:
> 1 fish — 3 to 4 MINUTES
> 2 fish — 5½ to 6 MINUTES
> 3 fish — 8 to 9 MINUTES

Shrimp is accented by the flavors of a sweet-sour sauce.

SWEET 'N SOUR SHRIMP

    ¼ **cup sugar**
    3 **tablespoons cornstarch**
    ½ **teaspoon ground ginger**
    1 **teaspoon paprika**
    2 **tablespoons soy sauce**
    ¼ **cup vinegar**
  1½ **cups (13¼-oz. can) undrained pineapple tidbits**
    3 **cups (12 oz.) frozen uncooked shrimp**
    3 **medium green or 1 small onion, sliced**
    2 **stalks celery, sliced**
    1 **green pepper, cut into strips**
    1 **large tomato, cut into small pieces**

Setting: HIGH

1. In 2-quart glass casserole, combine sugar, cornstarch, ginger, paprika, soy sauce and vinegar; mix well. Stir in pineapple, frozen shrimp, onions, celery and green pepper; cover.

2. MICROWAVE for 12 to 14 MINUTES or until shrimp is done. Stir in tomato and leave covered a few minutes to heat tomato.

4 to 5 Servings

TIPS If desired, 10-oz. pkg. frozen cooked shrimp can be used. MICROWAVE for 8 to 10 MINUTES or until vegetables are desired doneness.
● For crisp green pepper, add during last 5 MINUTES of cooking.

Scampi is in the same family as shrimp but usually a little larger. The easier-to-find shrimp can be used in this recipe.

WINE SCAMPI

    2 **tablespoons butter or margarine**
    1 **clove garlic, finely chopped**
    3 **tablespoons dry white wine**
    1 **package (10 oz.) frozen uncooked scampi, thawed**
      Parsley

Setting: HIGH

1. Combine butter, garlic and wine in 1½-quart glass casserole.

2. MICROWAVE for 1 to 2 MINUTES or until melted. Add scampi.

3. MICROWAVE for 4 MINUTES. Stir and MICRO-WAVE for about 2 MINUTES or until scampi turns pink. Garnish with snipped parsley. Let stand 5 minutes before serving.

2 to 3 Servings

TIP If you wish to reduce liquid after scampi is cooked, remove scampi to prevent toughening and MICROWAVE liquid, 2 to 3 MINUTES, or until reduced. Return scampi to liquid.

SHRIMP CURRY

    ¼ **cup butter or margarine**
    ¼ **cup chopped onion**
    ½ **cup chopped celery**
    2 **tablespoons chopped green pepper**
    3 **tablespoons all-purpose flour**
    2 **teaspoons curry powder**
    1 **teaspoon instant chicken bouillon**
    ½ **cup water**
    ½ **cup milk**
    1 **package (12 oz.) frozen uncooked shrimp, thawed**

Setting: HIGH

1. Combine butter, onion and celery in 2-quart glass casserole.

2. MICROWAVE for 2 to 3 MINUTES or until vegetables are partly cooked. Stir in remaining ingredients. Cover with glass lid.

3. MICROWAVE for 13 to 14 MINUTES or until shrimp turns pink. Serve over hot rice.

4 to 6 Servings

TIPS If serving curry with rice, cook rice in microwave oven while mixing together other ingredients. Cook curry while rice rests, covered.
● Condiments to pass with curry: toasted coconut, chopped peanuts, pickle relish, chunky sliced green onions, raisins or crumbled crisp bacon.

This makes an easy luncheon dish. You can cook it ahead and then just reheat for serving over toast points or patty shells. Lobster, crab, shrimp or a combination of these go well with the sauce.

NEWBURG

    ¼ **cup butter or margarine**
  1½ **tablespoons all-purpose flour**
    ½ **teaspoon salt**
  1½ **cups light cream**
    2 **egg yolks**
    ¼ **cup dry sherry or water**
    1 **package (12 oz.) cooked lobster, crab or shrimp**

Setting: HIGH

1. Place butter in 1½-quart glass casserole.

2. MICROWAVE for 1 to 2 MINUTES or until melted. Blend in flour and salt. Combine cream and egg yolks; mix well. Stir into flour mixture to form smooth paste. Add sherry and seafood. Cover with glass lid or plastic wrap.

3. MICROWAVE for 5 MINUTES. Stir and MICRO-WAVE for 4 to 5 MINUTES or until mixture thickens. Let stand, covered, 5 minutes before serving. Serve over toast points, patty shells or cooked rice.

5 to 6 Servings

TIP MICROWAVE on MEDIUM for about 1 MINUTE longer in each cooking step.

This will give you a good guide for reheating prebreaded scallops in the oven as well as an idea for a snappy and easy sauce to serve with scallops or other fish.

SCALLOPS WITH DEVILED SAUCE

- 2 packages (7 oz. each) frozen breaded scallops
- ¾ cup milk
- 2 teaspoons snipped chives
- 2 teaspoons Dijon mustard
- ¼ cup sour cream

Setting: HIGH

1. Place frozen scallops on glass serving platter.

2. MICROWAVE for 3 to 4 MINUTES or until piping hot. Combine milk, chives, mustard and sour cream in 2-cup glass measure; mix well.

3. MICROWAVE for 1 to 2 MINUTES or until mixture thickens slightly. Let stand, covered, 5 minutes. Pour sauce over scallops or into gravy boat to pass with scallops.

4 Servings

TIPS Substitute 1 teaspoon dry mustard for Dijon mustard.

• MICROWAVE on MEDIUM for 6 to 8 MINUTES in step 2 and 2 to 3 MINUTES in step 3.

SEAFOOD CREOLE

- 3 tablespoons butter or margarine
- 1 cup finely chopped onion
- ½ cup finely chopped green pepper
- ½ cup finely chopped celery
- 1 clove garlic, finely chopped
- 1½ tablespoons all-purpose flour
- 1 can (28 oz.) whole tomatoes, undrained
- 1 can (6½ oz.) chunk tuna, drained
- 1 can (6½ oz.) crabmeat, drained
- 1 can (4½ oz.) shrimp, drained
- 1 teaspoon salt
- 2 bay leaves
- ½ teaspoon leaf thyme
- ¼ teaspoon allspice
- 1 tablespoon Worcestershire sauce
- ¼ teaspoon Tabasco
- 2 tablespoons dried parsley flakes

Setting: HIGH

1. Combine butter, onion, green pepper, celery and garlic in 2-quart glass casserole; cover.

2. MICROWAVE for about 4 MINUTES or until vegetables are partly cooked. Blend in flour. Stir in remaining ingredients; recover.

3. MICROWAVE for 10 to 12 MINUTES or until hot. Let stand, covered, 5 minutes before serving.

6 to 8 Servings

TIP Serve over hot rice.

Scallops in a creamy wine sauce make a delicious main course or appetizer served in shells or small sauce dishes. You may find it convenient to make ahead and refrigerate or freeze for easy reheating.

COQUILLES ST. JACQUES

- ¼ cup butter or margarine
- ¼ cup chopped celery
- 1 can (4 oz.) sliced mushrooms, drained
- 2 medium green onions, sliced
- 2 tablespoons chopped green pepper
- 2 tablespoons all-purpose flour
- ½ teaspoon salt
- ⅛ teaspoon pepper
- 1 bay leaf
- ½ cup dry white wine
- 1 lb. sea scallops
- 1 tablespoon chopped pimento
- ¼ cup light cream
- 1 egg yolk

Buttered Bread Crumbs
- 2 tablespoons butter or margarine
- 2 tablespoons dry bread crumbs
- 2 tablespoons grated Parmesan cheese

Setting: HIGH

1. Combine butter, celery, mushrooms, onions and green pepper in 2-quart glass casserole.

2. MICROWAVE for 2 to 3 MINUTES or until onion is tender. Stir in flour, salt, pepper, bay leaf and wine; mix well. Add scallops and pimento.

3. MICROWAVE for 5 MINUTES. Stir and MICROWAVE for 1 to 2 MINUTES or until thickened. Mix together in small bowl, cream and egg yolk; stir into scallop mixture.

4. MICROWAVE for 1 to 2 MINUTES or until piping hot. Remove bay leaf. Spoon into 4 natural shells or 1-cup glass serving dishes.

5. Sprinkle about 1 tablespoon Buttered Bread Crumbs on each serving. MICROWAVE for 1 to 2 MINUTES or until heated through. Let stand, covered, 5 MINUTES before serving.

6. Buttered Bread Crumbs: Place 2 tablespoons butter in 1-cup glass measure.

7. MICROWAVE for about 1 MINUTE or until melted. Stir in bread crumbs and Parmesan cheese.

4 Servings

Bouillabaisse

Cooked on HIGH – even with clams – because the clams do not toughen when in a large amount of liquid and not overcooked.

BOUILLABAISSE

     4 **cups water**
     1 **can (8 oz.) tomato sauce**
    ½ **cup finely chopped onion**
     1 **clove garlic, finely chopped**
     2 **tablespoons dried parsley flakes**
  2½ **teaspoons salt**
     1 **teaspoon lemon juice**
    ¼ **teaspoon curry powder**
    ¼ **teaspoon pepper**
     1 **lb. fish fillets, cut into 2-inch pieces**
     1 **package (12 oz.) frozen shrimp, thawed**
     6 **ounces frozen crab or lobster meat, thawed**
     1 **pint oysters or clams**

Setting: HIGH

1. Pour water into 4-quart glass casserole; cover.

2. MICROWAVE for 10 to 12 MINUTES or until bubbly. Stir in remaining ingredients in order given. Recover and MICROWAVE for about 12 MINUTES. Stir and MICROWAVE for 8 to 10 MINUTES or until seafood is done. Let stand, covered, 5 minutes before serving.

10 to 12 Servings

TIPS The fish and seafood can be added either fresh or frozen. In using the frozen, you can add while still frozen and use the maximum cooking time. If they are thawed or fresh the minimal time will be about right.

● Any combination of fish or seafood can be used for this dish. Select the available kinds that are favorites. Cooking times may vary slightly but should fall within the range given. If some pieces are much larger than others, such as lobster tails, cut into smaller pieces.

LOBSTER TAILS

Setting: HIGH

1. Split each 9-ounce tail through top shell. Pull lobster meat out of shell; place on top, but leave connected to shell end. Brush with melted butter or margarine. Sprinkle with paprika. Arrange in 2-quart (12 x 7) glass baking dish. Cover with plastic wrap.

2. MICROWAVE:
     1 lobster tail — 4 to 5 MINUTES;
     2 lobster tails — 7 to 8 MINUTES;
     4 lobster tails — 11 to 12 MINUTES.
Let stand, covered, 5 minutes before serving.

FRESH LOBSTER

    ½ **cup water**
    ½ **teaspoon salt**
  1½ **lb. fresh lobster, pegged**

Setting: HIGH

1. Combine water and salt in 4-quart casserole.

2. MICROWAVE for 2 to 3 MINUTES or until water boils. Place lobster in casserole; cover.

3. MICROWAVE for 10 to 12 MINUTES or until shell turns red. Let stand, covered, for 2 minutes. Split tail; if meat is still translucent in center MICROWAVE for 1 to 2 more MINUTES. Serve with melted or drawn butter.

1 to 3 Servings

TIP A 1½-lb. live crab, such as Dungeoness, can be cooked as above using 3-quart casserole. Pry off shell after cooking.

SCALLOPS POULETTE

    ¼ **cup butter or margarine**
     1 **tablespoon finely chopped onion**
    ¼ **cup unsifted all-purpose flour**
    ½ **teaspoon salt**
    ⅛ **teaspoon pepper**
    ½ **cup dry white wine or chicken broth**
     1 **can (4 oz.) mushroom stems and pieces, drained**
     1 **package (12 oz.) frozen sea scallops, thawed**
     1 **bay leaf**
    ½ **cup light cream**
     1 **egg yolk**
     1 **teaspoon dried parsley flakes**

Settings: HIGH/DEFROST

1. Combine butter and onion in 2-quart glass casserole.

2. MICROWAVE on HIGH for 3 to 4 MINUTES or until onions are partly cooked. Blend in flour, salt and pepper. Stir in wine, mushrooms, scallops and bay leaf; cover.

3. MICROWAVE on DEFROST for 6 MINUTES. Stir and MICROWAVE on DEFROST for 6 to 7 MINUTES or until scallops are fork tender. Combine cream and egg yolk in small mixing bowl. Gradually stir into hot mixture. Recover.

4. MICROWAVE on DEFROST for 5 to 6 MINUTES or until hot. Let stand, covered, 5 minutes before serving. Add parsley and serve.

About 4 Servings

TIP MICROWAVE on MEDIUM for a total of 10 to 11 MINUTES in step 3 and 3 to 4 MINUTES in step 4.

The red color of crabmeat gives this luncheon dish or appetizer a very colorful appearance.

CRAB REGAL

 ¾ to 1 cup (6 to 8 oz.) drained and flaked cooked crabmeat
 ¼ to ½ cup shredded Cheddar or Swiss cheese
 2 tablespoons dry bread crumbs
 2 tablespoons chopped celery
 2 tablespoons salad dressing or mayonnaise
 2 tablespoons milk or cream
 1 tablespoon chopped pimento, if desired
 ½ teaspoon instant minced onion
 ½ teaspoon lemon juice
 ⅛ teaspoon salt
   Dash Pepper

Setting: HIGH

1. In 1-quart glass casserole or mixing bowl, combine all ingredients. Spoon into 2 individual casseroles, sauce dishes or shells.

2. MICROWAVE for 1½ to 2 MINUTES or until edges bubble.

2 Servings

TIPS It is easy to double or triple recipe, cooking 2 at a time.
• This dish can be made ahead and refrigerated. To reheat, MICROWAVE:

    1 dish   — 1 to 2 MINUTES
    2 dishes — 2 to 3 MINUTES
    3 dishes — 3 to 4 MINUTES
    4 dishes — 4 to 5 MINUTES

Fresh clams cooked in a small amount of water will actually be "steamed clams". Overcooking will toughen clams.

CLAMS OR OYSTERS IN THE SHELL

 ¼ cup water
 6 fresh clams or oysters, thoroughly washed

Setting: HIGH

1. In 2-quart glass casserole, bring water to a boil (45 sec.). Arrange clams evenly in casserole; cover.

2. MICROWAVE for 3 to 4 MINUTES. Let stand, covered, 1 to 2 minutes to finish cooking. Check for doneness (clam meat should be firm) and if necessary MICROWAVE longer, about 30 SECONDS.

2 Servings

TIP MICROWAVE on MEDIUM for 5 to 6 MINUTES.

SCALLOPED OYSTERS

 ½ cup butter or margarine
 1½ cups dry bread crumbs
 ½ cup grated Parmesan cheese
 ⅛ teaspoon pepper
   Ground mace
 2 cans (8 oz. each) oysters, undrained
 ¼ cup dry sherry or water

Setting: HIGH

1. Place butter in 4-cup glass measure.

2. MICROWAVE for 1 to 2 MINUTES or until melted. Blend in bread crumbs, cheese, pepper and mace. Arrange half of crumb mixture in bottom of 1½-quart (10 x 6) glass baking dish. Spoon oysters evenly over crumbs. Pour oyster liquid and sherry over all. Top with remaining crumbs.

3. MICROWAVE for 6 to 7 MINUTES or until oysters are hot. Let stand 5 minutes before serving.

4 to 6 Servings

TIPS Substitute canned whole clams for oysters.
• MICROWAVE on MEDIUM for 9 to 10 MINUTES in step 3.

This can be served as a main dish for a light lunch or as an appetizer for dinner. Cream of shrimp soup eliminates making a sauce.

SEAFOOD THERMIDOR

 1 can (10¾ oz.) condensed cream of shrimp soup
 1 can (4 oz.) sliced mushrooms, drained
 1 can (6½ oz.) cooked lobster meat, drained and diced
 ¼ cup milk
 ¼ teaspoon dry mustard
   Cayenne pepper
   Grated Parmesan cheese
   Dash paprika

Setting: HIGH

1. Combine all ingredients, except cheese and paprika, in large mixing bowl; mix well. Spoon into 4 individual glass casseroles or natural baking shells. Sprinkle with Parmesan cheese and paprika.

2. MICROWAVE 4 to 5 MINUTES or until bubbly. Let stand 5 minutes before serving.

About 4 Servings

TIPS To reheat 2 dishes from refrigerator, MICROWAVE, uncovered, 2 to 3 MINUTES.
• MICROWAVE on MEDIUM for 6 to 7 MINUTES.

MAIN COURSES **Poultry & Game Birds**

HOW TO DEFROST POULTRY

● Thaw poultry in its original wrapping including metal clip. Place in a large flat glass baking dish to catch drippings.

● Whole poultry and parts are thawed on DE-FROST. This defrosting technique sends enough heat into meat to warm and defrost center without starting cooking process at outer edges.

● Start whole birds thawing with breast side up. See chart for specific times.

● Poultry should be icy in center when taken from the microwave oven.

● Finish thawing by immersing poultry in cold water. If not completely thawed, poultry will take longer to cook and will not cook evenly.

● Remove loosened giblets from whole birds and set aside for gravy or soup broth.

POULTRY	WEIGHT	SETTING	APPROXIMATE TIME
CHICKEN Whole, fryer	2 to 3-lb.	DEFROST	16 to 20 min.
Whole, roasting	3 to 4-lb.	DEFROST	20 to 25 min.
Cut Up	2½ to 3-lb.	DEFROST	12 to 14 min.
Breasts	4 to 6 (½ lb. ea.)	DEFROST	12 to 15 min.
Drumsticks and Thighs	4 (½ lb. ea.)	DEFROST	6 to 8 min.
Drumsticks	about 1 lb.	DEFROST	5 to 7 min.
Thighs	about 1 lb.	DEFROST	5 to 7 min.
Wings	1½ lbs.	DEFROST	5 to 6 min.
Stewing Hen, cut up	2½ to 3-lb.	DEFROST	20 to 25 min.
Liver and/or Hearts	8 ozs. 2 lbs.	DEFROST	4 to 5 min. 7 to 9 min.
TURKEY Whole	8 to 12-lb.	DEFROST	20 min., rest 10 min.; turn over; 20 min. Stand in cold water about 1 hr.
	12 to 16-lb.	DEFROST	25 min., rest 10 min.; turn over; 25 min. Stand in cold water about 1½ hrs.
	16 to 20-lb.	DEFROST	20 min., rest 10 min.; turn over; 20 min., rest 10 min.; repeat once. Stand in cold water about 2 hrs.

(Continued, next page)

TURKEY (cont.) Breast, Bone-In	4 to 8-lb.	DEFROST	15 min.; rest 10 min.; turn over; 15 min. Stand in cold water about 10 min.
Drumsticks	1 to 2-lb. 2 to 3-lb.	DEFROST	12 to 15 min. 20 to 25 min.
Thigh	1 to 2-lb.	DEFROST	12 to 15 min.
Wings	2 to 3-lb.	DEFROST	15 to 20 min.
CAPON Whole	6 to 8-lb.	DEFROST	20 min., rest 10 min.; turn over; 20 min. Stand in cold water about 1 hr.
DUCKLING Whole	4 to 5-lb.	DEFROST	15 min., rest 10 min.; turn over; 15 min. Stand in cold water for about 30 min.
GOOSE Whole	9 to 11-lb.	DEFROST	25 min., rest 10 min.; turn over; 25 min. Stand in cold water about 1 hr.
PHEASANT Cut up	2 to 3-lb.	DEFROST	10 to 12 min.
ROCK CORNISH GAME HEN Whole	2 (12 oz. ea.) 4 (12 oz. ea.)	DEFROST	12 to 15 min. 15 to 20 min.

HOW TO COOK A FEW CHICKEN PIECES

- Microwave 1 tablespoon butter until melted.
- Roll chicken piece in melted butter, then in seasoned dry bread crumbs.
- Place chicken, skin side down, in glass pie plate or flat baking dish.
- Turn chicken piece(s) over halfway through cooking time.
- Microwave until fork tender.

CHICKEN PIECE	WEIGHT	SETTING	TIME
1 WING OR DRUMSTICK	4-oz.	HIGH	4 to 4½ min.
1 THIGH OR BREAST	5 to 6-oz.	HIGH	5 to 6 min.
3 INDIVIDUAL PIECES Assorted	14-oz.	HIGH	10 to 11 MIN.
1 THIGH-LEG (2 PIECES ATTACHED)	9-oz.	HIGH	7 to 8 min.
1 QUARTER	10-oz.	HIGH	8 to 9 min.

HOW TO COOK POULTRY

- Poultry should be completely thawed before cooking. See defrosting chart page 57.

- Season meat to taste before cooking.

- Place large whole poultry in 3-quart (13 x 9) glass baking dish; small whole birds and poultry pieces in 2-quart (12 x 7) glass baking dish.

- Use a microwave roasting rack in the dish when cooking whole birds.

- Arrange pieces of poultry with skin side up and thick edges toward outside of dish.

- Metal clip holding drumsticks may be left in place on large whole birds during cooking. Pop-out "doneness indicators" may be left in birds but will not indicate doneness in microwave cooking.

- Most whole poultry is cooked uncovered.

- When two different settings are mentioned, use HIGH during first cooking period; DEFROST during the second.

- Stuffing does not increase cooking time.

- Foil may be used to cover portions of the meat that appear to be drying during cooking. Do not allow foil to touch oven interior or the microwaves will arc and pit oven surfaces.

- Chicken and turkey pieces cooked without sauce or crumb coating should be covered during cooking and standing time. Use tightly-tucked plastic wrap or wax paper. Pierce wrap before removing it so steam escapes slowly and does not burn hands.

- Poultry weighing 10 pounds or less should be turned over once during cooking; when over 10 pounds, turn over three times.

- A microwave meat thermometer, registering 170°F. when bird comes from the oven, is an accurate test for doneness with whole birds. When a bird must be turned (Rock Cornish Game Hens are not), insert thermometer into thick part of the thigh after bird is turned the last time. DO NOT use a regular meat thermometer in a microwave oven.

- Other doneness tests: Meat and juices are no longer pink when bird is sliced between leg and body. Leg and thigh meat of small birds is tender when pinched. A conventional meat thermometer, inserted in thickest part of thigh meat after bird comes from oven, registers 170°F. at the end of the cooking time. It is a good idea to check doneness in both thighs in birds weighing 10 pounds or more.

- Poultry skin may be crisped by placing it under a conventional oven broiler for a few minutes before standing time.

- Standing time is ESSENTIAL to complete cooking. Allow whole birds or pieces totaling 10 pounds or less to stand 5 to 10 minutes after being taken from oven. Birds and pieces over 10 pounds should stand 10 to 15 minutes — internal temperature will rise 10°F. to 15°F.

- Cover whole birds tightly with foil during standing time. Cover cut-up poultry with glass lid, plastic wrap or wax paper.

POULTRY	WEIGHT	FIRST SETTING	SECOND SETTING	APPROXIMATE COOKING TIME
CHICKEN				
Whole, fryer	2 to 3-lb.	HIGH	HIGH	8 min. per lb.
Whole, roasting	3 to 4-lb.	HIGH	DEFROST	10 min. per lb.
Cut Up	2 to 3-lb.	HIGH	HIGH	8 min. per lb.
Parts	1 to 2 lbs.	HIGH	HIGH	8 min. per lb.
TURKEY				
Whole	8 to 10-lb.	HIGH	DEFROST	9 min. per lb.
	10 to 14-lb.	HIGH	DEFROST	10 min. per lb.
Breast, bone-in	4 to 5-lb.	HIGH	DEFROST	11 min. per lb.
Parts	2 to 3-lb.	HIGH	DEFROST	15 min. per lb.
CAPON				
Whole	6 to 8-lb.	HIGH	DEFROST	9 min. per lb.
DUCKLING				
Whole	4 to 5-lb.	HIGH	DEFROST	10 min. per lb.
GOOSE				
Whole	9 to 11-lb.	HIGH	DEFROST	10 min. per lb.
PHEASANT				
Cut Up	2 to 3-lb.	DEFROST	DEFROST	9 min. per lb.
ROCK CORNISH GAME HEN				
Whole	4 (12 oz. ea.)	HIGH	HIGH	9 min. per lb.

ROASTING CHICKEN AND TURKEY KEY: All whole birds are turned over during the cooking period to assure even cooking. During the first half of the cooking time, foil is used to cover the thinner parts of the bird (wing tips and end of legs) to prevent overcooking. However, do not use foil if it will touch the walls of the oven because it might cause pitting of the walls.

Roast up to 14-pound whole turkeys in a microwave oven. Start birds on HIGH to warm meat through; then continue cooking on DE-FROST to help meat cook evenly and stay juicy.

To keep the oven clean from spatters, you can loosely cover a bird with wax paper. All roasted birds rest on something to keep them out of the drippings. You can improvise your own device such as crisscrossed wooden spoons or overturned sauce dishes.

A microwave meat thermometer inserted in the thickest part of the thigh registers doneness at 170°F. at the end of the cooking time. Insert thermometer after bird is turned in the oven. DO NOT use conventional meat thermometer in a microwave oven.

Other doneness tests: Meat and juices are no longer pink when bird is sliced between leg and body. A conventional meat thermometer, inserted in thickest part of the thigh AFTER bird comes from oven, registers 170°F.

Standing time is essential to assure a well cooked bird. Follow directions carefully. Internal temperature will rise about 15°F. during standing time.

ROAST CHICKEN WITH ONIONS AND APPLES

4 to 4½-lb. whole roasting chicken
Salt
Pepper
1 medium apple, peeled, cored and quartered
1 medium onion, quartered
1 medium onion, chopped
1 cup applesauce

Settings: HIGH/DEFROST

1. Sprinkle body cavity with salt and pepper. Place quartered apple and onion in cavity. Tie legs together and wings to body. Place chicken, breast side down on microwave roasting rack, in 2-quart (12 x 7) glass baking dish.

2. MICROWAVE on HIGH for 20 MINUTES. Combine chopped onion and applesauce in medium bowl. Turn breast side up; pour on applesauce mixture.

3. MICROWAVE on DEFROST for 20 to 25 MINUTES or until microwave meat thermometer registers 170°F. Let stand, covered with foil, 5 to 10 MINUTES before serving.

4 to 6 Servings

Turkey is in the oven for an adequate time to get a golden brown skin. Because beginning temperatures and type of turkey may vary, we suggest using a thermometer to test doneness. Move thermometer from thigh to breast for a double doneness test. Turkey will be easiest to cook after you have a few weeks experience with the oven so you can best judge doneness. If you notice any dark brown spots developing on the breast bone, we would suggest covering the spots with foil as this indicates overcooking in these areas.

ROAST WHOLE TURKEY

12 lb. frozen turkey, thawed
Salt
Stuffing, if desired
Melted butter or margarine

Settings: HIGH/DEFROST

1. Wash completely thawed turkey; sat aside giblets. Sprinkle inside of cavity with salt. Stuff cavity and neck opening, if desired. Secure opening with toothpicks or metal skewers. Tie drumsticks together and wings to body with string.

2. Place bird, breast side down on microwave roasting rack, in 3-quart (13 x 9) glass baking dish. Brush with butter. (MICROWAVE 10 MINUTES per pound.)

3. MICROWAVE on HIGH for 30 MINUTES. Turn breast side up and continue cooking on HIGH for 30 MINUTES. Turn breast side down. Some areas may cook more rapidly than others; cover these with foil to slow down cooking.

4. MICROWAVE on DEFROST 30 MINUTES. Turn breast side up; insert microwave meat thermometer in thickest part of thigh, and MICROWAVE on DEFROST for 30 MINUTES or until thermometer registers 165°F. to 170°F. in thigh and 175°F. when inserted in breast meat. Let stand, covered with foil, 10 to 15 minutes before serving. Temperature will increase 10 to 15°F. during this time.

About 12 Servings

DUCK, GOOSE AND PHEASANT KEY: Duck, goose and pheasant microwave best when cooked on two power settings: HIGH and DEFROST. Fat rendered from the meat during cooking will spatter less with a lower setting — and these less tender meats have better texture when cooked slowly and gently.

Place whole birds, breast side down, on a microwave roasting rack which holds meat above fat and drippings.

Place rack in a flat glass baking dish.

Quartered or cut up birds are cooked without a rack in a glass casserole or baking dish with thick pieces and edges of meat toward the outside where they cook faster.

Turn birds as recipe specifies to assure even cooking.

Drain fat from pan halfway through cooking to prevent messy oven spatters and possible smoking.

Pheasant is often cooked in sauce and with a cover to keep the naturally dry meat moist.

Crisper outer skin results if birds are placed under a conventional oven broiler for a few minutes before standing time.

Whole birds are cooked if a microwave meat thermometer registers 170°F. when meat is taken from the oven. Cut-up or quartered birds should be fork tender.

Covering birds during standing time is important to complete cooking — follow recipe directions. Internal temperature will rise about 15°F.

See poultry charts at the beginning of this chapter for specific defrosting and cooking times.

ROAST GOOSE

    9 lb. frozen domestic goose, thawed
    1 teaspoon salt
    3 to 4 medium apples, quartered
    8 to 10 dried prunes
    1 teaspoon leaf marjoram

Settings: HIGH/DEFROST

1. Wash goose; remove giblets. Sprinkle inside of cavity with salt. Fill cavity with apples and prunes. Sprinkle with marjoram. Secure openings with toothpicks or metal skewers. Tie legs together and wings to body.

2. Place goose, breast side down on microwave roasting rack, in 3-quart (13 x 9) glass baking dish.

3. MICROWAVE on HIGH for 45 MINUTES. Turn goose breast side up.

4. MICROWAVE on DEFROST for 45 to 50 MINUTES or until microwave meat thermometer inserted in thickest part of thigh meat registers 170°F. Let stand, covered with foil, 10 minutes before serving.

About 10 Servings

TIP MICROWAVE on MEDIUM for same time in steps 3 AND 4.

The fat in duckling cooks out without the excessive spattering that is sometimes present in conventional cooking. The skin browns some and has some crispness; however, if you like crisper skin, you may prefer to put it under the broiler while you are cooking a vegetable in the oven.

DUCKLING A LA ORANGE

    4½ to 5-lb. duckling
    1 teaspoon salt
    2 unpeeled oranges, quartered
    1 clove garlic or ⅛ teaspoon instant minced garlic
    3 peppercorns
    3 to 4 tablespoons orange marmalade

Orange Sauce
    2 tablespoons packed brown sugar
    1 tablespoon cornstarch
    1 tablespoon grated orange peel
    ⅔ cup orange juice
    3 tablespoons duck drippings
    3 tablespoons Curacao, Cointreau or Grand Marnier

Settings: HIGH/DEFROST

1. Wash duckling and set aside giblets. Fasten neck skin with toothpicks or metal skewers.

2. Sprinkle inside of cavity with salt. Stuff main cavity with oranges, garlic and peppercorns. Close cavity securely with toothpicks or metal skewers.

3. Tie legs together and wings to body with string. Cover the ends of legs, tail and wings with small pieces of foil.

4. Place inverted saucers or microwave roasting rack in 2-quart (12 x 7) glass baking dish to hold duck out of juices. Place duck breast side down on saucers.

5. MICROWAVE on HIGH for 25 MINUTES. Remove duck using paper towels as hot pads to platter or cutting board. Drain juice. Remove foil pieces from duck. Turn duck breast side up.

6. MICROWAVE on DEFROST 25 MINUTES or until done. If necessary, cover with wax paper to prevent spattering. Spread skin with marmalade. MICROWAVE on HIGH 4 MINUTES, or for crisper skin, place under the broiler for a few minutes. Let stand while preparing orange sauce. Serve cut in half or quarters (kitchen shears work well) or carved like turkey with Orange Sauce spooned over meat.

Orange Sauce: In 2-cup glass measure combine brown sugar and cornstarch. Stir in orange peel, juice and drippings. MICROWAVE on HIGH for 3 to 4 MINUTES or until mixture boils and thickens. Stir in liqueur.

4 Servings

TIP MICROWAVE on MEDIUM for same times in steps 5 and 6.

It's very quick and simple to reduce the sauce in the oven after cooking the pheasant.

MANDARIN PHEASANT

- **1 pheasant (about 2 lb.), split in half**
- **1 cup (11-oz. can) undrained mandarin oranges**
- **1 tablespoon cornstarch**
- **1 teaspoon grated lemon peel**
- **1 tablespoon lemon juice**
- **½ teaspoon salt**

Setting: DEFROST

1. In 2 or 3-quart glass casserole, arrange pheasant skin side down. Sprinkle with salt. In 2-cup glass measure or bowl, combine liquid from oranges, cornstarch, lemon peel, lemon juice and salt.

2. MICROWAVE for 2 to 2½ MINUTES or until thickened, stirring once. Add oranges and pour mixture over pheasant.

3. MICROWAVE for 20 to 25 MINUTES or until pheasant is done, turning pheasant once. Remove pheasant to serving platter.

4. MICROWAVE remaining sauce, 5 to 6 MINUTES or until thickened. Spoon over pheasant.

2 Servings

TIPS This recipe can easily be doubled. MICRO-WAVE orange sauce 3 to 4 MINUTES; MICRO-WAVE pheasant in 2-quart (12 x 7) glass baking dish, 38 to 40 MINUTES, turning once.
- MICROWAVE on MEDIUM for 18 to 20 MINUTES in step 3.

PHEASANT IN MUSHROOM CREAM SAUCE

- **1 pheasant (about 2 lb.), cut into pieces**
- **¼ teaspoon salt**
- **Dash pepper**
- **2 tablespoons chopped onion**
- **½ cup sliced fresh or canned mushrooms**
- **Half of 10½-oz. can condensed cream of mushroom soup**
- **1 tablespoon cornstarch**
- **¼ cup sour cream**
- **Parsley**

Setting: DEFROST

1. In 2 or 3-quart glass casserole, arrange pheasant skin side down. Sprinkle with salt and pepper. Add onion, mushrooms and cornstarch mixed with cream of mushroom soup; cover.

2. MICROWAVE for 20 to 25 MINUTES or until pheasant is done, turning pheasant once. Stir in sour cream and garnish with parsley.

2 Servings

TIPS This recipe can easily be doubled. MICRO-WAVE covered, in 2-quart (12 x 7) glass baking dish, 36 to 38 MINUTES, turning once.
- MICROWAVE on MEDIUM for 18 to 20 MINUTES.

We've used a crunchy almond stuffing here for contrast with the hens; you may also like to try wild and white rice mix prepared as directed on package as stuffing. 4 hens will take about 30 minutes to cook plus 5 minutes standing time.

STUFFED CORNISH GAME HENS

- **¼ cup butter or margarine**
- **1 teaspoon paprika**
- **4 whole Rock Cornish Game Hens (12 oz. each)**
- **1 teaspoon salt**
- **Almond stuffing**

Setting: HIGH

1. Place butter and paprika in 2-cup glass measure.

2. MICROWAVE for about 1½ MINUTES or until melted; set aside.

3. Salt body cavities of hens. Fill each hen with stuffing. Tie legs together and wings to body. Arrange, breast side up and drumsticks toward center of microwave roasting rack, in 2-quart (12 x 7) glass baking dish. Brush with seasoned melted butter.

4. MICROWAVE for 30 to 35 MINUTES or until microwave meat thermometer registers 170°F. Let stand 5 minutes before serving.

4 Servings

TIPS For variety, use water chestnuts for almonds in stuffing and brush with a glaze of 2 tablespoons butter, 2 tablespoons soy sauce and 2 tablespoons dark corn syrup.
- Do not use meat thermometer in oven when cooking.

ALMOND STUFFING

- **¾ cup butter or margarine**
- **½ cup chopped celery**
- **¼ cup chopped onion**
- **½ cup chopped almonds**
- **4 cups soft bread cubes**
- **1 tablespoon dried parsley flakes**
- **¼ teaspoon salt**
- **1 teaspoon instant chicken bouillon**
- **⅓ cup water**

Setting: HIGH

1. Combine butter, celery and onion in medium mixing bowl.

2. MICROWAVE for 3 to 4 MINUTES or until vegetables are partly cooked. Stir in remaining ingredients; mix well. Stuff poultry.

Stuffs 4 Cornish Hens or 4 to 5-lb. Roasting Chicken

TIP MICROWAVE on MEDIUM for 4 to 5 MINUTES.

Pictured, top to bottom: Stuffed Cornish Game Hens, this page, Orange Burgundy Chicken, page 65, Speedy Chicken Stew, page 65.

TANGY CORNISH HENS

    2 cornish hens, split in half
    1 cup (8-oz. can) undrained crushed
       pineapple
   ¼ cup packed brown sugar
    1 tablespoon cornstarch
    2 tablespoons lemon juice
    1 tablespoon prepared mustard
    1 tablespoon soy sauce

Setting: HIGH

1. Arrange hens in 2-quart (12 x 7) glass baking dish, tucking giblets under hens, if desired. Combine remaining ingredients and spoon over hens; cover.

2. MICROWAVE for 18 to 20 MINUTES or until done, spooning sauce over hens during last half of cooking time. If additional browning is desired, place under broiler. Serve with rice.

4 Servings

TIP Pineapple tidbits can be used for crushed pineapple.

An easy cornish hen and wild rice dish that cooks in just 30 minutes. Since the rice takes longer to cook than the hens, it is cooked partially before adding the hens.

CORNISH HEN AND RICE BAKE

    1 package (6 oz.) white and wild rice mix
   ½ cup (1 stalk) chopped celery
   ½ cup (4-oz. can) drained mushroom
       stems and pieces
  1¾ cups water
   ¼ cup butter or margarine
    2 cornish hens (1 lb. each)
    2 tablespoons butter or margarine

Setting: HIGH

1. In 2-quart (12 x 7) glass baking dish, combine uncooked rice mix (with seasonings), celery, mushrooms and water. Dot top with ¼ cup butter; cover.

2. MICROWAVE for 10 MINUTES.

3. Meanwhile, cut cornish hens in half lengthwise down side of breast-bone (kitchen shears work well). Arrange on top of rice, tucking giblets and neck under each half. Brush with 2 tablespoons butter; Cover.

4. MICROWAVE for 15 to 18 MINUTES or until done.

4 Servings

TIP If desired, reserve 2 teaspoons of seasonings from rice mix and add to butter for brushing hens.

We used the domestic rabbit that is available frozen. If you have wild rabbit, we would suggest marinating it in the sauce overnight before cooking. This will help tenderize the meat.

RABBIT IN SAVORY SAUCE

    2 to 2½-lb. rabbit, cut up
    1 onion, sliced
    1 stalk celery, sliced
   ⅓ cup red wine
    1 can (10½ oz.) condensed golden
       mushroom soup
   ½ teaspoon salt
    1 clove garlic, minced, or ⅛ teaspoon
       instant minced garlic
    1 teaspoon Worcestershire sauce
   ½ bay leaf, crumbled

Setting: HIGH

1. In 2-quart (12 x 7) glass baking dish, arrange rabbit. Top with onion and celery. Pour wine over pieces. Combine soup with salt, garlic, Worcestershire sauce and bay leaf. Spoon over rabbit; cover.

2. MICROWAVE for 35 to 36 MINUTES or until done.

4 to 5 Servings

TIP MICROWAVE on MEDIUM for 40 to 45 MINUTES.

STEWED CHICKEN KEY: Stewed chicken is similar to soup. Microwave first in HIGH to heat quickly; then reduce to DEFROST to tenderize the tougher meat with slow cooking.

OLD-FASHIONED CHICKEN 'N NOODLES

    1 cup chopped celery
    3 green onions, chopped
    1 medium tomato, quartered
    1 tablespoon dried parsley flakes
    2 teaspoons salt
       Dash pepper
  2½ lbs. stewing chicken, cut up
    3 cups water
  1½ cups uncooked egg noodles

Settings: HIGH/DEFROST

1. Combine all ingredients, except noodles, in 3-quart glass casserole. Cover with glass lid or plastic wrap.

2. MICROWAVE on HIGH for 15 MINUTES. Turn chicken pieces over.

3. MICROWAVE on DEFROST for 50 to 60 MINUTES or until chicken is fork tender. Remove chicken from broth; stir in noodles; recover, and MICROWAVE on DEFROST for 10 to 12 MINUTES or until noodles are tender. Remove chicken from bones. Return chicken meat to broth; recover, and MICROWAVE on DEFROST for 3 to 4 MINUTES or until hot. Let stand, covered, 5 minutes before serving.

4 to 6 Servings

FRYING CHICKEN KEY: Most of the recipes have a one step method that simplifies the preparation and enhances flavors. Microwave all chicken and parts on HIGH. If additional browning is desired, chicken may be browned in a flame proof dish or brown under a broiler just before serving. The larger pieces of a chicken are cut to make all the parts more even in size. When arranging chicken pieces, put the larger part of each piece toward the outside of the cooking dish and the smaller part toward the center to aid even cooking.

We suggest using a frying chicken to make a delicious stew because a stewing chicken will remain too tough during the relatively short cooking time.

IMPORTANT: Before you begin refer to the "Beginning to Cook" section for basic technique and this example recipe:

Chicken Atop Rice ....**Page 28**

If you like crisper chicken skin, just place the chicken dish under the broiler while you cook a vegetable in the oven.

ORANGE BURGUNDY CHICKEN

    2½ to 3-lb. frying chicken, cut up
    ½ cup orange marmalade
    ½ cup orange juice
    ½ cup dry red wine
    2 tablespoons cornstarch
    2 tablespoons packed brown sugar
    1 tablespoon lemon juice
    1 teaspoon salt

Setting: HIGH

1. Arrange chicken pieces, skin side down and thick edges toward outside, in 2-quart (12 x 7) glass baking dish. Combine remaining ingredients in medium mixing bowl; pour over chicken; cover.

2. MICROWAVE for 20 MINUTES. Turn chicken over and MICROWAVE for 5 to 6 MINUTES or until chicken is fork tender. Let stand 5 minutes before serving.

4 to 6 Servings

TIPS For half recipe, use 2-quart (8 x 8) baking dish and MICROWAVE for 20 MINUTES.
● A 1¼ to 1½-lb turkey thigh can be used with half this sauce. MICROWAVE in 1½-quart glass covered casserole 15 MINUTES or until done, occasionally spooning sauce over turkey.

We found the flavor as good as with stewing chicken cooked conventionally.

SPEEDY CHICKEN STEW

    2½ to 3-lb. frying chicken, cut up
    2 stalks celery, cut into 1-inch pieces
    1 medium onion, sliced
    1 bay leaf
    4 peppercorns
    1 tablespoon salt
    3 cubes or teaspoons chicken bouillon
    3 cups water
    4 carrots, cut into thin slices
    ¼ cup all-purpose flour

Dumplings
    1½ cups unsifted all-purpose flour
    2 teaspoons baking powder
    ½ teaspoon salt
    1 teaspoon parsley flakes
    ⅔ cup milk
    1 egg, slightly beaten
    2 tablespoons oil

Setting: HIGH

1. In 4-quart glass casserole or Dutch oven, combine fryer, celery, onion, bay leaf, peppercorns, salt, bouillon and water; cover.

2. MICROWAVE for 24 MINUTES, stirring once. Add carrots. Combine ¼ cup flour with ½ cup water. Stir into chicken mixture; recover.

3. MICROWAVE for 8 MINUTES. (Meanwhile, prepare dumplings.)

4. Remove bay leaf and peppercorns; if desired, remove meat from bone at this point. Spoon dumplings by rounded tablespoons onto hot chicken mixture; cover.

5. MICROWAVE for 6 to 8 MINUTES or until dumplings are no longer doughy on underside.

Dumplings: In mixing bowl, combine flour, baking powder, salt and parsley flakes. Combine milk, egg and oil; add to dry ingredients and mix just until moistened. (Mixture will be soft.)

4 to 6 Servings

TIPS For stewed chicken without vegetables and dumplings, MICROWAVE chicken 28 minutes or until tender.
● For variety, add ½ cup raisins and ⅛ teaspoon nutmeg to flour mixture for dumplings.

CHICKEN MAGNIFICO

>   2½ to 3-lb. frying chicken, cut up
>   1 can (10½ oz.) condensed Cheddar
>   cheese soup
>   1 cup (8-oz. can) undrained stewed
>   tomatoes
>   ¼ cup instant minced onion or 1 cup
>   chopped onion
>   1 teaspoon leaf basil
>   ½ teaspoon salt
>   ⅛ teaspoon pepper
>   2 oz. (½ cup) chopped ham
>   Paprika

Setting: HIGH

1. Cut larger pieces of chicken in half for uniform size. Arrange skin side up in 2-quart (12 x 7) glass baking dish.

2. Combine remaining ingredients except paprika. Spoon over chicken. Sprinkle generously with paprika; cover.

3. MICROWAVE for 28 to 30 MINUTES or until chicken is done.

4 to 5 Servings

TIP If you do not have ham on hand, it can be omitted. Other luncheon meats or 1 tablespoon bacon-flavored bits can be used, if desired.

An easy chicken dish with rich, golden flavor and color from mushroom soup. It cooks in just 30 minutes.

GOLDEN CHICKEN

>   2½ to 3-lb. frying chicken, cut up
>   1 stalk (½ cup) celery, chopped
>   1 teaspoon salt
>   1 can (10½ oz.) condensed golden
>   mushroom soup

Setting: HIGH

1. Cut larger pieces of chicken in half for uniform size. Arrange skin side up in 2-quart (12 x 7) glass baking dish. Sprinkle with celery and salt. Spoon soup over top of chicken; cover.

2. MICROWAVE for 28 to 30 MINUTES or until chicken is done.

5 to 6 Servings

TIPS A 2 to 2½-lb. turkey breast can be used with half this sauce. MICROWAVE in 2-quart covered glass casserole for about 20 MINUTES or until done, occasionally spooning sauce over turkey.
● MICROWAVE on MEDIUM for 35 to 38 MINUTES.

Bamboo shoots and water chestnuts add a crunchy texture.

ORIENTAL CHICKEN

>   2½ to 3-lb. frying chicken, cut up
>   ¼ teaspoon salt
>   ⅛ teaspoon pepper
>   ½ cup chicken broth or bouillon*
>   ¼ cup soy sauce
>   1 medium onion, cut into wedges
>   1 tablespoon cornstarch
>   1 tablespoon sugar
>   2 tablespoons water
>   ¾ cup (5-oz. can) drained bamboo shoots
>   ⅔ cup (5-oz. can) drained and sliced
>   water chestnuts

Setting: HIGH

1. Cut larger pieces of chicken in half for uniform size. In 2-quart (12 x 7) glass baking dish, combine salt, pepper, chicken broth, soy sauce and onion. Place chicken in dish, skin side down; cover.

2. MICROWAVE for 30 to 32 MINUTES, turning chicken over once. Remove chicken to serving platter.

3. Combine cornstarch, sugar and water. Add to juices; cover.

4. MICROWAVE for 1½ to 2 MINUTES, stirring once. Add bamboo shoots and water chestnuts.

5. MICROWAVE for 2 to 3 MINUTES or until hot, stirring once. Serve over rice along with chicken.

4 to 6 Servings

TIP *For bouillon you can add 1 chicken bouillon cube or ½ teaspoon instant chicken bouillon to ½ cup water.

A mild, tomato-flavored chicken dish. Canned soups make this traditional dish very easy.

CHICKEN MARENGO

>   2½ to 3-lb. frying chicken, cut up
>   1 can (10½ oz.) condensed golden
>   mushroom soup
>   1 can (10¾ oz.) condensed tomato soup
>   1 clove garlic, minced, or ⅛ teaspoon
>   garlic powder
>   1 lb. (about 16) small whole onions or
>   1⅔ cups (1-lb. can) drained pearl onions

Setting: HIGH

1. In 2 or 3-quart glass casserole, combine all ingredients; cover.

2. MICROWAVE for 28 to 30 MINUTES, stirring once. If desired, thicken sauce with 1 to 2 teaspoons cornstarch dissolved in 2 tablespoons water.

4 to 6 Servings

TIP MICROWAVE on MEDIUM for 35 to 38 MINUTES.

CHICKEN BASQUE

2½ to 3-lb. frying chicken, cut up
¾ cup chopped onion
1 clove garlic, crushed, or ⅛ teaspoon garlic powder
1⅓ cups (two 4-oz. cans) undrained mushroom stems and pieces or 1 lb. fresh mushrooms
3 cups (1 lb. 12-oz. can) undrained tomatoes, broken up
1 cup vermouth or dry white wine
1 teaspoon salt
¼ teaspoon pepper
½ teaspoon each powdered basil and thyme
1 bay leaf, crumbled

Setting: HIGH

1. Cut larger pieces of chicken in half for uniform size. Combine all ingredients in 4-quart glass casserole; cover.

2. MICROWAVE for 30 to 32 MINUTES or until done, stirring once. If desired, thicken sauce with 1 tablespoon cornstarch.

4 to 6 Servings

TIP MICROWAVE on MEDIUM for 35 to 38 MINUTES.

Cook the vegetable in the oven just before you add the bananas and nuts to the chicken.

ISLANDER CHICKEN

2½ to 3-lb. frying chicken, cut up
1 can (6 oz.) frozen orange juice concentrate, thawed
1 tablespoon cornstarch
1 teaspoon salt
¼ teaspoon cinnamon
1 tablespoon lime or lemon juice
2 bananas, sliced
½ cup chopped cashew or macadamia nuts

Setting: HIGH

1. Cut larger pieces of chicken in half for uniform size. Arrange skin side up in 2-quart (12 x 7) glass baking dish. Combine juice concentrate, cornstarch, salt, cinnamon and lime juice. Pour over chicken; cover.

2. MICROWAVE for 28 to 30 MINUTES or until chicken is done, spooning sauce over chicken during last half of cooking time. Add bananas and nuts. MICROWAVE for 1½ to 2 MINUTES.

4 to 5 Servings

TIPS If browner chicken is desired, place under broiler a few minutes before adding bananas and nuts.
• If fixing ahead, add bananas and nuts just before serving because bananas are easy to overcook and the nuts lose their crunchy texture.

This sauce is mild flavored; increase the oregano and garlic if you prefer a zestier sauce.

CHICKEN CACCIATORE

2½ to 3-lb. frying chicken, cut up
2 cups (16-oz. can) tomato sauce
¾ cup (6-oz. can) tomato paste
2 tablespoons instant minced onion or ½ cup chopped onion
1 teaspoon salt
1¼ teaspoons leaf oregano
½ teaspoon garlic powder or 2 cloves garlic
¼ teaspoon pepper
¼ teaspoon powdered thyme
2 cups water

Setting: HIGH

1. Cut larger pieces of chicken in half for uniform size and set aside. Combine remaining ingredients in 4-quart glass casserole or Dutch oven. Stir in chicken pieces, coating with sauce; cover.

2. MICROWAVE for 40 to 45 MINUTES or until chicken is done, stirring once. Serve plain or over spaghetti.

4 to 6 Servings

TIP If desired, use ¼ cup red wine for part of water.

The microwave oven can be used to partially cook chicken before placing on the grill to reduce the total cooking time and to prevent the barbecued chicken being too brown on the outside before the center of the pieces are done.

CHICKEN FOR BARBECUING

Setting: HIGH

1. Arrange a 2½ to 3-lb. cut up frying chicken in 2-quart (12 x 7) glass baking dish with larger pieces toward outside of dish.

2. MICROWAVE for 15 MINUTES.

3. Dip pieces in favorite barbecue sauce and grill over hot coals 15 to 20 MINUTES, turning occasionally until chicken is done and browned.

4 to 6 Servings

TIP This same idea can be used when broiling chicken.

ORANGE GLAZED CHICKEN

 2½ to 3-lb. frying chicken, cut up
  1 can (6 oz.) frozen orange juice
   concentrate, thawed
  ½ cup (4-oz. can) drained mushroom
   stems and pieces
  ½ tablespoon cornstarch
  1 teaspoon dry or prepared mustard
 1½ teaspoons paprika

Setting: HIGH

1. Cut larger pieces of chicken in half for uniform size. Arrange chicken in 2-quart (12 x 7) glass baking dish. Combine juice concentrate, mushrooms, cornstarch, mustard and paprika. Spoon over pieces of chicken; cover.

2. MICROWAVE for 28 to 30 MINUTES or until chicken is done, spooning glaze over chicken during last 10 minutes of cooking.

          4 to 6 Servings

TIP MICROWAVE on MEDIUM for 35 to 38 MINUTES.

We found the chicken breast bone did not affect cooking time.

CHICKEN BREASTS IN WINE SAUCE

  4 chicken breasts, skinned and boned,
   if desired
  ½ teaspoon salt
 Pepper
  ½ cup (4-oz. can) drained mushroom
   stems and pieces
  3 medium carrots, thinly sliced
  ¼ cup white wine or milk
  1 can (10½ oz.) condensed cream of
   chicken soup
 Parsley

Setting: HIGH

1. Arrange chicken breasts in 1½-quart (10 x 6 or 8-inch round) glass baking dish. Sprinkle with salt and pepper. Top with mushrooms, carrots and wine. Spoon soup over top, spreading to cover; cover.

2. MICROWAVE 15 to 18 MINUTES or until carrots and chicken are done. Garnish with parsley. Serve with rice or noodles.

           4 Servings

TIP MICROWAVE on MEDIUM for 26 to 28 MINUTES.

This recipe was given to us by a microwave oven owner. She likes to serve it to guests with asparagus spears garnished with pimento. Ready to serve in 20 minutes.

CHICKEN DOUBLE

  ½ cup slivered or sliced almonds
  4 slices bacon
  4 chicken breasts, skinned and boned,
   if desired
  1 can (10½ oz.) condensed cream of
   chicken soup
  2 tablespoons sherry or white wine,
   if desired

Setting: HIGH

1. Toast almonds by spreading in thin layer in 2-quart (12 x 7) glass baking dish.

2. MICROWAVE for 4 to 5 MINUTES or until toasted, stirring 4 times. Remove from dish.

3. MICROWAVE bacon in dish between layers of paper towel, 1½ to 2 MINUTES or until still limp. Discard paper towels and wrap 1 piece of bacon around each chicken breast. Arrange in baking dish; cover.

4. MICROWAVE for 10 to 12 MINUTES or until chicken is done. Mix soup with sherry and juices from chicken. Spoon over top of chicken. Cover and return to oven.

5. MICROWAVE for 3 to 4 MINUTES or until soup is hot. Top with toasted almonds. Serve on bed of rice.

           4 Servings

TIP To make ahead, toast almonds, microwave bacon and wrap chicken breasts. Refrigerate until ready to cook.

TURKEY NOODLE BAKE

  1 can (10¾ oz.) condensed cream of
   chicken soup
  ¼ cup water
  2 cups cubed cooked turkey
  1 cup chopped celery
  ½ cup coarsely chopped nuts
  ¼ cup chopped onion
  1 tablespoon chopped pimento
  1 can (3 oz.) chow mein noodles

Setting: HIGH

1. Combine all ingredients, including 1 cup chow mein noodles, in 2-quart glass casserole. Mix well. Cover with glass lid.

2. MICROWAVE for 8 to 10 MINUTES or until hot. Let stand, covered, 5 minutes. Sprinkle top with remaining noodles and serve.

          About 4 Servings

Pictured, clockwise: Turkey Noodle Bake, this page, Turkey Sandwiches topped with peas and cheese, Easy Chicken Rice, page 70, and Roast Turkey, page 60, as cooked totally in the microwave oven.

EASY CHICKEN RICE

    1 can (10½ oz.) condensed chicken broth
    1 teaspoon soy sauce
    ⅓ cup finely chopped onion
    1 cup quick-cooking rice
    1 cup cubed cooked chicken
    1 can (7 oz.) cut green beans, drained
    1 can (5 oz.) water chestnuts, drained
      and sliced

Setting: HIGH

1. Combine all ingredients in 2-quart glass casserole. Cover with glass lid.

2. MICROWAVE for 8 to 10 MINUTES or until hot. Let stand, covered, 5 minutes before serving.

About 4 Servings

TIP You can use 1¼ cups water and either 2 chicken bouillon cubes or 1 teaspoon chicken stock base.

HUNTINGTON CHICKEN

    1 cup chicken stock
    ½ cup milk or light cream
    1½ cups uncooked noodles
    2 to 3 cups cubed cooked chicken or
      turkey
    2 tablespoons chopped pimento
    ½ teaspoon salt
    ⅛ teaspoon pepper
    1 cup (4-oz. pkg.) shredded Cheddar
      cheese

Setting: HIGH

1. In 1½ or 2-quart glass casserole, combine all ingredients except cheese; cover.

2. MICROWAVE for 15 to 18 MINUTES or until noodles are tender. Stir in cheese.

6 Servings

TIPS You can use 1 cup water and either 2 chicken bouillon cubes or 1 teaspoon chicken stock base.
• MICROWAVE ON MEDIUM of 24 to 26 MINUTES.

TURKEY DIVAN

    2 packages (10 oz. each) frozen broccoli
      spears
    6 to 8 slices cooked turkey
    1½ cups shredded process American cheese
    1 can (10¾ oz.) condensed cream of
      chicken soup
    1 can (3½ oz.) French-fried onion rings

Setting: HIGH

1. Place frozen broccoli in 2-quart (12 x 7) glass baking dish; cover.

2. MICROWAVE for about 10 MINUTES or until partly cooked; arrange in dish. Top with turkey slices and cheese. Spoon soup over all; recover.

3. MICROWAVE for 10 MINUTES. Place onion rings on top and MICROWAVE for 1 to 2 MINUTES or until onions are hot.

4 to 6 Servings

Here is one recipe for turkey stuffing...you may have another that you prefer. Cooking times will not be affected by dressing.

SAVORY MUSHROOM STUFFING

    ½ cup butter or margarine
    ½ cup chopped onion or 2 tablespoons
      instant minced onion
    1 cup chopped celery
    1 cup (8-oz. can) drained mushroom
      stems and pieces
    8 cups dry bread cubes
    2 tablespoons parsley flakes
    1 teaspoon salt
    2 teaspoons poultry seasoning or
      ground sage
    ¼ teaspoon pepper
    ½ cup broth or water

Setting: HIGH

1. In large glass bowl, combine butter, onion and celery.

2. MICROWAVE for 5 to 6 MINUTES or until onion is tender. Stir in remaining ingredients, mixing well.

Stuffing for 12 to 15-lb. Turkey

TIP MICROWAVE on MEDIUM for 6 to 8 MINUTES.

STUFFING FOR CHICKEN

    ¼ cup butter or margarine
    ¼ cup chopped onion or 1 tablespoon
      instant minced onion
    ½ cup (1 stalk) chopped celery
    4 cups (4 slices) soft bread cubes
    ½ teaspoon salt
    ½ teaspoon poultry seasoning
    ¼ cup broth or water

Setting: HIGH

1. In glass mixing bowl, combine butter, onion and celery.

2. MICROWAVE for 3 to 4 MINUTES, stirring once. Stir in bread cubes, salt, seasoning and broth.

*Stuffing for 1 Roasting Chicken
or 4 Cornish Game Hens*

TIP MICROWAVE on MEDIUM for 4 to 5 MINUTES.

MAIN COURSES **Meat Charts**

HOW TO DEFROST MEAT

- Thaw meat in its original wrapping. Place wrapped meat in a flat glass baking dish to catch drippings.
- Meat is thawed on DEFROST setting. Meat weighing 4 pounds and over can be thawed on MEDIUM setting by reducing times in chart below.
- Turn large cuts during defrosting as specified in chart.

- Meat should be icy in center when removed from oven. Edges will begin cooking if microwaves thaw meat completely.
- Standing time in package is necessary to complete thawing.

CUT	WEIGHT	APPROXIMATE DEFROSTING TIME	APPROXIMATE STANDING TIME (at room temperature)
BEEF			
Rib roast, rolled	7 to 8-lb.	10 min; turn. Repeat 3 times.	2 hrs.
	3 to 4-lb.	25 to 30 min.	1 hr.
Rib Roast, standing	5 to 6-lb.	10 min; turn. Repeat 3 times.	2 hrs.
Sirloin Tip Roast	4 to 5-lb.	10 min.; turn. Repeat 2 times.	2 hrs.
Rump Roast, boneless	6 to 7-lb.	12 min.; turn; 10 to 12 min.	2 hrs.
	3 to 4-lb.	15 to 20 min.	1 hr.
Rump Roast, bone in	3 to 4-lb.	15 to 20 min.	1 hr.
Chuck Arm Roast	4 to 4½-lb.	15 to 20 min.	10 min.
Chuck Roast	3 to 4-lb.	10 to 12 min.	10 min.
Beef Blade Roast	2¾ to 3¼-lb.	15 to 18 min.	5 min.
Rib Eye Steak	2 to 3-lb.	7 to 8 min.	5 min.
Sirloin Steak	1¾ to 2-lb.	10 to 12 min.	5 min.
Round Steak	1¾ to 3-lb.	10 to 12 min.	5 min.
Flank Steak	1¼ to 1½-lb.	7 to 9 min.	5 min.
Cubed Steak	8 oz.	2 to 3 min.	5 min.
Short Ribs	2 to 3 lbs.	7 to 8 min.	5 min.
Stew Meat	1¾ to 2 lbs.	7 to 8 min.	5 min.
Ground beef	1 lb.	7 to 8 min.	5 min.
	2 lbs.	15 to 18 min.	5 min.
Brisket, fresh	3¼ to 3½-lb.	12 to 15 min.	1 hr.
Brisket, corned	2¾ to 3-lb.	12 to 14 min.	30 min.

(Continued, next page)

CUT	WEIGHT	APPROXIMATE DEFROSTING TIME	APPROXIMATE STANDING TIME (at room temperature)
VARIETY MEATS			
Liver	8 ozs.	4 to 5 min.	5 min.
	1 lb.	5 to 6 min.	5 min.
Tongue	2¼ to 2½-lb.	6 min.; turn; 6 min.	5 min.
Kidney	2-lb.	5 to 6 min.	5 min.
PORK			
Loin Roast, boneless	4 to 5-lb.	12 min.; turn; 4 to 5 min.	1 hr.
Loin Roast, center rib	4 to 5-lb.	12 min.; turn 4 to 5 min.	1 hr.
Tenderloin	1¾ to 2-lb.	10 to 12 min.	5 min.
Loin Chops, 1-in. thick	3 to 3½ lbs.	8 to 10 min.	10 min.
Chops, ½-in. thick	1½ lbs.	8 to 10 min.	5 min.
Blade Steak	1¼ to 1½-lb.	4 to 6 min.	5 min.
Shoulder steak	2½-lb.	12 to 15 min.	5 min.
Spareribs, country style	2 to 3 lbs.	12 to 15 min.	5 min.
Spareribs	2¾ to 3 lbs.	12 to 15 min.	5 min.
Cubed	1½ lbs.	6 to 8 min.	5 min.
Hocks	1 to 2 lbs.	6 to 8 min.	5 min.
Ground, fresh	1 lb.	6 to 8 min.	5 min.
Ground, ham	1 lb.	6 to 8 min.	5 min.
LAMB			
Leg Roast	4 to 4½-lb.	15 min.; turn; 15 min.	1 hr.
Shoulder Roast	3¼ to 3½-lb.	15 min.; turn; 6 to 8 min.	1 hr.
Steaks	2 to 2½ lbs.	6 to 8 min.	5 min.
Spareribs	2¼ to 2½ lbs.	6 to 8 min.	5 min.
Shanks	1 lb.	4 to 6 min.	5 min.
Cubed	1 lb.	6 to 7 min.	5 min.
Ground	1 lb.	4 to 6 min.	5 min.
Patties	1½ lbs.	6 to 8 min.	5 min.

CUT	WEIGHT	APPROXIMATE DEFROSTING TIME	APPROXIMATE STANDING TIME (at room temperature)
VEAL Rump Roast, bone in	2½ to 3-lb. 5 to 6-lb.	8 to 12 min. 8 min.; turn; 6 to 7 min.	30 min. 1 hr.
Chops	1 to 2 lbs.	10 to 12 min.	5 min.
Steak	1 lb.	6 to 7 min.	5 min.
Ground	1 lb.	4 to 6 min.	5 min.
VENISON Rump Roast, bone in	3 to 3½-lb.	10 to 12 min.	1 hr.
Chops	1¼ lbs.	6 to 7 min.	5 min.
RABBIT Cut up	2 to 2½-lb.	15 to 18 min.	5 min.

HOW TO ROAST MEATS

• Microwave fresh or completely thawed frozen meat. See defrosting chart page 71.

• Season meat to taste. Place meat, fat side down on microwave roasting rack, in 2-quart (12 x 7) glass baking dish.

• Microwave on "first setting" for half of the total cooking time.

• Turn meat, fat side up. Meat weighing 7 pounds or over should be turned 3 times during cooking.

• Microwave on "second setting" for second half of cooking time. Check for desired doneness as specified in chart.

• Use a microwave meat thermometer in a microwave oven during cooking. DO NOT use a conventional meat thermometer in a microwave oven; insert this kind as soon as meat comes from oven.

• Let meat stand, covered with foil, about 10 minutes before serving. Temperature will rise about 15°F. during standing time as meat continues to cook to final desired doneness.

CUT AND WEIGHT	FIRST SETTING	SECOND SETTING	DONENESS WHEN MEAT COMES FROM OVEN	APPROXIMATE COOKING TIME
BEEF Rib Roast, rolled 3 to 4-lb.	HIGH	DEFROST	rare — 125°F. medium — 145°F. well done — 155°F.	9 to 10 min. per lb. 11 to 12 min. per lb. 13 to 14 min. per lb.
Rib Roast, standing 5 to 6-lb.	HIGH	DEFROST	rare — 125°F. medium — 145°F. well done — 155°F.	8 to 9 min. per lb. 9 to 10 min. per lb. 11 to 12 min. per lb.
Sirloin Tip Roast 4 to 5-lb.	HIGH	DEFROST	rare — 125°F. medium — 145°F. well done — 155°F.	9 to 10 min. per lb. 11 to 12 min. per lb. 13 to 14 min. per lb.

(Continued, next page)

CUT AND WEIGHT	FIRST SETTING	SECOND SETTING	DONENESS WHEN MEAT COMES FROM OVEN	APPROXIMATE COOKING TIME
Rump Roast, boneless 3 to 4-lb.	DEFROST	DEFROST	rare — 125°F. medium — 145°F. well done — 155°F.	12 to 13 min. per lb. 14 to 15 min. per lb. 16 to 17 min. per lb.
Rump Roast, bone in 3 to 4-lb.	DEFROST	DEFROST	rare — 125°F. medium — 145°F. well done — 155°F.	12 to 13 min. per lb. 14 to 15 min. per lb. 16 to 17 min. per lb.
PORK Loin Roast, boneless 4 to 5-lb.	HIGH	DEFROST	well done — 155°F.	11 to 12 min. per lb
Loin Roast, center rib cut 4 to 5-lb.	HIGH	DEFROST	well done — 155°F.	11 to 12 min. per lb.
Ham, boneless, ready to eat 2 to 3-lb. 4 to 5-lb. 6 to 8-lb.	DEFROST DEFROST DEFROST	DEFROST DEFROST DEFROST	heated — 120°F. heated — 120°F. heated — 120°F.	14 to 15 min. per lb. 13 to 14 min. per lb. 11 to 12 min. per lb.
Ham, shank of leg, ready to eat 7 to 8-lb.	DEFROST	DEFROST	heated — 120°F.	10 to 11 min. per lb.
Ham, canned 3-lb. 5-lb.	DEFROST DEFROST	DEFROST DEFROST	heated — 120°F. heated — 120°F.	12 to 13 min. per lb. 10 to 11 min. per lb.
LAMB Leg Roast 4 to 4½-lb.	DEFROST	DEFROST	well done — 165°F.	12 to 13 min. per lb.
Shoulder Roast, bone in 3 to 3½-lb.	DEFROST	DEFROST	well done — 155°F.	11 to 12 min. per lb.
VEAL Rump Roast, bone in 2½ to 3-lb.	DEFROST	DEFROST	well done —155°F.	21 to 22 min. per lb.
VENISON Rump Roast, bone in 3 to 3½-lb.	DEFROST	DEFROST	well done — 155°F.	14 to 15 min. per lb.

TIP All meats roasted on DEFROST setting can be cooked on MEDIUM setting; reduce times by about 2 min. per lb.

Pictured, clockwise: Ranch Meat Loaf, page 29, Ground Beef Patties, page 81, with Tater Tots, Beef-Stuffed Peppers, page 82, and Lasagna, page 81.

MAIN COURSES **Beef**

BRAISED BEEF KEY: Pieces, strips and cubes of less tender beef, such as round and chuck, microwave into flavorful entrées. Use Microwave HIGH for quick cooking and then DEFROST for flavorful blending of sauces which provide the moisture needed to tenderize meat.

Although shortribs are from the beef rib, high fat and bone content, plus sauce and vegetable additions, make them suitable to the braising and draining technique used for less tender meat cuts.

Note that cooking times vary with cut of beef, shape of pieces and other ingredients added to the recipe.

Meat should be completely thawed before cooking. See defrosting chart page 71.

Score pieces of meat that must be rolled or which need tenderizing. Do this by making shallow criss-cross cuts on both sides of the meat with a sharp knife.

Cover less tender meat during cooking and standing time to trap steam, hasten cooking and tenderize. Place meat in a glass baking dish or casserole with fitted glass lid, plastic wrap or wax paper stretched tightly across top of dish. Pierce plastic wrap before removing it to prevent steam burns.

Stir or rearrange meat during cooking as recipe directs to assure even cooking.

Drain, when directed, to remove excess fat and moisture.

When planning to adapt a favorite dish, use a similar recipe in this section as a model. Note that less moisture and fat need to be added in microwave meat cooking.

SAUCY POT ROAST

   3 to 4-lb. pot roast, 1½ inches thick
   1 envelope onion soup mix
   1 can (10¾ oz.) condensed cream of
     mushroom soup
   ¼ cup water

Settings: HIGH/DEFROST

1. Place roast in 3-quart glass casserole. Sprinkle with soup mix. Spoon mushroom soup over top. Add water; cover.

2. MICROWAVE on HIGH for 10 MINUTES.

3. MICROWAVE on DEFROST for 30 MINUTES. Turn meat over.

4. MICROWAVE on DEFROST for 20 MINUTES; turn meat over.

5. MICROWAVE on DEFROST for 20 MINUTES more, or until tender. Skim fat from sauce and serve sauce with roast.

6 to 8 Servings

SWISS STEAK

   2 tablespoons butter or margarine
   2 tablespoons all-purpose flour
   1 teaspoon salt
   ¼ teaspoon pepper
   ¼ teaspoon dry mustard
   1½ to 2-lb. boneless beef round steak,
     cut into serving pieces
   1 medium onion, sliced
   ¼ cup packed brown sugar
   ½ cup catsup

Settings: HIGH/DEFROST

1. Place butter in 2-quart (12 x 7) glass baking dish.

2. MICROWAVE on HIGH for 1 MINUTE or until melted. Combine flour, salt, pepper and mustard in plate. Coat meat in seasoned flour. Arrange seasoned meat in melted butter. Cover with glass lid or plastic wrap.

3. MICROWAVE on HIGH for about 5 MINUTES or until no longer pink. Turn meat over. Place onion rings on top. Combine catsup and brown sugar in 2-cup measure. Pour over meat. Cover with plastic wrap.

4. MICROWAVE on DEFROST for 20 MINUTES. Rearrange meat; recover, and MICROWAVE on DEFROST for 20 to 25 MINUTES or until fork tender. Let stand, covered, 5 minutes before serving.

About 4 Servings

CORNED BEEF 'N CABBAGE DINNER

   2¾ to 3-lb. corned beef brisket with
     seasonings
   1½ cups water
   2 medium onions, quartered
   3 carrots, sliced
   3 potatoes, quartered
   1 cabbage, cut into 8 wedges

Settings: HIGH/DEFROST

1. Place corned beef brisket in 3-quart glass casserole; add water, and sprinkle with seasonings included with meat. Cover with glass lid or plastic wrap.

2. MICROWAVE on HIGH for 10 to 12 MINUTES or until boiling. Turn meat over.

3. MICROWAVE on DEFROST for about 1½ hours or until fork tender. Turn meat over; add remaining ingredients; recover.

4. MICROWAVE on DEFROST for 30 to 45 MINUTES or until vegetables are tender. Let stand, covered, 5 minutes before serving.

About 6 Servings

BEEF STROGANOFF

¼ cup butter or margarine
4 medium onions, thinly sliced
1 tablespoon dry mustard
1 tablespoon sugar
2 teaspoons salt
1 teaspoon pepper
2 cans (4 oz. each) mushroom stems and pieces, drained
2 to 2¼-lb. boneless beef round steak, cut into thin strips
1 cup sour cream
Hot buttered noodles

Settings: HIGH/DEFROST

1. Combine butter, onion, dry mustard, sugar, salt and pepper in 3-quart glass casserole; cover.

2. MICROWAVE on HIGH for about 10 MINUTES stirring twice. Stir in beef; recover.

3. MICROWAVE on HIGH for about 6 MINUTES or until no longer pink. Stir in mushrooms; recover.

4. MICROWAVE on DEFROST for 20 MINUTES. Mix in sour cream; recover, and MICROWAVE on DEFROST for 4 to 5 MINUTES or until heated through. Serve with buttered noodles. Let stand, covered, 5 minutes before serving.

6 to 8 Servings

Scoring and sprinkling with tenderizer helps tenderize this flank steak before it is cooked in the oven. Overcooking will toughen steak.

STUFFED FLANK ROLL UP

1 beef flank steak (1 to 1½ lbs.)
Meat tenderizer
1½ cups soft bread cubes
¼ cup chopped onion or 1 tablespoon instant minced onion
½ cup chopped celery
1 tablespoon parsley flakes
½ teaspoon powdered sage or thyme
Dash pepper
2 tablespoons water or red wine
1 cup water
1 teaspoon or cube beef bouillon

Setting: DEFROST

1. Score both sides of steak diagonally, about 1 inch apart. Sprinkle both sides with meat tenderizer.

2. Combine bread cubes, onion, celery, parsley, sage, pepper and 2 tablespoons water.

3. Place stuffing down center of steak, lengthwise. Roll and tie steak with string. Place seam side down in 1½-quart (8 x 4) glass loaf dish; cover.

4. MICROWAVE on DEFROST for 20 MINUTES. Pour soup over meat. Sprinkle with snipped parsley and MICROWAVE for 4 to 5 MINUTES or until fork tender. Let stand, covered, 5 minutes before serving.

4 to 6 Servings

BEEF RAGOUT

1½ lbs. beef stew meat
1 medium onion, sliced
½ cup water
½ cup red wine
1 teaspoon salt
1 cube or teaspoon beef bouillon
1 bay leaf
¼ cup water
2 tablespoons all-purpose flour
4 medium carrots, peeled and sliced
2 stalks celery sliced

Settings: HIGH/DEFROST

1. In 1½-quart glass casserole combine meat, onion, ½ cup water, the wine, salt, bouillon and bay leaf; cover.

2. MICROWAVE on HIGH for 5 MINUTES, or until mixture is steaming hot, stirring once.

3. MICROWAVE on DEFROST for 20 MINUTES, stirring once.

4. Combine ¼ cup water with the flour. Stir into meat mixture. Stir in carrots and celery.

5. MICROWAVE on DEFROST for 20 to 30 MINUTES or until vegetables are desired doneness. Serve stew over potatoes or noodles.

5 to 6 Servings

TIPS If you prefer to omit the wine, increase water to 1 cup and add 2 tablespoons vinegar.
● You may wish to prebrown the meat on microwave browning grill before adding it to the casserole. The browning will add flavor to the sauce.

BEEF BOURGUIGNON

1½ to 1¾-lb. beef sirloin steak, cut into 1½-inch cubes
¼ teaspoon salt
2 tablespoons all-purpose flour
1 envelope (1¼ oz.) dehydrated onion soup mix
⅔ cup dry red wine
1 can (4 oz.) mushroom stems and pieces, drained
1 green pepper, cut into strips
1 can (16 oz.) whole onions, drained

Settings: HIGH/DEFROST

1. Combine steak cubes, salt, flour, soup mix and wine in 2-quart glass casserole. Cover with glass lid or plastic wrap.

2. MICROWAVE on HIGH for about 5 MINUTES or until no longer pink. Stir in remaining ingredients; recover.

3. MICROWAVE on DEFROST for 12 to 15 MINUTES or until fork tender. Let stand, covered, 5 minutes before serving.

About 6 Servings

QUICK-COOK TENDER BEEF STEAK KEY:
Tender steak, such as sirloin and tenderized minute steaks, cook fast and retain full flavor on Microwave HIGH.

The microwave browning grill accessory can be used to sear these steaks on HIGH as directed in the manufacturer's instruction booklet.

Frozen steak should be completely thawed before cooking. See defrosting chart page 71.

Cook tender beef steak directly on the microwave browning grill when called for in a recipe. Other cooking dishes used must be glass. Covers should be fitted glass lids, plastic wrap or wax paper. Pierce plastic wrap before removing it to prevent steam burns.

Stir, turn or rearrange steak as called for in a recipe to assure even cooking.

Standing time, when called for, is important. It assures complete cooking.

These tender steak recipes are models for favorites from a homemaker's recipe box.

ORIENTAL STIR-FRIED STEAK

   1 **lb. beef sirloin steak,
     cut into thin slices**
   ½ **tablespoon sugar**
   2 **tablespoons dry sherry**
   2 **tablespoons soy sauce**
   ¼ **cup sliced green onions**
   1 **cup sliced fresh mushrooms**
   1 **can (8½ oz.) bamboo shoots, drained**

Setting: HIGH

1. Combine steak, sugar, sherry and soy sauce. Cover and refrigerate 1 hour, stirring occasionally. Drain meat on paper towel (save marinade).

2. Preheat microwave browning grill as directed in manufacturers instruction booklet.

3. Add bamboo shoots to marinade. Add meat to grill. Top with onions and mushrooms.

4. MICROWAVE for 3 MINUTES, stirring twice. Add bamboo shoots and soy sauce mixture.

5. MICROWAVE 30 to 45 SECONDS or until heated through and meat is desired doneness. Serve with rice.

                               4 to 5 Servings

RIB STEAKS ON MICROWAVE BROWNING GRILL

   2 **beef rib steaks (1 lb. each),
     trim off fat**
   2 **tablespoons butter or margarine,
     if desired**
Salt
Pepper

Setting: HIGH

1. Preheat microwave browning grill in oven as directed in instruction booklet. Place butter on hot grill to melt. Place steaks on hot grill.

2. MICROWAVE for 4 MINUTES. Turn steaks over and MICROWAVE for 3 to 4 MINUTES or to desired doneness.

                                  2 Steaks

A traditional favorite made easy in the microwave oven. Use a shallow dish that will be attractive on the table. Prepare and assemble ingredients in advance for quick 10 minute cooking.

SUKIYAKI

  1½ **to 2-lb. beef sirloin steak,
     cut into thin strips**
   ½ **cup soy sauce**
   ½ **cup water**
   3 **tablespoons sugar**
   1 **can (4 oz.) mushroom stems and
     pieces, drained**
   ½ **cup sliced green onion**
   1 **can (5 oz.) water chestnuts, drained
     and sliced**
   1 **can (5 oz.) bamboo shoots, drained**
   1 **can (16 oz.) bean sprouts, drained**

Setting: HIGH

1. Combine steak, soy sauce, water and sugar in 3-quart (13 x 9) glass baking dish; cover. Marinate 3 to 4 hours at room temperature.

2. Place remaining ingredients in rows across meat and sauce with mushrooms and onions in center rows; recover.

3. MICROWAVE for 10 to 12 MINUTES. Let stand, covered, 2 minutes before serving.

                                4 to 6 Servings

Pictured, top: Rolled Rib Roast, page 80.

Pictured, bottom: Beef Bourguignon, page 77 and Sukiyaki, above.

ROAST BEEF KEY: Microwave tender beef roasts, such as sirloin tip and rib, on Microwave HIGH during first half of cooking time. This setting heats meat through quickly. Microwave on DEFROST during final cooking period so meat stays tender and is thoroughly cooked.

Microwave less tender beef roasts, such as rump roast, on DEFROST. Lower settings allow longer cooking to tenderize meat.

Season meat to taste. Place, fat side down on microwave roasting rack, in a flat glass baking dish. Rack keeps meat above drippings.

Beef roasts weighing 7 pounds or over should be turned over 3 times to assure even cooking.

Cook roasts to desired doneness using a microwave meat thermometer and the meat doneness chart on page 73 as a guide.

Note that the 10-minute standing time is very important because meat continues to cook after it comes from the oven and internal temperature should rise about 15°F. Cover dish of meat with foil during standing time to hold in heat.

A microwave meat thermometer can be used in the oven during cooking. Insert it after meat is turned the last time. DO NOT use a conventional meat thermometer in a microwave oven. Check doneness with this kind of thermometer by inserting it as soon as roast comes from the oven.

GROUND BEEF KEY: Ground beef, mainstay of American dinner tables, microwaves on HIGH.

Meat should be completely thawed before cooking.

Cook ground beef patties uncovered, on a microwave browning grill, a glass pie plate, dinner plate or serving platter (without silver or other metal trim).

Microwave most other ground beef dishes in glass casseroles or baking dishes with fitted glass lids, tight coverings of plastic or wax paper.

Drain off excess fat and moisture as directed in a recipe, to preserve flavor and sauce consistency.

Rearrange or stir ground beef dishes thoroughly when called for in a recipe so the entire mixture cooks evenly.

Follow standing time directions carefully. Food continues to cook after it comes from a microwave oven.

IMPORTANT: Before you begin, refer to the "Beginning to Cook" section for basic technique and these example recipes:

ROLLED PRIME RIB ROAST WITH MADEIRA SAUCE

> 3 to 4-lb. rolled beef rib roast
> 1 teaspoon salt
> ¼ teaspoon pepper

Madeira Sauce
> 1 teaspoon salt
> ½ teaspoon pepper
> 1 can (10½ oz.) condensed beef broth
> ¼ cup Madeira wine

Settings: HIGH/DEFROST

1. Place roast, fat side down on microwave roasting rack in 2-quart (12 x 7) glass casserole. Season with salt and pepper.

2. MICROWAVE on HIGH for 18 MINUTES. Turn fat side up.

3. MICROWAVE on DEFROST for 14 to 18 MINUTES or until rare doneness. Let stand, covered with foil, 10 minutes before serving. Serve with Madeira Sauce.

4. Madeira Sauce: Combine all ingredients in 2-cup measure. Stir into hot meat drippings; mix well.

9 to 12 Servings

TIPS STANDING RIB ROAST and BONELESS SIRLOIN TIP ROAST: Use same technique as above. See meat roasting chart, page 73, for time and doneness tests.

● MICROWAVE on MEDIUM for 12 to 16 MINUTES in step 3.

GROUND BEEF PATTIES ON MICROWAVE BROWNING GRILL

> 1 lb. ground beef
> 1 teaspoon salt
> ¼ teaspoon pepper
> 1 tablespoon finely chopped onion

Setting: HIGH

1. Combine all ingredients in medium glass mixing bowl; mix well. Shape into 4 patties. Preheat microwave browning grill in oven as directed in instruction booklet. Place patties on browning grill.

2. MICROWAVE for 2 MINUTES. Turn patties over and MICROWAVE for 2½ to 3 MINUTES or to desired doneness.

4 Patties

TIPS Make FRENCH-STYLE PATTIES by basting meat with ¼ cup dry red wine after first cooking time. Top with 1 can (4 oz.) mushroom stems and pieces, drained, and MICROWAVE for 3 to 4 MINUTES or until desired doneness. Sprinkle with snipped parsley.

● Make CHEDDAR CHEESE PATTIES. Top each patty with 2 tablespoons shredded Cheddar cheese and 1 teaspoon catsup after first cooking time. Microwave as directed in basic recipe.

HOW TO COOK GROUND BEEF PATTIES

- Season 1 pound ground beef with 1 teaspoon salt and ¼ teaspoon pepper. Shape patties.
- Place patty(ies) on 9-inch glass pie plate, dinner plate or platter without silver or other metal trim.
- MICROWAVE on HIGH. Turn once halfway through cooking period.
- When serving, surround patties with hot cooked rice or mashed potatoes to absorb flavorful meat juices — or if preferred, drain on paper towel.

PATTIES	WEIGHT	SETTING	MINUTES
1	4-oz.	HIGH	2 to 2½
2	4-oz. ea.	HIGH	3 to 3½
4	4-oz. ea.	HIGH	4½ to 5
6	4-oz. ea.	HIGH	6½ to 7

Since there is no real time saving with cooking spaghetti in the microwave oven, you may find it more convenient to cook it conventionally while the sauce cooks in the oven. If you have a favorite sauce recipe, use this as a timing guide for a similar amount of sauce.

OH! SO GOOD SPAGHETTI

- **2 lbs. ground beef**
- **¼ cup finely chopped onion**
- **1 can (16 oz.) whole tomatoes**
- **1 can (6 oz.) tomato paste**
- **1 can (8 oz.) tomato sauce**
- **1 tablespoon dried parsley flakes**
- **½ teaspoon Worcestershire sauce**
- **¼ teaspoon garlic salt**
- **¼ teaspoon leaf oregano**
- **Salt**
- **Pepper**
- **Grated Parmesan cheese**

Setting: HIGH

1. Crumble ground beef into 4-quart glass casserole. Stir in onion.

2. MICROWAVE for 7 MINUTES; drain. Stir in remaining ingredients, except cheese; cover.

3. MICROWAVE for 9 to 10 MINUTES or until meat absorbs juices. Serve with hot cooked spaghetti. Sprinkle Parmesan cheese on top of each serving.

6 to 8 Servings

TIPS If you like a wine flavored sauce, use ¼ cup red wine for part of the water.
- If desired, add a 4-oz. can mushroom stems and pieces, using the liquid for part of the water.
- MICROWAVE on MEDIUM for 15 to 20 MINUTES in step 3.

LASAGNA

- **1 lb. ground beef**
- **1 teaspoon salt**
- **1 package (1 oz.) spaghetti sauce mix**
- **1 can (16 oz.) tomato sauce**
- **1 can (4 oz.) mushroom stems and pieces, drained**
- **1 package (8 oz.) lasagna noodles, cooked**
- **1 carton (12 oz.) creamed cottage cheese**
- **1 package (6 oz.) sliced Mozzarella cheese**
- **½ cup grated Parmesan cheese**

Settings: HIGH/DEFROST

1. Crumble ground beef in 2-quart (12 x 7) glass baking dish; cover.

2. MICROWAVE on HIGH for 5 MINUTES. Drain and stir in salt, spaghetti sauce mix, tomato sauce and mushrooms; mix well. Assemble in 2-quart (12 x 7) glass baking dish by layers: ⅓ cooked noodles, ⅓ meat mixture, ½ cottage cheese and ½ Mozzarella cheese. Repeat layers. On third layer of noodles, spread last ⅓ of meat mixture and sprinkle with Parmesan cheese; cover.

3. MICROWAVE on DEFROST for 20 to 25 MINUTES or until hot in center. Let stand, covered, 5 minutes before serving.

6 to 8 Servings

TIPS Recipe can be assembled in two 2-quart (8 x 8) or two 1½-quart (10 x 6) baking dishes. For these sizes it is easier to assemble in 2 layers and sprinkle Parmesan cheese on top of Mozzarella. You can freeze one dish for use at a later time. When ready to serve just MICROWAVE on DEFROST, covered with wax paper for 20 to 25 MINUTES or until hot.
- MICROWAVE on MEDIUM for 15 to 18 MINUTES in step 3.

CHILI

- **1 lb. ground beef**
- **1 medium onion, finely chopped**
- **2 teaspoons chili powder**
- **1½ teaspoons salt**
- **1 teaspoon prepared mustard**
- **1 clove garlic, finely chopped**
- **1 can (15½ oz.) kidney beans, drained**
- **1 can (16 oz.) tomatoes**

Settings: HIGH/DEFROST

1. Crumble ground beef in 2-quart glass casserole. Stir in onion; cover.

2. MICROWAVE on HIGH for 5 MINUTES. Drain and stir in remaining ingredients; recover.

3. MICROWAVE on DEFROST for 15 to 20 MINUTES or until hot. Let stand, covered, 5 minutes before serving.

4 to 6 Servings

TIP MICROWAVE on MEDIUM for 12 to 14 MINUTES in step 3.

STUFFED CABBAGE ROLLS

- **1 large head cabbage, cored**
- **½ cup water**
- **1½ lbs. ground beef**
- **½ cup finely chopped onion**
- **½ cup quick-cooking rice**
- **1 egg**
- **1 teaspoon Worcestershire sauce**
- **½ teaspoon leaf basil**
- **1 teaspoon salt**
- **¼ teaspoon pepper**
- **1 can (8 oz.) tomato sauce**

Setting: HIGH

1. Place cabbage in 2-quart glass casserole. Pour water in bottom of dish; cover.

2. MICROWAVE for 8 to 10 MINUTES or until cabbage is partly cooked; set aside. Crumble ground beef in medium mixing bowl. Stir in remaining ingredients, except tomato sauce. Remove 12 cabbage leaves from partly cooked cabbage. Place an equal amount of meat mixture in each leaf. Roll up and secure with toothpick. Place in 2-quart (12 x 7) glass baking dish; cover.

3. MICROWAVE for 13 to 15 MINUTES. Pour tomato sauce over cabbage rolls. Recover and MICROWAVE for 2 to 3 MINUTES or until hot. Let stand, covered, 5 minutes before serving.

About 6 Servings

We found we could cook stuffed peppers without first precooking peppers and rice.

BEEF-STUFFED PEPPERS

- **3 large sweet green peppers, cut in half lenghwise**
- **1 lb. ground beef**
- **1 cup quick-cooking rolled oats**
- **1 egg, slightly beaten**
- **1 small onion, finely chopped**
- **1 can (8 oz.) tomato sauce**
- **1 tablespoon Worcestershire sauce**
- **1 teaspoon salt**
- **⅓ cup water**

Setting: HIGH

1. Place peppers in 2-quart (12 x 7) glass baking dish; set aside. Combine remaining ingredients, except water, in medium bowl; mix well. Spoon meat mixture into green pepper halves. Pour water in bottom of dish; cover.

2. MICROWAVE for 12 to 15 MINUTES or until done. Let stand, covered, 5 minutes before serving.

About 6 Servings

TIPS Top with catsup or chili sauce.
- Reheat frozen stuffed peppers on HIGH
  - 3 peppers — 7 MINUTES
  - 6 peppers — 10 MINUTES, 30 SECONDS
- MICROWAVE on MEDIUM for 22 to 24 MINUTES.

A hearty chili and corn flavored casserole to serve a hungry family.

MEXICAN BEEF 'N DUMPLINGS

- **2 lbs. ground beef**
- **2 to 3 teaspoons chili powder**
- **1½ teaspoons salt**
- **1 small onion, chopped, or 2 tablespoons instant minced onion**
- **2 cups (16-oz. can) tomato sauce with onion, celery and green pepper**
- **2 cups (1-lb. can) undrained tomatoes**
- **1½ cups (16-oz. can) drained whole kernel corn**

Dumplings
- **1 cup pancake mix**
- **½ cup cornmeal**
- **½ cup water**
- **2 tablespoons cooking oil**
- **1 egg**

Setting: HIGH

1. In 3-quart glass casserole, crumble ground beef. Sprinkle with chili powder.

2. MICROWAVE for 5 MINUTES, stirring once. Stir in salt, onion, tomato sauce, tomatoes and corn; cover.

3. MICROWAVE for 5 to 6 MINUTES or until mixture boils.

4. Meanwhile, prepare **Dumplings** by combining pancake mix, cornmeal, water, oil and egg; mix until well combined. When mixture boils; spoon dumplings on top of mixture; cover.

5. MICROWAVE for 7 to 8 MINUTES or until center dumpling is no longer doughy underneath. Let stand, covered, a couple minutes before serving.

8 Servings

TIPS For half a recipe, use 2-quart glass casserole, microwave as directed and for Dumplings use 1 egg and 2 tablespoons water and MICROWAVE for 5 MINUTES.
- Regular tomato sauce can be used, adding ½ cup chopped celery and ¼ cup chopped green pepper.

SWEDISH MEATBALLS WITH GRAVY

- 1 **egg, slightly beaten**
- 1 **lb. ground beef**
- 1 **slice bread, crumbled**
- ¼ **cup cream or milk**
- ½ **cup (1 med.) chopped onion or**
  2 tablespoons instant minced onion
- ½ **teaspoon salt**
- ¼ **teaspoon pepper**
- ¼ **teaspoon mace or allspice, if desired**
- 1 **can (10¾ oz.) condensed beef gravy**

Setting: HIGH

1. In 1½-quart (8-inch round) glass baking dish, combine all ingredients except gravy. Shape into 8 to 10 meatballs, arranging in same dish.

2. MICROWAVE for 5 MINUTES, turning and rearranging once. Drain fat. Spoon gravy over meatballs; cover.

3. MICROWAVE for 3 MINUTES or until heated through.

4 Servings

TIPS Gravy mix can be used for canned gravy. Just sprinkle partially cooked meatballs with gravy mix and stir in ½ cup water (half red wine can be used) and cook as directed, stirring once.
- Canned soups can also be used for gravy. Meatballs are good with cream of chicken, mushroom or celery soup.

An unusual combination of ingredients for a new twist to the traditional meatball. Our taste panel especially liked the flavors.

SAUCY ORIENTAL MEATBALLS

- 1 **lb. lean ground beef**
- ½ **cup (5-oz. can) chopped water**
  chestnuts
- ½ **teaspoon salt**
- 1 **tablespoon prepared horseradish**
- ½ **cup orange marmalade**
- ⅛ **teaspoon instant minced garlic or**
  garlic powder
- 1½ **tablespoons all-purpose flour**
- 2 **tablespoons soy sauce**
- 1 **tablespoon lemon juice**

Setting: HIGH

1. In 1½-quart (8-inch round) glass baking dish, combine ground beef, water chestnuts, salt and horseradish. Form into 1-inch meatballs, arranging in same baking dish.

2. Combine marmalade, garlic, flour, soy sauce and lemon juice. Spoon over meatballs; cover.

3. MICROWAVE for 7 to 8 MINUTES, rearranging and turning once. Serve with rice.

4 Servings

TIP These flavors would make tasty appetizer meatballs; serve on toothpicks from chafing dish.

A speedy 10 minute Chow Mein made with ground beef. If you prefer, use chow mein meat (coarsely ground pork and veal) instead of ground beef.

GROUND BEEF CHOW MEIN

- 1 **lb. ground beef**
- ½ **cup (4-oz. can) drained mushroom**
  stems and pieces
- ½ **teaspoon ground ginger**
- 2 **tablespoons soy sauce**
- 1 **package (⅝ oz.) brown gravy mix**
- 1 **medium onion, sliced, or 1 tablespoon**
  instant minced onion
- 1 **cup (2 stalks) sliced celery**
- 2 **cups (1-lb. can) undrained chow mein**
  vegetables

Setting: HIGH

1. In 1½ or 2-quart glass casserole, crumble ground beef. Stir in mushrooms, ginger and soy sauce. Sprinkle with gravy mix; cover.

2. MICROWAVE for 5 MINUTES. Stir in onion, celery and chow mein vegetables; recover.

3. MICROWAVE for 5 to 6 MINUTES or until vegetables are desired doneness, stirring occasionally. Serve with rice or chow mein noodles.

4 to 5 Servings

TIPS If chow mein vegetables are drained, add 1 cup water.
- MICROWAVE on MEDIUM for 7 to 8 MINUTES in step 3.

HOW TO HEAT PRECOOKED REFRIGERATED MAIN DISHES

- Reheat main dishes in glass casseroles filled about ⅔ full.
- Cover with glass lid or plastic wrap.
- MICROWAVE on HIGH until hot.
- Stir once halfway through cooking.
- Let stand, covered, 5 minutes before serving.

GLASS CASSEROLE	SETTING	APPROXIMATE MINUTES
1-qt.	HIGH	6 to 8
1½-qt.	HIGH	10 to 12
2-qt.	HIGH	12 to 15
3-qt.	HIGH	14 to 17

MAIN COURSES **Ham & Pork**

CURED PORK KEY: Ham, Canadian bacon, smoked pork chops — all these cured meats come from the market partially or fully cooked. This means they'll microwave evenly on DEFROST.

Ground ham, however, can be cooked more quickly on Microwave HIGH.

Cook large pieces of cured ham on a microwave roasting rack set in a flat glass baking dish.

Microwave smaller cuts of cured pork in a glass baking dish or casserole. Cover, when specified, with glass lid, plastic wrap or wax paper to speed heating and cooking.

Some dishes do not require covering because a roasting technique is employed. Do cover these dishes with foil during standing time to assure thorough heating and cooking.

Turn larger pieces of meat over during cooking.

If an area on a roast appears to be drying during cooking, cover it with foil. Do not let foil touch oven surface or arching and pitting may result.

IMPORTANT: Before you begin, refer to the "Beginning to Cook" section for basic technique and these example recipes:

Bacon 15
Canadian Bacon 15

SCALLOPED HAM 'N CABBAGE

   4 cups (½ med. head) shredded cabbage
   2 tablespoons all-purpose flour
   ½ teaspoon caraway seed or ¼ teaspoon nutmeg
   1 cup milk
   3 cups (1 lb.) cubed cooked ham
      French-fried onion rings, if desired

Settings: HIGH/DEFROST

1. In 2-quart glass casserole, mix cabbage with flour and caraway seed. Stir in milk and ham; cover.

2. MICROWAVE on HIGH for 5 MINUTES.

3. MICROWAVE on DEFROST for 10 to 12 MINUTES or until cabbage is desired doneness. Top with onion rings just before serving.

4 to 5 Servings

TIP MICROWAVE on MEDIUM for a total time of 12 to 14 MINUTES.

These will heat most evenly if rolls are placed in spoke fashion on a round plate, with the larger stalk ends of asparagus toward outer edge.

HAM-ASPARAGUS HOLLANDAISE

   1 package (1⅝ oz.) hollandaise sauce mix or ⅔ cup prepared hollandaise sauce
   3 tablespoons (half of 3-oz. pkg.) cream cheese
   ¼ cup mayonnaise or salad dressing
   1 package (10 oz.) frozen asparagus spears
   8 slices (two 4-oz. pkgs.) boiled ham
      Slivered toasted almonds, if desired

Setting: HIGH

1. In 2-cup glass measure, prepare hollandaise sauce mix according to package directions.

2. MICROWAVE for 2½ to 3 MINUTES or until mixture boils, stirring 3 times.

3. In small glass bowl, MICROWAVE cream cheese for 10 SECONDS; blend in mayonnaise. Remove wax or foil overwrap from asparagus and place package in oven.

4. MICROWAVE for 2 MINUTES. Open package and rearrange asparagus. Close package.

5. MICROWAVE for 4 MINUTES. Spread cream cheese mixture on ham slices. Divide asparagus spears among ham slices. Roll up, securing with toothpick. Place rolls on serving platter.

6. MICROWAVE for 1 MINUTE. Pour sauce over rolls and MICROWAVE for 2 to 3 MINUTES or until hot. Garnish with almonds.

4 to 5 Servings

TIP To heat 1 roll that has been refrigerated, MICROWAVE 45 SECONDS; 2 rolls, MICROWAVE 1 MINUTE.

SMOKED PORK CHOPS

Setting: DEFROST

1. Arrange chops in shallow baking dish or platter. If desired, brush with honey or orange marmalade; cover.

2. MICROWAVE until edges of meat begin to sizzle:

      3 chops — 6 to 6½ MINUTES
      4 chops — 7 to 8 MINUTES
      5 chops — 8 to 10 MINUTES

Pictured, top to bottom: Country Barbecued Ribs, page 89, (combination of microwave cooking and grilling), Stuffed Pork Chops, page 88, Sweet and Sour Pork, page 88, Baked Ham, page 75, (garnish with cloves), Stuffed Pork Tenderloin, page 89, (garnish with kumquats).

HAM LOAF

3 eggs, slightly beaten
1½ lbs. ground cooked ham
½ cup (½ slice) soft bread cubes
¼ cup firmly packed brown sugar
1 tablespoon chopped onion or
  1 teaspoon instant minced onion
2 tablespoons chopped green pepper
  if desired
1½ tablespoons prepared mustard
¼ cup milk

Setting: HIGH

1. In mixing bowl, combine all ingredients. Press mixture into 1½-quart (8 x 4) glass loaf dish; cover.

2. MICROWAVE for 12 to 15 MINUTES or until done. Let stand a few minutes before slicing and serving.

4 to 6 Servings

TIPS For individual ham loaves, place ½ cup mixture in about nine 5 or 6-oz. custard cups. MICROWAVE, uncovered:

1 cup — 2 to 2½ MINUTES
2 cups — 3 to 3½ MINUTES
3 cups — 4 to 4½ MINUTES
4 cups — 5 to 5½ MINUTES

Invert onto serving plate.
• Loaf can be topped before cooking with mixture of ¾ cup drained crushed pineapple and 2 tablespoons brown sugar. For individual loaves, place 1 tablespoon of this mixture in bottom of each custard cup.
• MICROWAVE on MEDIUM for 16 to 18 MINUTES.

An especially colorful and tasty dress up for ham. You can serve a ham slice more economically by buying a ready-to-eat boneless ham, cutting a slice and then using the remainder for other recipes.

FESTIVE HAM SLICE

1 ham slice, cut 1 inch thick (2¼ lbs.)
½ cup whole cranberry sauce
½ orange, sliced and quartered
Whole cloves

Setting: DEFROST

1. Place ham slice in shallow glass baking dish or platter; cover.

2. MICROWAVE for 8 MINUTES. Spoon cranberry sauce over top of ham. Insert a clove in each orange piece and arrange on cranberry sauce.

3. MICROWAVE for 3 to 4 MINUTES or until hot.

6 to 8 Servings

TIPS Cherry pie filling can be used for cranberry sauce.
• For other ham slice thicknesses cook: ½ inch thick — 5 minutes; then, 2 minutes.
1½ inch thick — 10 minutes; then, 4 minutes. Increase or decrease sauce as desired.
• MICROWAVE on MEDIUM for 6 MINUTES in step 2.

This recipe calls for the popular, ready-to-eat ham. Since this ham is already cooked, time to reach serving temperature is all that is necessary.

PINEAPPLE GLAZED HAM

1 small ready-to-eat ham
  (2½ to 3½ lbs.)
⅓ cup packed brown sugar
⅓ cup drained crushed pineapple
1 teaspoon dry mustard
8 to 10 whole cloves, if desired

Setting: DEFROST

1. In shallow glass baking dish, place ham fat side down on microwave roasting rack.

2. MICROWAVE for 18 MINUTES. Turn ham fat side up.

3. MICROWAVE for 18 to 20 MINUTES.

4. Combine brown sugar, pineapple and mustard. Slash fat at 1-inch intervals and insert cloves in fat. Spoon pineapple mixture over ham.

5. MICROWAVE for 6 to 8 MINUTES, or until meat thermometer registers 120°F. (do not leave thermometer in oven when cooking). Let stand, covered with foil, 10 minutes.

About 8 Servings

TIPS If one end of ham is smaller, cover with foil during first half of cooking time.
• For an easy glaze, try brushing the ham with apple or currant jelly, orange marmalade, or a combination of ⅓ cup drained crushed pineapple.
• MICROWAVE on MEDIUM for 12 to 13 MINUTES per pound.

This recipe is very easy to double for larger amounts. One of our consumer testers wrapped these in foil after cooking the roll-ups and took them on a picnic. She found them to be a nice change from sandwiches.

SWISS HAM ROLL-UPS

15 frozen tater tots
4 slices (4-oz. pkg.) boiled ham
2 slices (half 8-oz. pkg.) Swiss cheese
¼ cup sour cream

Setting: HIGH

1. MICROWAVE tater tots on paper plate or towel, for 1½ to 2 MINUTES or until thawed.

2. Place ½ slice of cheese on each ham slice. Spread each cheese slice with sour cream. Place 3 tater tots inside each ham-cheese slice and roll-up, fastening with toothpick. Place on serving platter.

3. MICROWAVE for 2 to 2½ MINUTES or until hot.

4 Roll-ups (2 Servings)

TIP To heat 1 roll, MICROWAVE 45 SECONDS; 2 rolls, MICROWAVE 1 MINUTE, 15 SECONDS.

ORANGE GLAZED CANADIAN BACON

1½ lbs. Canadian-style bacon
¼ cup orange marmalade
Dash dry mustard

Setting: DEFROST

1. Cut bacon into 8 slices (about ½ inch thick). Place in 2-quart (12 x 7) glass baking dish. Spread about 1 teaspoon marmalade on each slice. Sprinkle with dry mustard.

2. MICROWAVE for 12 to 15 MINUTES or until hot. Let stand 5 minutes before serving.

About 6 Servings

BARBECUED PORK CHOPS

4 loin or rib pork chops, cut ½ inch thick
¾ cup barbecue sauce
½ cup (1 med.) chopped onion or 2 tablespoons instant minced onion
1 clove garlic, minced or ⅛ teaspoon instant minced garlic
⅛ teaspoon pepper

Setting: DEFROST

1. Arrange chops in single layer in 2-quart (8 x 8) or 1½-quart (10 x 6) glass baking dish. Combine remaining ingredients and pour over chops; cover.

2. MICROWAVE for 15 to 18 MINUTES or until done, occasionally spooning sauce over chops.

4 Servings

TIP For 6 chops, use 2-quart (12 x 7) glass baking dish, increase barbecue sauce to 1 cup and increase cooking time to 20 minutes.

GERMAN-STYLE SMOKED CHOPS

2 cups (1-lb. can) drained sauerkraut
1 small onion, chopped or 1 tablespoon instant minced onion
2 medium apples, chopped
1 tablespoon sugar
4 smoked pork chops
½ cup water

Settings: HIGH/DEFROST

1. In 2-quart (8 x 8) glass baking dish, mix together half of sauerkraut, onion, apple, and sugar. Top with chops; layer remaining sauerkraut, onion, apple and sugar over chops. Mix this layer lightly to distribute ingredients. Pour water over mixture; cover.

2. MICROWAVE on HIGH for 5 MINUTES.

3. MICROWAVE on DEFROST for 6 to 8 MINUTES or until apple is tender.

4 Servings

HAM 'N NOODLE BAKE

1½ cups water
1 cup noodles, uncooked
1 cup cubed cooked ham
1 cup cooked or canned cut green beans
1 can (10½ oz.) condensed cream of celery soup
¼ teaspoon dry mustard
⅛ teaspoon pepper
⅓ to ½ cup milk
Buttered bread crumbs or French-fried onion rings

Settings: HIGH/DEFROST

1. In 2-quart glass casserole, MICROWAVE water on HIGH for 3 MINUTES. Add noodles.

2. MICROWAVE on DEFROST for about 10 MINUTES. Let stand, covered, 5 minutes and drain.

3. Add ham, green beans, soup, mustard, pepper and milk; cover.

4. MICROWAVE on HIGH for 3 to 4 MINUTES or until hot, stirring once. Top with crumbs just before serving.

4 Servings

TIP Casserole can be made ahead by cooking noodles and adding remaining ingredients. Refrigerate. Just before serving, MICROWAVE on HIGH for 6 to 8 MINUTES or until hot, stirring once.

HAM 'N YAM STACKS

4 to 6 medium yams or sweet potatoes
2 tablespoons packed brown sugar
½ tablespoon cornstarch
⅛ teaspoon cinnamon
1 cup (8-oz. can) undrained crushed pineapple
1 tablespoon lemon juice
6 slices (1 serving each) cooked ham

Settings: HIGH/DEFROST

1. Cook yams as directed on page 117. Meanwhile, prepare sauce by combining in 2-cup glass measure, brown sugar, cornstarch, cinnamon, pineapple and lemon juice.

2. MICROWAVE on HIGH for 3 to 4 MINUTES, stirring occasionally until mixture boils and thickens.

3. Arrange ham on serving platter; cool yams enough to handle. Peel yams, slice or leave whole and arrange on top of ham. Spoon sauce over each serving.

4. MICROWAVE on DEFROST for 6 to 7 MINUTES or until heated through.

6 Servings

TIPS For individual servings, MICROWAVE for 1 MINUTE if room temperature; 2 MINUTES if refrigerated temperature.

• If desired, use canned yams or sweet potatoes and omit step of cooking yams.

ROAST FRESH PORK KEY: A microwave oven cooks large pork cuts thoroughly — keeps them tender and juicy. Start cooking on Microwave HIGH to heat meat through quickly. Lower setting to DEFROST during last half of cooking to assure evenly done meat.

Thaw meat completely before cooking. See defrosting chart on page 71.

Boneless and bone-in roasts cook in about the same time in open flat glass baking dishes. Place meat on a microwave roasting rack to hold it above drippings.

Microwave roasts, fat side down first; turn smaller roasts over halfway through cooking. If roast weighs 7 pounds or more, turn it over 3 times during cooking.

Pork is removed from the oven when internal temperature reaches 160°F. so meat does not overcook. Insert a microwave meat thermometer in roast center when meat is turned the last time.

Let meat stand, covered with foil, to finish cooking and raise internal temperature about 15°F. Pork is done when internal temperature reaches 170°F.

Other doneness tests: When roast center is cut, juices run clear and meat is no longer pink. Or a conventional meat thermometer may be inserted after meat is taken from the oven. DO NOT use this thermometer in a microwave oven.

Smaller pork cuts are done when meat is no longer pink and juices run clear. Thorough cooking is important but do not overcook.

SWEET AND SOUR PORK

  1½ **lbs. cubed lean pork**
    2 **tablespoons cornstarch**
    3 **tablespoons soy sauce**
   ¼ **cup packed brown sugar**
   ¼ **cup vinegar**
    1 **teaspoon salt**
   ¼ **teaspoon ground ginger**
    1 **can (13¼ oz.) pineapple chunks, undrained**
    1 **small onion, thinly sliced**
    1 **medium green pepper, cut into strips**

Settings: HIGH/DEFROST

1. Toss together pork and cornstarch in 2-quart glass casserole. Stir in remaining ingredients, except green pepper. Cover with glass lid.

2. MICROWAVE on HIGH for 10 MINUTES. Stir in green pepper. Recover.

3. MICROWAVE on DEFROST for 25 to 30 MINUTES or until fork tender. Let stand, covered, 5 minutes before serving.

4 to 6 Servings

TIP MICROWAVE on MEDIUM for 25 MINUTES in step 2 and 5 to 10 MINUTES in step 3.

CENTER RIB PORK ROAST WITH CHERRY SAUCE

    4 **to 5-lb. pork loin center rib roast**

Cherry Sauce
   ½ **cup cherry preserves**
   ¼ **cup dark corn syrup**
    2 **tablespoons vinegar**
   ⅛ **teaspoon salt**
   ⅛ **teaspoon nutmeg**
   ⅛ **teaspoon cinnamon**
   ⅛ **teaspoon ground cloves**
     Dash pepper

Settings: HIGH/DEFROST

1. Place roast, fat side down on microwave roasting rack, in 2-quart (12 x 7) glass baking dish.

2. MICROWAVE on HIGH for 27 MINUTES. Turn fat side up.

3. MICROWAVE on DEFROST for 22 to 26 MINUTES or until microwave meat thermometer inserted in center of meat reaches 160°F. Let stand, covered with foil, 15 minutes before serving or until internal temperature reaches 170°F. Slash pork roast between ribs; place on serving platter. Pour hot Cherry Sauce over meat.

4. Cherry Sauce: Combine all ingredients in 2-cup glass measure.

5. MICROWAVE on HIGH for 3 to 4 MINUTES or until bubbly.

6 to 8 Servings

TIPS BONELESS PORK ROAST: Use same technique as above. See meat roasting chart, page 73, for time and doneness tests.
● MICROWAVE on MEDIUM for 20 to 24 MINUTES in step 3.

STUFFED PORK CHOPS

   ½ **cup milk**
   ¼ **cup butter or margarine**
    2 **cups dry seasoned bread stuffing**
    1 **envelope (⅝ oz.) brown gravy mix**
    8 **thin rib pork chops (about 1½ lbs.), trim off fat**

Settings: HIGH/DEFROST

1. Combine milk and butter in medium glass mixing bowl.

2. MICROWAVE on HIGH for 2 to 3 MINUTES until butter is melted. Stir in bread stuffing and mix well; set aside. Sprinkle one side of 4 chops with half of dry gravy mix; place seasoned side down in 2-quart (8 x 8) glass baking dish. Spoon dressing on top of each chop. Place remaining chops on top of dressing. Sprinkle with remaining gravy mix; cover.

3. MICROWAVE on DEFROST for 15 to 18 MINUTES or until fork tender. Let stand, covered, 5 minutes before serving.

About 4 Servings

Ribs begin cooking in the microwave oven and then are quickly finished on the grill. This idea can be used with other meats that normally need long grilling times.

COUNTRY BARBECUED RIBS

1½ to 2 lbs. country-style ribs

Sauce
- ¼ cup catsup
- ¼ cup chili sauce or tomato sauce
- 1 tablespoon brown sugar
- 2 tablespoons chopped onion or
  1½ teaspoons instant minced onion
- ½ teaspoon salt
- ⅛ teaspoon garlic powder or instant minced garlic
- 1 teaspoon dry or prepared mustard
- ½ tablespoon Worcestershire sauce
- Dash Tabasco sauce
- 1 slice lemon or 1 teaspoon lemon juice

Setting: HIGH

1. Cut ribs into one-rib pieces. Arrange in 2-quart (8 x 8) glass baking dish (place larger pieces around edge); cover.

2. MICROWAVE for 12 MINUTES or until partially cooked, rearranging halfway through cooking time.

3. Meanwhile, in 1-cup measure, combine ingredients for **Sauce**; mix well. Remove ribs from oven; drain.

4. MICROWAVE sauce 1 to 1½ MINUTES or until mixture boils, stirring once. Pour over ribs, turning to coat or dip each rib into sauce to coat.

5. Cool and refrigerate until ready to grill or grill immediately.

6. Grill over hot coals for 15 to 20 minutes, turning occasionally until ribs are browned and heated through.

3 to 4 Servings

TIP Ribs can be broiled as well as grilled.

HOW TO COOK PORK CHOPS ON A MICROWAVE BROWNING GRILL

- Preheat microwave browning grill in oven on HIGH as directed in manufacturer's instruction booklet.
- Place chop(s) on preheated browning grill.
- Turn once half way through cooking.
- Let stand 3 minutes on hot microwave browning grill before serving.

PORK CHOPS	WEIGHT	SETTING	MINUTES
1 (½-in. thick)	3-oz.	HIGH	3½ to 4
2 (½-in. thick)	3-oz. ea.	HIGH	5 to 6

STUFFED PORK TENDERLOIN

- ¼ cup butter or margarine
- ¼ cup sesame seed
- ½ cup (1 stalk) chopped celery
- 2 tablespoons chopped onion or
  2 teaspoons instant minced onion
- 3 slices bread, cubed
- 1 teaspoon salt
- ½ teaspoon poultry seasoning or thyme
- 1 teaspoon Worcestershire sauce
- 2 pork tenderloins, about 1¼ lbs. each

Settings: HIGH/DEFROST

1. In glass mixing bowl, combine butter, sesame seed, celery and onion.

2. MICROWAVE on HIGH for 3 MINUTES, stirring occasionally. Mix in bread, salt, poultry seasoning and Worcestershire sauce.

3. Cut each pork tenderloin almost through lengthwise, flatten slightly. To keep meat out of juices, invert a saucer in bottom of 2-quart (12 x 7) glass baking dish. Lay one of flattened tenderloins, cut-side up, in baking dish. (For ease in tying, place about 4 pieces of string at intervals under tenderloin.)

4. Spoon bread stuffing onto tenderloin. Top with other tenderloin, cut-side down with wide end over narrow end of bottom piece. Bring string around tenderloins, tying to hold together.

5. MICROWAVE on DEFROST for 25 MINUTES, turn dish, MICROWAVE on DEFROST for 12 to 15 MINUTES or until done. Cover loosely with foil and let stand 10 to 15 minutes.

6 Servings

TIP If desired, use 2 cups seasoned bread cubes for bread, salt and poultry seasoning.

SHERRY GLAZED SPARERIBS

- 2 lbs. spareribs, cut into 1-inch pieces
- ¼ cup firmly packed brown sugar
- 1 tablespoon cornstarch
- 3 tablespoons soy sauce
- ¼ cup sherry
- ¼ cup orange juice

Settings: HIGH/DEFROST

1. Arrange ribs in 2-quart (12 x 7) glass baking dish; cover.

2. MICROWAVE on HIGH for 5 MINUTES. Drain juices and rearrange ribs. Combine brown sugar and cornstarch; mix in remaining ingredients. Pour over ribs; recover.

3. MICROWAVE on DEFROST for 30 to 40 MINUTES or until done, occasionally turning and rearranging ribs in pan. Pour off excess fat before serving. If desired, garnish with orange slices, cut in half.

4 Servings

TIP Microwave on MEDIUM for 20 to 25 MINUTES in step 3.

MAIN COURSES **Sausage & Luncheon Meats**

SAUSAGE AND LUNCHEON MEATS KEY: Luncheon meats and sausages (except fresh pork sausage) are already cooked. MICRO-WAVE them on HIGH to bring them to a serving temperature. To avoid overcooking, the meat is sometimes added toward the end of the cooking time when it is part of a longer cooking casserole. It is not necessary to score the outer edge of sausage before cooking it. Sausage combinations are good make aheads for individual servings that can be kept on hand in the refrigerator as a quickly heated meal or snack.

IMPORTANT: Before you begin, refer to the "Beginning to Cook" section for basic technique and these example recipes:

Hot Dogs 18
Wieners in the Round 21

Be sure metal skewers will fit in the oven without touching the walls. Keep the larger foods toward the ends and the smaller foods toward the center.

BOLOGNA KABOBS

    1 **ring (16 oz.) bologna, cut into ¾-inch chunks**
    1 **can (8¼ oz.) pineapple chunks, drained**
    1 **can (16 oz.) whole potatoes, drained**
    1 **green pepper, cut into 1-inch pieces**
      Pitted ripe olives
  ¼ **cup orange marmalade**
      Cherry tomatoes

Setting: HIGH

1. Alternate bologna slices, pineapple chunks, potatoes, green pepper and olives on metal kabob skewers. Arrange on microwave roasting rack in 2-quart (12 x 7) glass baking dish. Spread marmalade over kabobs.

2. MICROWAVE for 8 to 9 MINUTES or until hot. Spear tomatoes on ends just before serving.

About 4 Servings

TIPS Cooked sweet potatoes can be used for canned whole potatoes.
● Cooked ham, cut into 1-inch cubes, can be used for bologna.
● Popsicle sticks make handy skewers for using in the oven.
● MICROWAVE on MEDIUM for 12 to 14 MINUTES in step 2.

Here is a quick and tasty way to make German potato salad using dehydrated hash brown potatoes. Do not use a paper towel under the bacon because you need the bacon drippings for the salad. Mix it together early in the day and then cook just before serving to heat the salad and bologna.

BOLOGNA AND GERMAN POTATO SALAD

    4 **slices bacon**
  1⅓ **cups hash brown potatoes**
  1⅔ **cups water**
    1 **teaspoon parsley flakes**
  ¼ **teaspoon salt**
    2 **teaspoons instant minced onion or 3 green onions, sliced**
    2 **tablespoons sugar**
    1 **tablespoon flour**
  ¼ **cup water**
  ¼ **cup white vinegar**
    1 **ring (12 oz.) bologna**

Setting: HIGH

1. Place bacon in 2-quart glass casserole; cover.

2. MICROWAVE for 2½ to 3 MINUTES or until crisp. Remove bacon, leaving extra drippings in casserole. Add potatoes and 1⅔ cups water; cover.

3. MICROWAVE for 6 MINUTES. Stir in crumbled bacon and remaining ingredients except bologna, mixing well. Arrange evenly in casserole. Top with ring of bologna; recover.

4. MICROWAVE for 4½ to 5 MINUTES.

3 to 4 Servings

TIPS If desired, use 12 oz. (¾ lb.) wieners for bologna. For best heating, arrange spoke fashion around edge of casserole, cutting in half crosswise if necessary. Since wieners are smaller than bologna, reduce final cooking period to 3 minutes.
● MICROWAVE on MEDIUM for 6 to 7 MINUTES in step 4.

Pictured: Bologna Kabobs, page 90, (see recipe for use of metal skewers), served on rice, and Stuffed Cabbage Rolls, page 82.

BOLOGNA ROLL UPS

Sliced Bologna
Onion dip, cream cheese or sour cream
Strips of cheese or pickle

Setting: HIGH

1. Spread about ½ tablespoon dip down center of each slice of bologna. Top with a cheese or pickle strip. Roll up, fastening with toothpicks. Place on serving platter.

2. MICROWAVE 8 roll ups for 2 to 2½ MINUTES or until hot.

8 Roll Ups

TIPS For 4 roll ups, MICROWAVE 1 MINUTE. If desired, place roll ups (before heating) in wiener buns. Heat 1 roll up, in a bun, 25 to 30 SECONDS or until hot.
● Bologna can be spread with mustard and filled with leftover mashed potato or other thick casserole mixtures. Heat 2½ to 3 minutes, or until hot.
● MICROWAVE on MEDIUM for 3 to 4 MINUTES in step 2.

Bratwurst will cook in the oven, but will lack browning. Unless serving bratwurst in a bun, you will probably prefer to place them on the grill or under the broiler for browning.

BRATWURST IN BEER

6 uncooked bratwurst (about 1 lb.)
½ cup finely chopped onion
2 tablespoons butter or margarine
1 can (12 oz.) beer, room temperature

Setting: DEFROST

1. Place bratwurst in 8-inch round glass baking dish. Add remaining ingredients. Cover with plastic wrap.

2. MICROWAVE for 7 to 8 MINUTES or until done. Let stand, covered, 5 minutes before serving.

About 3 Servings

TIPS These can be microwaved and left to marinate in beer up to 12 hours.
● Try this same idea with equal amounts of Knackwurst or Metwurst.
● MICROWAVE on MEDIUM for 5 to 6 MINUTES.

BRATWURST

Setting: HIGH

1. Preheat microwave browning grill as directed in manufacturer's instructions booklet.

2. Arrange 4 precooked bratwurst on grill.

3. MICROWAVE for 1 MINUTE. Turn bratwurst.

4. MICROWAVE for 2 MINUTES. Turn and MICROWAVE for 1 to 1½ MINUTES.

TIPS For 2 bratwurst, MICROWAVE for 1 MINUTE, turn and MICROWAVE 1 MINUTE more.
● With fresh bratwurst, MICROWAVE 2 bratwurst 1 MINUTE longer; MICROWAVE 4 bratwurst 2 MINUTES longer.

WIENERS-IN-A-BLANKET

> 1 can (8 oz.) refrigerated biscuits
> Mustard or catsup
> 5 wieners
> 2 tablespoons butter or margarine, melted
> Sesame or poppy seed, if desired

Setting: HIGH

1. Separate biscuit dough into 10 biscuits. Flatten each into oval shape about 3 inches long. Spread with mustard or catsup to within ½ inch of edge.

2. Cut wieners in half crosswise. Place one piece in each biscuit. Wrap biscuit around wieners, sealing edges by pinching firmly together. Dip in butter to coat all sides. Sprinkle with seeds.

3. Preheat microwave browning grill as directed in manufacturer's instruction booklet.

4. Place wrapped wieners on grill. Turn biscuits ⅓ rd over before returning to oven.

5. MICROWAVE for 1 MINUTE. Turn another ⅓ turn. MICROWAVE for 2 MINUTES longer or until biscuits are done.

10 Small Sandwiches

CHEESE-IN-A-BLANKET

Substitute sticks of cheese 3 inches long by ⅜-inch thick, for wiener halves. Reduce final cooking to 1½ minutes.

TIP For even cooking, transfer biscuits from edge to center when turning the second time.

CORN 'N WIENERS

> ⅓ cup chopped onion or 1 tablespoon instant minced onion
> ⅓ cup sliced green pepper
> 2 tablespoons butter or margarine
> 2 cans (12 oz. each) whole kernel corn, drained
> ⅔ cup pitted black olives, cut in half
> ⅓ cup shredded Swiss cheese
> 6 wieners, cut into ½-inch slices
> 2 to 3 tablespoons catsup
> Grated Parmesan cheese

Setting: HIGH

1. In 2-quart glass casserole, combine onion, green pepper and butter; cover.

2. MICROWAVE for 3 MINUTES or until tender, stirring once. Stir in corn, olives, Swiss cheese and wieners; recover.

3. MICROWAVE for 5 MINUTES, stirring once. Spoon catsup over casserole and sprinkle with Parmesan cheese; cover.

4. MICROWAVE for 2 to 3 MINUTES or until cheese is melted.

6 Servings

TIP MICROWAVE on MEDIUM for 7 to 8 MINUTES in step 3.

These wieners can be served over buns as a sandwich or on toothpicks as an appetizer.

BARBECUED WIENERS

> 1 package (⅝ oz.) home-style gravy mix
> 1 cup water
> 1 tablespoon instant minced onion or ¼ cup chopped onion
> 1 cup catsup
> 1 tablespoon prepared mustard
> 10 wieners, cut into ½-inch slices

Setting: HIGH

1. In 1-quart glass casserole, combine gravy mix, water and onion.

2. MICROWAVE for 3 MINUTES, stirring twice. Add catsup, mustard and wieners; cover.

3. MICROWAVE for 6 MINUTES or until hot, stirring once.

5 Servings

TIPS This dish can be refrigerated and reheated, MICROWAVE, covered, for 7 MINUTES or until hot, stirring twice.
● MICROWAVE on MEDIUM for 8 to 9 MINUTES in step 3.

BEANS 'N KRAUT

> **1 lb. wieners (10)**
> **1 can (31 oz.) pork and beans**
> **¼ cup chili sauce**
> **1 can (16 oz.) sauerkraut, drained**
> **1 teaspoon caraway seeds**

Setting: HIGH

1. Cut half of wieners into ¼-inch slices. Combine with pork and beans and chili sauce in 2-quart glass casserole. Spread sauerkraut on top. Sprinkle with caraway seeds. Cover with glass lid or plastic wrap.

2. MICROWAVE for 10 MINUTES. Arrange remaining wieners on top, spoke fashion. Recover and MICROWAVE for 4 to 5 MINUTES or until heated through.

3 to 4 Servings

TIP MICROWAVE on MEDIUM for 6 to 7 MINUTES in last cooking period.

WIENERS

Setting: HIGH

1. Place wieners on serving plate.

2. MICROWAVE uncovered, until wieners are hot:
   1 wiener — 30 to 35 SECONDS
   2 wieners — 45 to 50 SECONDS
   3 wieners — 1 to 1½ MINUTES
   4 wieners — 1½ to 2 MINUTES
   6 wieners — 2 to 2½ MINUTES
   10 wieners — 3 to 3½ MINUTES

TIP MICROWAVE on MEDIUM for a little longer.

Beans, Kraut and Wieners

We found those who normally don't care for sauerkraut were pleasantly surprised with this dish. This is good served with baked potatoes. Start cooking the sauerkraut first, then cook potatoes before the final heating of wieners.

SAVORY KRAUT 'N WIENERS

> **¼ cup butter or margarine**
> **1 stalk celery, sliced**
> **1 small onion, sliced**
> **¼ cup sugar**
> **1 cube or teaspoon beef bouillon**
> **¼ teaspoon ground ginger**
> **1½ tablespoons cornstarch**
> **1 tablespoon chopped pimento, if desired**
> **2 tablespoons vinegar**
> **1½ cups water**
> **2 cups (1-lb. can) sauerkraut (drain, using liquid for part of water)**
> **4 to 8 wieners**

Setting: HIGH

1. In 2-quart glass casserole, combine butter, celery and onion.

2. MICROWAVE for 2 MINUTES, stirring after butter melts. Stir in sugar, bouillon, ginger and cornstarch. Add pimento, vinegar, water and sauerkraut; mix well and cover.

3. MICROWAVE for 5 MINUTES, stirring occasionally. Arrange wieners on top; cover.

4. MICROWAVE for 2 MINUTES or until heated through.

4 to 5 Servings

TIP For 2 servings, microwave half of ingredients in 1-quart glass casserole. MICROWAVE about 3 MINUTES and then after adding wieners, 1½ to 2 MINUTES.

Here's a hot potato salad turned into a main dish with sauerkraut and cocktail franks.

FRANK 'N POTATO SALAD

> **4 cups (2 lbs.) prepared potato salad**
> **1 cup (8-oz. can) drained sauerkraut**
> **½ lb. cocktail franks**
> **½ teaspoon salt**
> **½ teaspoon caraway seed**
> **Paprika**

Setting: HIGH

1. In 1½ or 2-quart glass casserole, combine all ingredients except paprika; cover.

2. MICROWAVE for 7 to 8 MINUTES or until hot, stirring once. Sprinkle with paprika before serving.

6 Servings

TIP MICROWAVE on MEDIUM for 9 to 10 MINUTES in step 2.

HOW TO COOK PORK SAUSAGE ON MICROWAVE BROWNING GRILL

• Preheat microwave browning grill in oven on HIGH as directed in manufacturer's instructions.

• Place sausage on preheated grill.

• Microwave on HIGH. Turn sausage over and rearrange halfway through cooking.

• Cook fresh pork sausage until no longer pink in center.

• Brown precooked sausage until hot; serve.

PORK SAUSAGE	SETTING	MINUTES
FRESH LINKS 8-oz. pkg.	HIGH	6 to 6½
PRECOOKED LINKS OR PATTIES 8-oz. pkg.		
Frozen	HIGH	3 to 3½
Refrigerated	HIGH	1½ to 2

HOW TO MICROWAVE PRECOOKED PORK SAUSAGE

• Place sausage links or patties on paper napkin or paper towel on glass plate.

• Microwave on HIGH until hot; serve.

PORK SAUSAGE	SETTING	TIME
PRECOOKED LINKS OR PATTIES Frozen:		
2	HIGH	1 to 1½ min.
3	HIGH	1¾ to 2 min.
4	HIGH	2 to 2½ min.
Refrigerated: 2	HIGH	15 to 30 sec.
3	HIGH	30 to 45 sec.
4	HIGH	1 to 1½ min.

ORANGE GLAZED LUNCHEON LOAF

> 1 can (12 oz.) luncheon meat
> 4 thin orange slices, cut in half
> 8 whole cloves
> ¼ cup orange marmalade
> 1 teaspoon all-purpose flour
> ⅛ teaspoon dry mustard or ¼ teaspoon prepared mustard

Setting: HIGH

1. Place meat in 2-quart (8 x 8) or 1½-quart (8-inch round) glass baking dish. Cut half way through meat into 8 slices. Insert orange slice between each slice and clove in top of each slice.

2. In 1-cup glass measure, combine orange marmalade, flour and mustard.

3. MICROWAVE for 1 MINUTE. Stir and spread over meat. Cover loosely with wax paper.

4. MICROWAVE for 5 to 6 MINUTES or until glaze begins to bubble around edges.

4 Servings

TIPS Pineapple slices, cut in half may be used for orange slices.
• MICROWAVE on MEDIUM for 7 to 8 MINUTES in step 4.

Cheese is added near the end of the cooking time to avoid stringiness.

SMOKIE MUSHROOM SUPPER

> 1 medium onion (½ cup), chopped
> 1 can (10½ oz.) condensed cream of mushroom soup
> ⅔ cup (4-oz. can) undrained mushroom stems and pieces
> 1½ cups (12-oz. can) undrained corn with red and green peppers
> 1 cup quick-cooking rice, uncooked
> 2 eggs, beaten
> ¼ cup milk
> 1 package (10 oz.) smokie links
> 1 cup (4 oz.) shredded Monterey Jack cheese

Setting: HIGH

1. In 2-quart glass casserole, MICROWAVE for 2 to 2½ MINUTES or until tender.

2. Add soup, mushrooms, corn, rice, eggs and milk. Reserve 4 smokie links and cut remaining links into ½-inch slices; stir into casserole mixture; cover.

3. MICROWAVE for 12 to 13 MINUTES or until rice is tender, stirring once. Stir in cheese until melted. Cut reserved smokie links in half and arrange spoke fashion on top of casserole; recover.

4. MICROWAVE for 2 to 3 MINUTES or until links are hot.

6 to 8 Servings

MAIN COURSES **Other Meats**

VEAL KEY: Veal, meat from specially fed beef calves, is delicately flavored and textured. Cook larger roasts on DEFROST to gently cook and retain tenderness. Check meat chart for roasting times.

Small cuts of veal cook quickly enough to retain flavor and texture. Use the DEFROST setting throughout cooking.

Ground veal, as with ground beef and pork, cooks well on a higher setting — HIGH in this case.

Roast large cuts of veal on a microwave roasting rack set in a glass baking dish to catch drippings — see meat roasting chart. Braise large bone-in cuts. Use Braised Veal Rump Roast recipe, this page, as a guide.

Cook smaller veal cuts in a flat glass baking dish or casserole. Cover tightly with a glass lid, plastic wrap or wax paper to preserve meat's juiciness. Pierce plastic wrap before removing it to prevent steam burns.

Turn meat when specified to assure even cooking.

Remove veal from the oven when it is fork tender.

Follow standing time directions carefully so meat cooks completely.

BRAISED VEAL RUMP ROAST

 2½ to 3-lb. bone-in veal rump roast
 1 can (10¾ oz.) condensed beef and
   barley vegetable soup
 1 teaspoon salt
 ¼ teaspoon pepper
 1 tablespoon dried parsley flakes
 ½ teaspoon leaf thyme
 1 bay leaf
 2 tablespoons all-purpose flour

Setting: DEFROST

1. Place roast, fat side down, in 3-quart glass casserole. Cover with glass lid or plastic wrap.

2. MICROWAVE for 32 MINUTES. Turn meat over. Drain juice into measuring cup; set aside. Add remaining ingredients, except flour; recover.

3. MICROWAVE for 32 to 36 MINUTES or until fork tender. Let stand, covered, 5 minutes before serving. Remove roast to platter. Blend flour with juice drained from roast. Stir into hot seasoned meat drippings; mix well.

4. MICROWAVE for 2 to 3 MINUTES or until thickened. Serve gravy over toast.

About 4 Servings

This makes a convenient dish for company, because it is easy to assemble ahead for quick finishing in the microwave oven just before serving. Since the tomato sauce is very flavorful, serve with a mild vegetable such as corn or green beans.

VEAL PARMIGIANA

 1 egg, slightly beaten
 ¼ teaspoon salt
 2 tablespoons cornflake crumbs
 ⅓ cup grated Parmesan cheese
 1 lb. veal cutlets or boneless round steak
 2 tablespoons oil
 1 medium onion, chopped
 4 oz. (1 cup) sliced or shredded
   Mozzarella cheese
 1 cup (8-oz. can) tomato sauce
 Pepper
 ⅛ teaspoon leaf oregano or Italian
   seasoning
 Parmesan cheese

Settings: HIGH/DEFROST

1. In shallow dish, beat egg with salt. Combine crumbs and ⅓ cup Parmesan cheese on shallow plate or wax paper. Cut veal into 4 serving pieces and pound to make ¼ inch thick.

2. Dip veal in egg, then in crumb mixture, coating well.

3. Brown over medium high heat in oil in fry pan until golden brown, turning to brown both sides. Arrange in 1½-quart (10 x 6) glass baking dish, adding drippings from fry pan.

4. While meat is browning, MICROWAVE on HIGH onion in small glass sauce dish, for 2 to 3 MINUTES or until tender. Sprinkle onion over meat in baking dish. Top with cheese slices, then spoon tomato sauce over top. Sprinkle with pepper and oregano; cover.

5. MICROWAVE on DEFROST for 10 to 12 MINUTES or until bubbly. Sprinkle with Parmesan cheese; cover.

6. MICROWAVE on HIGH for 1 MINUTE to melt cheese.

4 Servings

TIPS To make ahead, assemble in baking dish and refrigerate. Since mixture is cold, increase cooking time to 18 MINUTES.

● Beef round steak, cut ¼ inch thick, can be used for veal.

● MICROWAVE on MEDIUM for 8 to 10 MINUTES in step 5.

VEAL GOULASH

- 1 lb. boneless veal cubes
- 1 package (⅝ oz.) brown gravy mix
- 1 medium onion (½ cup), chopped
- 2 stalks celery, chopped
- 2 tablespoons all-purpose flour
- 1½ cups water
- ¼ cup sherry
- 1 teaspoon paprika
- ½ teaspoon salt
- ⅛ teaspoon instant minced garlic or
  1 clove garlic, minced
- 1 teaspoon Worcestershire sauce

Settings: HIGH/DEFROST

1. In 1½ or 2-quart glass casserole, combine veal, gravy mix, onion and celery.

2. MICROWAVE on HIGH for 5 MINUTES. Stir in remaining ingredients, mixing well; cover.

3. MICROWAVE on DEFROST for 15 to 18 MINUTES or until veal is done, stirring occasionally. Let stand a few minutes before serving over noodles or potatoes.

3 to 4 Servings

TIPS Sherry can be omitted, increasing water to 1¾ cups.
● MICROWAVE on MEDIUM for 12 to 15 MINUTES in step 3.

LAMB KEY: Today's lamb is marketed at a young age, so flavor will be delicate and meat tender. Microwave cooking on DEFROST retains these key qualities.

Lamb should be completely thawed before cooking in a microwave oven.

Cook larger roasts, uncovered, on a microwave roasting rack. Set rack in shallow glass baking dish to catch drippings. Turn roasts as specified in roasting chart on page 73, to make certain meat cooks evenly.

Lamb steaks may be cooked uncovered, too, because they cook so quickly. Other small cuts of lamb should be covered to assure complete cooking plus tenderness. Microwave in glass casseroles or baking dishes covered tightly with glass lids, plastic wrap or wax paper. Pierce plastic wrap before removing it to prevent steam burns.

A microwave meat thermometer is the most accurate doneness test for large cuts. It should register 165°F. when meat comes from the oven. Foil covering during standing time allows internal temperature to rise about 15°F. and complete cooking. Small cuts of lamb are done when meat is fork tender.

Pictured, top to bottom: Garlic Glazed Lamb Roast, this page, Veal Parmigiana, page 95, Liver Bacon and Onions, page 99, and Curried Lamb Meatballs, page 98.

LAMB SHANKS

- 2 tablespoons all-purpose flour
- 1 teaspoon salt
- ½ teaspoon pepper
- ¼ teaspoon garlic salt
- 4 lamb shanks (2½ to 3 lbs.)
- ½ cup chopped onion
- 1 cup thinly sliced carrots
- 1 tablespoon dried parsley flakes
- ½ teaspoon leaf rosemary
- 1 teaspoon salt
- 1 can (10½ oz.) condensed beef consommé

Settings: HIGH/DEFROST

1. Combine flour, salt, pepper and garlic salt in 9-inch glass pie dish. Roll lamb shanks in seasoned flour; place in 2-quart (12 x 7) glass baking dish; cover.

2. MICROWAVE on HIGH for 20 MINUTES. Turn meat over. Stir in remaining ingredients; recover.

3. MICROWAVE on DEFROST for 20 to 25 MINUTES or until fork tender.

About 4 Servings

TIP MICROWAVE on MEDIUM for 25 MINUTES in step 2 and 15 to 20 MINUTES in step 3.

A garlic glaze enhances the flavor of lamb. The roast will be a very pleasing brown color when done.

GARLIC GLAZED LAMB ROAST

- cup dry sherry
- 1 tablespoon paprika
- ½ teaspoon leaf basil
- 2 tablespoons soy sauce
- 2 tablespoons oil
- 3 cloves garlic, minced, or ⅜ teaspoon instant minced garlic
- 4-lb. leg of lamb roast, boned

Setting: DEFROST

1. In 1-cup glass measure, combine all ingredients except roast.

2. MICROWAVE for about 1 MINUTE or until mixture is warm. Place roast on microwave roasting rack or small casserole cover in 2-quart (12 x 7) glass baking dish. Baste roast with garlic glaze.

3. MICROWAVE for 20 MINUTES. Turn roast and baste with additional garlic glaze.

4. MICROWAVE for 20 to 25 MINUTES or until meat thermometer registers 165°F. basting several times with garlic glaze. Let stand, covered with foil, 10 minutes or until internal temperature reaches 180°F.

6 to 8 Servings

TIP MICROWAVE on MEDIUM a total of 10 MINUTES per lb.

CURRIED LAMB MEATBALLS

  1 lb. ground lamb
  1 clove garlic, finely chopped
  1 medium onion, sliced
  1 stalk celery, sliced
  2 tablespoons all-purpose flour
1½ teaspoons curry powder
  1 teaspoon salt
  2 teaspoons instant chicken bouillon
  ¼ cup chutney
  1 teaspoon prepared mustard
  ¾ cup water

Settings: HIGH/DEFROST

1. Combine ground lamb and garlic in medium mixing bowl; mix well. Shape into 16 to 18 (1-inch) lamb balls. Place in 2-quart (12 x 7) glass baking dish. Add onion and celery; cover.

2. MICROWAVE on HIGH for 5 MINUTES. Combine remaining ingredients in 4-cup measure; mix well. Drain and rearrange lamb balls; pour on sauce; recover.

3. MICROWAVE on DEFROST for 8 to 10 MINUTES or until hot. Let stand, covered, 5 minutes before serving.

About 4 Servings

TIP MICROWAVE on MEDIUM for same times in step 2 and 3.

Since lamb is young tender meat, it does not need long cooking to tenderize. The meat is cooked for a short time with gravy mix to aid in browning the meat and sauce.

EASY LAMB STEW

  1 lb. boneless lamb stew meat
  1 package (⅝ oz.) brown gravy mix
  ½ teaspoon sugar
  2 tablespoons all-purpose flour
  1 teaspoon salt
  ⅛ teaspoon pepper
  ⅛ teaspoon instant minced garlic or
    1 clove garlic, minced
  1 teaspoon Worcestershire sauce
  1 cup water
  ½ cup red wine
  3 medium carrots, cut into ½-inch pieces
  2 stalks celery, cut into 1-inch pieces
  2 medium potatoes, cut into 1-inch cubes

Settings: HIGH/DEFROST

1. In 2 or 3-quart glass casserole, combine lamb, gravy mix and sugar.

2. MICROWAVE on HIGH for 5 MINUTES. Stir in remaining ingredients, mixing well; cover.

3. MICROWAVE on DEFROST for 35 to 45 MINUTES or until vegetables and meat are desired doneness, stirring occasionally.

4 Servings

LAMB PATTIES WITH PLUM SAUCE

1 lb. ground lamb
½ teaspoon salt
⅛ teaspoon pepper
½ cup plum preserves
2 teaspoons lemon juice

Setting: HIGH

1. In 2-quart (8 x 8) glass baking dish, combine lamb, salt and pepper. Shape into 4 patties and arrange in same baking dish.

2. MICROWAVE for 3 MINUTES. Drain and turn patties; top with plum preserves and sprinkle with lemon juice.

3. MICROWAVE for 2 to 3 MINUTES or until lamb is no longer pink. Spoon sauce from baking dish over patties before serving.

4 Servings

TIP MICROWAVE on MEDIUM for 4 MINUTES in step 2 and 3 to 4 MINUTES in step 3.

> **VARIETY MEAT KEY:** A homemaker's concern for top notch nutrition means liver, tongue and kidney dishes should become microwave oven favorites. DEFROST setting retains the fine texture and outstanding flavor of these low-fat meats. Liver is especially delicate and needs gentle cooking to prevent "popping."
>
> Microwave meat that is completely thawed.
>
> All variety meats are cooked, covered, in glass casseroles or baking dishes. Cover dishes tightly with glass lids, plastic wrap or wax paper. Pierce plastic wrap before removing it to prevent steam burns.
>
> Liver should be cooked quickly — only until meat loses its pink color. Do not overcook. Cooked liver slices may be reheated on DEFROST.
>
> Standing times are essential to tender evenly-cooked variety meats — observe these carefully.

FRIED LIVER AND BACON

2 slices bacon
½ lb. baby beef liver, cut in ⅜ inch
  slices

Setting: HIGH

1. Preheat microwave browning grill as directed in manufacturer's instruction booklet.

2. Lightly grease grill by placing bacon on grill and turning several times. Place bacon along edge of grill. Arrange liver slices in center.

3. MICROWAVE for 1 MINUTE; turn liver over.

4. MICROWAVE for 1½ to 2 MINUTES or until liver is desired doneness. If necessary, place bacon on paper towel and MICROWAVE for 15 to 30 SECONDS or until desired crispness.

2 to 3 Servings

When cooking liver in the oven, tender liver such as baby beef liver cooks best. With beef liver there is some connective tissue that may take long, slow cooking to tenderize. For best tenderness and juiciness, cook liver just until it loses its pinkness on the inside.

LIVER BACON AND ONIONS

> **4 slices bacon**
> **2 medium onions, sliced**
> **1 lb. baby beef liver, sliced**
> **Salt**
> **Pepper**

Settings: HIGH/DEFROST

1. Place bacon between paper napkin or towel in 2-quart (12 x 7) glass baking dish.

2. MICROWAVE on HIGH for 4 to 4½ MINUTES or until crisp. Remove bacon and drain. Coat liver slices with bacon drippings. Arrange in baking dish. Add onions. Cover with plastic wrap.

3. MICROWAVE on DEFROST for 12 to 14 MINUTES or until meat loses pink color. Crumble bacon on top. Let stand, covered, 5 minutes before serving.

About 4 Servings

> **VENISON KEY:** Venison roasts, steaks and chops microwave on DEFROST to juicy tenderness.
>
> Venison stew cooks with the typical microwave stew technique — first HIGH, then DEFROST.
>
> All meat should be completely thawed or it will take longer to cook. See defrosting chart page 71.
>
> Large venison cuts roast well on a microwave roasting rack in an open flat glass dish. Turn larger cuts to assure even cooking.
>
> Smaller venison cuts are cooked in glass casseroles or baking dishes covered tightly with glass lids, plastic wrap or wax paper. Pierce plastic wrap before removing it to prevent steam burns.
>
> Venison is often marinated and/or cooked in sauce becuase it sometimes has a strong flavor. These methods are particularly suited to microwave cooking and produce especially good results — quickly.
>
> Drain meat when called for to remove excess moisture and fat.
>
> Meat continues to cook and heat after it is removed from the oven. Standing time allows cooking to finish gently.

VENISON STEW

> **1½ lbs. venison stew meat, cubed**
> **2 tablespoons all-purpose flour**
> **2 tablespoons butter or margarine**
> **1 cup finely chopped carrots**
> **1 medium onion, chopped**
> **1 tablespoon dried parsley flakes**
> **1 teaspoon salt**
> **½ teaspoon garlic salt**
> **½ teaspoon Italian seasoning**
> **¼ teaspoon pepper**
> **1 cup water**
> **1 can (8 oz.) tomato sauce**
> **1 can (10¾ oz.) condensed cream of mushroom soup**

Settings: HIGH/DEFROST

1. Coat meat with flour. Place butter and meat in 2-quart glass casserole. Cover with glass lid or plastic wrap.

2. MICROWAVE on HIGH for about 10 MINUTES or until meat is no longer pink. Stir in remaining ingredients; recover.

3. MICROWAVE on DEFROST for 30 MINUTES. Stir and MICROWAVE on DEFROST for 15 to 20 MINUTES or until meat is fork tender. Let stand, covered, 5 minutes before serving.

4 to 6 Servings

TIP Serve atop wild rice.

Draining removes excess fat and moisture.

SAVORY VENISON CHOPS

> **6 venison chops (1½ to 2 lbs.), trim off fat**
> **1 medium onion, finely chopped**
> **¼ cup chopped celery**
> **¼ cup chopped green pepper**
> **¼ cup chili sauce**
> **¼ cup dry sherry or water**
> **1 teaspoon salt**
> **¼ teaspoon pepper**

Setting: DEFROST

1. Place chops, onion, celery and green pepper in 2-quart (12 x 7) glass baking dish. Cover with plastic wrap.

2. MICROWAVE on DEFROST for 15 MINUTES. Drain and turn meat over. Combine remaining ingredients in 4-cup measure. Pour over chops; recover.

3. MICROWAVE on DEFROST for 15 to 20 MINUTES. Let stand, covered, 5 minutes before serving.

3 to 4 Servings

TIPS Serve with zucchini and tossed green salad.
● MICROWAVE on MEDIUM for 10 MINUTES and then 10 to 15 MINUTES.

MAIN COURSES Eggs & Cheese

HOW TO SCRAMBLE EGGS

- Break eggs into soup bowl or 20-ounce glass casserole (1-quart size for 4, 5 or 6 eggs). Do not use dishes with silver, gold or other metal trim.
- Add milk and beat together with a fork.
- Add butter and other seasonings to taste.
- Cover with glass lid or plastic wrap.

- MICROWAVE on HIGH or MEDIUM setting. Stir 6 or more eggs once during cooking period.
- Stir gently with fork before serving.
- If cooking scrambled eggs a while before serving, undercook slightly and warm on HIGH when served.
- Soak cooking dish immediately after emptying for easiest clean-up.

NO. OF EGGS	BUTTER MARGARINE	MILK	APPROX. TIME ON HIGH	OR	APPROX. TIME ON MEDIUM
1	1 tsp.	1 tbsp.	45 sec.		1 to 1½ min.
2	2 tsps.	3 tbsps.	1 to 1¼ min.		2 to 2½ min.
4	4 tsps.	4 tbsps.	2½ to 3 min.		4½ to 5 min.
6	2 tbsps.	6 tbsps.	3½ to 4 min.		4 min.; stir 2½ to 3½ min.

TIP As with conventional cooking, egg dishes may be difficult to wash after standing. We found using a vegetable spray-on coating on the dish before cooking made cleaning easier. If you wish to omit melting butter, just cut it in pieces and add along with milk.

HOW TO POACH EGGS

- When poaching 1 to 3 eggs, use individual 6-ounce glass custard cups. Poach 4 eggs in a 1-quart glass casserole.
- Bring water and ¼ teaspoon vinegar to boil on HIGH.
- Break eggs carefully into hot water.

- Cover tightly with glass lid or plastic wrap.
- MICROWAVE eggs in boiling water on HIGH.
- Let stand, covered, 1 minute before serving.
- To poach eggs in bouillon, omit vinegar; use ½ cup water per egg plus 1 cube or teaspoon chicken bouillon. Stir after heating to dissolve bouillion.

WATER	GLASS CONTAINER	WATER SETTING AND TIME	EGGS	EGG SETTING AND TIME
¼ CUP	6-oz. custard cup	HIGH 1½ to 2 min.	1	HIGH 25 to 30 sec.
¼ CUP EA.	6-oz. custard cups	HIGH 2 to 2½ min.	2	HIGH 1 min.
1 CUP	1-qt. casserole	HIGH 2½ to 3 min.	4	HIGH 1½ to 2½ min.

TIPS The eggs don't need stirring until ⅔ cooked because little coagulation of the egg has taken place before that time.
- To reheat refrigerated eggs on serving plate, MICROWAVE on HIGH, covered with bowl:
  1 egg — 30 SECONDS
  2 eggs — 45 SECONDS
  3 eggs — 1 MINUTE, 10 SECONDS
  4 eggs (2 eggs/plate) — 1 MINUTE, 45 SECONDS

HOW TO FRY EGGS ON A MICROWAVE BROWNING GRILL

• Preheat microwave browning grill as directed in browner's instruction booklet on HIGH.

• Melt 1 teaspoon butter on microwave browning grill.

• Break egg(s) on browning grill.

• MICROWAVE on HIGH.

NO. OF EGGS	SETTING	MINUTES
1	HIGH	30 to 40 sec.
2	HIGH	1 to 1½ min.
4	HIGH	1½ to 2 min.

For these times, we used extra large eggs that were at refrigerator temperature. The cooking time is especially critical when preparing eggs that do not have the white and yolk mixed together.

HOW TO BAKE EGGS

• Break each egg into a buttered 10-ounce glass custard cup.

• Cover with plastic wrap.

• MICROWAVE on HIGH or MEDIUM setting.

• Let stand, covered, 1 minute before serving.

NO. OF EGGS	APPROX. TIME ON HIGH	OR	APPROX. TIME ON MEDIUM
1	30 to 35 sec.		35 to 40 sec.
2	1 min.		1 to 1¼ min.
4	1½ to 2 min.		2 to 2¼ min.

TIPS The composition of egg is such that the yolk has the highest fat content. Microwave energy tends to cook the yolk before the white. By covering the egg during cooking, the egg can be taken out before the white is completely set; the trapped steam will finish cooking the white during standing.

• An overcooked egg can be cut up and used as a hard-cooked egg in salads or sauces.

EGG KEY: MICROWAVE on HIGH or MEDIUM settings. Yolk has a high fat content which tends to make it cook faster than egg white. Covering the dish with plastic wrap for a baked egg holds in the heat to finish cooking the white without overcooking the yolk during the standing time. It is easiest to cook scrambled eggs because the yolk and white are mixed together before cooking. Stirring while cooking scrambled eggs prevents overcooking on the outside edges.

Eggs cooked in your oven will give you far more flexible breakfasts. One or two servings can be fixed at a time or you can undercook a larger amount and then reheat as needed.

We have not included directions for hard boiled eggs because eggs cooked in the shell might explode, due to pressure created within the shell by such rapid cooking. This could possibly happen even after eggs are removed from the oven.

When developing recipes, we have used extra large eggs from the refrigerator. If you use smaller eggs or ones at room temperature, you may need to decrease the time very slightly. It is quite normal to hear popping noise while eggs are cooking.

HERB OMELET

  1 tablespoon butter or margarine
  3 eggs
  3 tablespoons water
  ¼ teaspoon salt
  ⅛ teaspoon pepper
  ¼ teaspoon leaf basil

Setting: HIGH

1. Place butter in 9-inch glass pie plate.

2. MICROWAVE for about ½ MINUTE or until melted. Beat remaining ingredients into melted butter. Cover with plastic wrap.

3. MICROWAVE for 1 MINUTE. Stir lightly; recover, and MICROWAVE for 1 to 1½ MINUTES or until almost set in center. Let stand, covered, 2 minutes before serving.

1 to 2 Servings

TIPS For 2 egg omelet, use ½ tablespoon butter, 2 eggs, 2 tablespoons milk, ⅛ teaspoon salt and dash pepper. MICROWAVE in 8-inch pie pan 45 SECONDS; stir; MICROWAVE for 1¼ MINUTES.

• For 4 egg omelet, use 1 tablespoon butter, 4 eggs, 4 tablespoons milk, ¼ teaspoon salt, dash pepper. MICROWAVE in 10-inch pie pan 1½ minutes; stir; MICROWAVE 1¼ minutes.

• MICROWAVE on MEDIUM for 2 MINUTES, then 1 to 1½ MINUTES in step 3.

Bacon on paper towel, muffin in a double cupcake liner and scrambled eggs cooked in glass measuring cup.

MINI-CHILE RELLANOS

   1 **can (2 oz.) whole Jalapeño (green) chiles**
     Cheese (Jack, Cheddar or American)
   3 **eggs, separated**
 1½ **tablespoons all-purpose flour**
   1 **tablespoon oil**

Setting: HIGH

1. Rinse chilies, being careful to remove all seeds. Stuff with sticks of cheese. Set aside.

2. Beat egg whites in small mixing bowl until stiff peaks form. In small bowl, beat yolks with flour. Fold yolk mixture with egg whites.

3. Preheat microwave browning grill for 2 MINUTES. Spread 1 tablespoon cooking oil on browner. Spoon about ¼ cup batter onto each end of browner. Place 1 stuffed chile, on half of batter.

4. MICROWAVE for 30 SECONDS. Fold in half over chile and MICROWAVE for 15 to 20 SECONDS or until set. Repeat to use all batter. (Reheating of browning grill takes 30 SECONDS.)

                        6 Servings

TIPS ITALIAN OMELETS-Substitute diced, cooked Italian sausage or pepperoni and shredded mozzarella cheese for stuffed chiles.
● FRENCH OMELETS-Substitute crumbled bleu cheese and bacon for stuffed chiles.
● SWISS OMELETS-Substitute sauteed mushroom slices and shredded Swiss cheese for stuffed chiles.
● SWEET-STUFF OMELET-Substitue 1 teaspoon strawberry or raspberry preserves and chopped nuts for stuffed chiles. Sprinkle powdered sugar on top.

DENVER BRUNCH SANDWICH

   8 **slices bacon**
   6 **eggs**
 ⅓ **cup milk**
 ½ **cup mayonnaise or salad dressing**
 ¼ **cup chopped pimento**
 ¼ **cup chopped green pepper**
 ¼ **teaspoon salt**
    Tomato slices

Setting: HIGH

1. Place bacon slices between paper napkin or paper towels in 1½-quart (10 x 6) glass baking dish.

2. MICROWAVE for 7 to 9 MINUTES or until bacon is crisp. Remove bacon; drain drippings; crumble bacon; set aside. Combine eggs, milk and mayonnaise in medium mixing bowl; beat well with rotary beater. Stir in bacon and remaining ingredients. Pour into baking dish; cover.

3. MICROWAVE for 5 to 6 MINUTES or until center is almost set. Garnish with tomato slices. Let stand, covered, 5 minutes before serving.

                    4 to 6 Servings

TIP MICROWAVE on MEDIUM for 6 to 7 MINUTES in step 3.

Prepare the Hollandaise sauce before the rest of this recipe and simply reheat 30 to 45 seconds.

EGGS BENEDICT

   1 **package (10 oz.) frozen asparagus spears**
   4 **English muffins, split and toasted**
   4 **slices ham, ⅛ to ¼ inch thick**
   4 **poached eggs**
   1 **recipe (⅔ cup) Hollandaise sauce (page 136)**

Setting: HIGH

1. Remove wax or foil overwrap and place package of frozen asparagus in oven; MICROWAVE for 3 MINUTES. Open carton and rearrange, moving center spears to outside. Close carton and MICROWAVE for 2 MINUTES. Drain on paper towel.

2. Using 4 luncheon plates, arrange one English muffin and one ham slice on each plate; divide asparagus evenly and arrange on ham.

3. MICROWAVE 2 plates at a time, 1½ to 2 MINUTES or until ham is hot. Carefully place poached eggs on asparagus and top with hot Hollandaise sauce. Serve immediately.

                        4 Servings

TIP You may find it easier to poach the eggs conventionally because you'll have less egg breakage when placing on asparagus. This will also free the oven for preparation of asparagus and Hollandaise sauce.

BACON AND EGG CASSEROLE

   6 **hard-cooked eggs**
   6 **slices bacon**
   2 **tablespoons butter or margarine**
   2 **tablespoons all-purpose flour**
 ½ **teaspoon salt**
   1 **cup milk**
 ¼ **teaspoon pepper**
 ⅛ **teaspoon dry or prepared mustard**
    Half of 3½-oz. can French-fried onion rings

Setting: HIGH

1. Cook eggs conventionally. In 2-quart glass casserole or baking dish, MICROWAVE bacon between layers of paper towel until crisp, about 4 MINUTES. Remove bacon, paper towels and excess drippings from dish.

2. Melt butter in same baking dish (20 sec.). Stir in flour and salt until smooth. Gradually add milk, stirring constantly.

3. MICROWAVE for 3 to 4 MINUTES or until thickened, stirring occasionally. Stir in pepper and mustard.

4. Peel and quarter hard cooked eggs; arrange in the sauce. Crumble bacon and sprinkle over eggs.

5. MICROWAVE for 2 to 3 MINUTES or until hot. Add onion rings and MICROWAVE for 1 MINUTE.

                        4 Servings

BRUNCH SPECIAL

> 1 **package (12 oz.) frozen hash brown potatoes**
> ⅓ **cup sour cream**
> ⅓ **cup milk**
> ½ **teaspoon salt**
> 1 **tablespoon snipped chives**
> 4 **slices Canadian style bacon**
> 4 **eggs**

Setting: HIGH

1. Place potatoes in 2-quart (8 x 8) glass baking dish; cover.

2. MICROWAVE for 6 to 7 MINUTES or until partly cooked. Blend in sour cream, milk, salt and chives. Place bacon slices down center of dish. Make two hollows in potatoes on each side of bacon. Break 1 egg into each indentation; recover.

3. MICROWAVE for 4 to 5 MINUTES or until eggs are cooked to desired doneness. Let stand, covered, 2 minutes before serving.

About 4 Servings

TIP MICROWAVE on MEDIUM for 6 to 8 MINUTES in step 3.

EGG FOO YONG SCRAMBLE

> 6 **eggs**
> 1 **can (16 oz.) bean sprouts, drained**
> ½ **cup chopped onion or 2 tablespoons instant minced onion**
> ¼ **cup chopped green pepper**
> 2 **tablespoons soy sauce**
> 2 **tablespoons butter or margarine**

Setting: HIGH

1. In 1½ or 2-quart glass casserole, beat eggs. Stir in remaining ingredients; cover.

2. MICROWAVE for 5½ to 6 MINUTES or until eggs are almost set, stirring twice during last half of cooking time. Let stand, covered, 1 to 2 minutes before serving.

4 to 5 Servings

TIP MICROWAVE on MEDIUM for 8 to 9 MINUTES.

Pictured, top to bottom: Brunch Special, this page, Denver Brunch Special, page 102, and Welsh Rarebit, page 105, served over toast and garnished with nutmeg.

HOW TO SOFTEN CREAM CHEESE AND SPREADS

• Remove foil wrapper from cream cheese and place in glass bowl or dish to be used in recipe.

• Cheese spreads may be warmed in their original containers after the cap is removed — or in a glass or pottery serving dish which has no silver or other metal trim.

• MICROWAVE on WARM until cheese is soft.

ITEM	SIZE	SETTING	MINUTES
CREAM CHEESE	3-oz. pkg.	WARM	2 to 2½
	8-oz. pkg.	WARM	4 to 5
CHEESE SPREAD	8-oz. container	WARM	2 to 2½

TIP MICROWAVE on DEFROST for about half of time suggested in chart.

> **CHEESE KEY:** MICROWAVE cheese recipes on HIGH or MEDIUM setting. Custard recipes like Quiche Lorraine cook best on DEFROST. Different types of cheese often can be interchanged, according to personal tastes. Cheese is overcooked if it has become rubbery.

Cover keeps both cheese and macaroni tender and moist.

TRADITIONAL MACARONI WITH CHEESE

    2 tablespoons butter or margarine
    ¼ cup finely chopped onion
    2 cups shredded process American cheese
    ¾ cup milk
    1 teaspoon salt
    ⅛ teaspoon pepper
    4 cups cooked elbow macaroni

Setting: HIGH

1. Place butter and onion in 2-quart glass casserole.

2. MICROWAVE for about 2 MINUTES or until onion is partly cooked. Stir in remaining ingredients. Cover with glass lid.

3. MICROWAVE for 3 MINUTES. Stir lightly; recover, and MICROWAVE for 3 to 4 MINUTES or until piping hot. Let stand, covered, 5 minutes before serving.

About 6 Servings

TIP MICROWAVE on MEDIUM for 4 MINUTES, then 4 to 5 MINUTES in step 3.

This cheese and shrimp dish is assembled several hours ahead to allow the custard-milk mixture to soak into the bread. Try it for brunch or lunch – just put it in the oven about 18 minutes before serving time.

CHEESE AND SHRIMP BAKE

    8 slices bread
    1 or 2 cans (4½ oz. each)
      shrimp, drained
    ½ cup (1 stalk) chopped celery
    2 tablespoons chopped onion
    1 can (10¾ oz.) condensed cream
      of mushroom soup
    2 tablespoons lemon juice
    ½ teaspoon Worcestershire sauce
    4 oz. shredded or sliced American,
      Cheddar or Swiss cheese
    ¾ cup milk
    3 eggs
    ¼ cup butter or margarine

Settings: DEFROST/HIGH

1. If desired trim crusts from bread. (Use crust for dressing on croutons.) Arrange 4 slices of bread on bottom of ungreased 2-quart (8 x 8) glass baking dish. Top with shrimp, celery and onion.

2. Combine soup with lemon juice and Worcestershire sauce; spoon over shrimp. Top with cheese and remaining 4 slices of bread.

3. Beat together milk and eggs; pour over sandwich mixture. Cut butter into pieces and place on top; cover with plastic wrap and refrigerate 6 to 12 hours or overnight.

4. To cook, loosen plastic wrap slightly and MICROWAVE on DEFROST for 12 MINUTES.

5. MICROWAVE on HIGH about 6 MINUTES, or until hot and bubbly in center.

4 Servings

With regular cooking, a Quiche overcooks at the edge before the center is set. Now the automatic defroster makes it possible to cook it in the microwave oven.

QUICHE LORRAINE

   8 slices bacon
   9 -inch Baked Pastry Shell
   3 eggs
   1 teaspoon salt
   Dash pepper
   Dash nutmeg
   1 cup milk
   ⅔ cup (5⅓-fl. oz. can) evaporated milk
   1½ cups (6 oz.) shredded Swiss cheese

Settings: HIGH/DEFROST

1. Arrange bacon in glass baking dish. MICRO-WAVE on HIGH for 5 MINUTES or until crisp; drain.

2. Beat together eggs, salt, pepper and nutmeg. Measure milk into 4-cup glass measure. Add evaporated milk.

3. MICROWAVE on HIGH for 3 MINUTES or until hot. Arrange cheese in bottom of pastry shell. Crumble bacon over top. Add hot milk to egg mixture; beat well. Pour into pastry shell.

4. MICROWAVE on HIGH for 2 MINUTES, then MICROWAVE on DEFROST for 4 MINUTES. Carefully move cooked outer portion of filling to center.

5. MICROWAVE on DEFROST for 12 MINUTES, or until knife inserted near center comes out clean. Let stand 10 minutes before cutting into wedges.

5 to 6 Servings

Serve this as rarebit over toast, or use in a fondue dish for dipping cubes of bread. It reheats easily in the microwave oven.

WELSH RAREBIT

   2 eggs
   1 cup beer
   2 cups (10 oz.) cubed American cheese
   2 tablespoons butter or margarine
   1 teaspoon dry or prepared mustard
   1 teaspoon Worcestershire sauce
   4 drops Tabasco sauce

Setting: HIGH

1. In 1-quart glass casserole, beat eggs. Stir in remaining ingredients.

2. MICROWAVE for 5 to 6 MINUTES or until cheese is melted and mixture thickened, stirring about once every minute.

3. Beat with beater or wire whip to make smooth. Serve over toast.

4 Servings

TIPS For heartier servings, top toast with slices of turkey or chicken before adding sauce.
● Other types of processed cheese can be used.
● MICROWAVE on MEDIUM for 7 to 8 MINUTES.

ONE-STEP MACARONI & CHEESE

   1 cup uncooked macaroni
   2 tablespoons all-purpose flour
   ¼ cup chopped onion or 1 tablespoon
      instant minced onion
   ½ teaspoon salt
   Dash Tabasco sauce
   1 cup milk
   ¾ cup water
   2 tablespoons butter or margarine
   1 cup (4 oz.) cubed or shredded cheese

Settings: HIGH/DEFROST

1. In 1½ or 2-quart glass casserole, combine macaroni, flour, onion, salt and Tabasco sauce. Stir in milk and water; add butter; cover.

2. MICROWAVE on HIGH for 3 to 4 MINUTES or until milk is steaming hot. Stir mixture.

3. MICROWAVE on DEFROST for 12 to 14 MINUTES, or until macaroni is just about tender, stirring occasionally. Stir in cheese. Let stand, covered, 3 to 5 minutes to finish cooking macaroni and to melt cheese.

3 to 4 Servings

TIP For additional color and flavor, add 2 tablespoons chopped pimento, 2 tablespoons chopped parsley or 1 teaspoon dry mustard.

Defrost setting allows cheese to melt without overcooking.

CREAMY SMOOTH CHEESE FONDUE

   1½ cups dry sherry
   5 cups shredded process American Cheese
   2 tablespoons cornstarch
   ¼ teaspoon dry mustard
   ⅛ teaspoon garlic salt
   1 loaf French bread

Settings: HIGH/DEFROST

1. Pour sherry into 2-cup glass measure.

2. MICROWAVE on HIGH for 4 to 5 MINUTES or until very hot but not boiling. Toss remaining ingredients together, except bread, in 3-quart glass mixing bowl. Pour hot sherry over cheese mixture; stir to blend well.

3. MICROWAVE on DEFROST for 3 MINUTES. Stir and MICROWAVE on DEFROST for 3 to 4 MINUTES or until hot. Beat mixture until smooth. Serve hot with chunks of French bread.

About 4 Cups Fondue

MAIN COURSES Soup & Sandwiches

HOW TO COOK DEHYDRATED SOUP MIX

- Pour water into glass casserole or 8-ounce mugs. Add soup mix if directed on package and heat. Heat water, only, if package directs.
- Cover containers with glass lids, saucers or plastic wrap.
- MICROWAVE on HIGH until liquid is hot and bubbly.

- Stir in dry mix and continue cooking if package specified that mix is added after water boils.
- MICROWAVE most soups on HIGH until hot.
- MICROWAVE soups with dehydrated rice or noodles on DEFROST until rice or noodles are tender.
- Let stand, covered, 5 minutes before serving.

SOUP	AMOUNT	GLASS CONTAINER	WATER	SETTING	MINUTES
CUP O' SOUP					
any kind	1 envelope	1 (8-oz.) mug	⅔ cup	HIGH	2 to 2½
1½-oz. pkg. with	2 envelopes	2 (8-oz.) mugs	⅔ cup ea.	HIGH	3 to 3½
4 envelopes	4 envelopes	4 (8-oz.) mugs	⅔ cup ea.	HIGH	6 to 7
SOUP MIX					
without rice or noodles 2¾-oz. pkg. with 2 envelopes	1 envelope	2-qt. casserole	4 cups	HIGH add mix; HIGH	8 to 10 4 to 5
with rice or noodles 3½-oz. pkg. with 2 envelopes	1 envelope	2-qt. casserole	3 cups	HIGH add mix; DEFROST	7 to 8 5 to 6
5-oz. pkg.		2-qt. casserole	5 cups	HIGH add mix; DEFROST	9 to 10 10 to 12

HOW TO HEAT CANNED SOUP

- Pour soup into 1½-quart glass casserole.
- Add milk or water as directed on can.
- Cover with glass lid or plastic wrap.
- MICROWAVE on HIGH until hot — except mushroom soup which heats on DEFROST to prevent "popping."
- Stir when taken from oven.
- Let stand, covered, 3 minutes before serving.

SOUP	SETTING	MINUTES
DILUTED		
Broth 10¾-oz.	HIGH	3 to 4
Tomato, Cream Noodle or Vegetable		
10¾-oz.	HIGH	5 to 6
26-oz.	HIGH	8 to 9
Mushroom 10¾-oz.	DEFROST	8 to 10
UNDILUTED		
Chunky Vegetable, Noodle or Split Pea and Ham		
10¾-oz.	HIGH	2½ to 3½
19-oz.	HIGH	5 to 7

After filling serving dishes, you can heat soup until it is piping hot before placing on the table. This is especially handy for guest dinners where the soup sometimes cools before everyone is at the table and ready to eat.

FRENCH ONION SOUP

    2 large or 3 medium onions, sliced
    ¼ cup butter or margarine
    4 cups water
    6 cubes or teaspoons beef bouillon
    ½ teaspoon paprika
    1 teaspoon Worcestershire sauce
    Dash pepper
    4 to 6 slices French bread, toasted
    Grated Parmesan cheese

Setting: HIGH

1. In 4-quart glass casserole or Dutch oven, combine onions and butter.

2. MICROWAVE for 7 to 8 MINUTES or until onions are limp, stirring occasionally. Add water, bouillon, paprika, Worcestershire sauce and pepper; cover.

3. MICROWAVE for 7 to 8 MINUTES or until hot and bubbly. Place in 4 to 6 individual soup bowls. Top with toasted bread and sprinkle generously with cheese.

4. MICROWAVE 2 bowls at a time, about 30 SECONDS to melt cheese.

4 to 6 Servings

TIPS For a rich, wine flavor, use ½ cup white wine or sherry for part of water.
• To make several hours ahead, cook onion and add remaining ingredients except bread. Let stand at room temperature. About 10 minutes before serving, MICROWAVE for 7 MINUTES or until hot and bubbly and continue as directed.

This very basic potato soup will be a family favorite. Soup and a sandwich will make a complete lunch.

POTATO SOUP

    3 cups cubed potatoes
    ¼ cup finely chopped onion
    ½ teaspoon salt
    1½ cups water
    2 tablespoons all-purpose flour
    ½ cup milk
    1½ cups milk

Setting: HIGH

1. Combine potatoes, onion, salt and water in 2-quart glass casserole. Cover with glass lid.

2. MICROWAVE for 12 to 15 MINUTES or until potatoes are tender. Blend flour with ½ cup milk to make smooth paste. Stir in 1½ cups milk. Stir into potato mixture and MICROWAVE for 4 to 5 MINUTES or until thickened.

About 4 Servings

Add a sandwich with this soup for a complete meal. Leftovers can be added easily to make an even heartier soup.

CHEESY CLAM CHOWDER

    1 package (10 oz.) frozen mixed vegetables
    1 can (10¾ oz.) condensed clam chowder
    1 soup can milk
    1 cup shredded Cheddar cheese

Setting: DEFROST

1. Combine all ingredients in 2-quart glass casserole. Cover with glass lid.

2. MICROWAVE for 15 MINUTES. Stir; recover, and MICROWAVE for 12 to 13 MINUTES or until piping hot.

4 to 6 Servings

TIPS For a heartier soup, cubes of cooked meat or other vegetables can be added. Increase cooking time 1 minute for each ½ cup of additional ingredients.
• MICROWAVE on MEDIUM for 12 MINUTES and then 10 to 12 MINUTES.

CLAM CHOWDER

    2 slices bacon
    2 cans (6½ oz. each) minced clams,
      undrained
    1 large potato, finely chopped
    ¼ cup chopped onion
    1 medium carrot, thinly sliced
    2 tablespoons all-purpose flour
    ⅓ cup milk
    1 cup milk
    1 teaspoon salt
    Dash pepper
    Parsley

Setting: HIGH

1. Place bacon slices in 2-quart glass casserole.

2. MICROWAVE for 2 to 2½ MINUTES or until crisp. Remove bacon; crumble, and set aside. Add clam liquid, potato, onion and carrot to bacon drippings; cover.

3. MICROWAVE for 8 to 10 MINUTES or until vegetables are partly cooked. Blend flour with ⅓ cup milk. Stir into cooked vegetable mixture. Mix in 1 cup milk, salt, pepper and clams; recover.

4. MICROWAVE for 4 MINUTES. Stir and MICROWAVE for 2 to 3 MINUTES or until mixture comes to a boil. Let stand, covered, 3 minutes. Garnish with crumbled bacon and parsley and serve.

3 to 4 Servings

TIP MICROWAVE on MEDIUM for 5 MINUTES and then 3 to 4 MINUTES in step 3.

Since lentils cook relatively quickly for a dried pea or bean, they can be cooked with the microwave oven in the same time it takes to cook a ham hock.

HAM AND LENTIL SOUP

    1 cup dry lentils
    1 ham hock (1¼ to 1½ lbs.)
    1 medium onion, sliced
    1 carrot, sliced
    ¼ teaspoon pepper
    1 tablespoon Worcestershire sauce
    6 cups water

Settings: HIGH/DEFROST

1. In 3-quart glass casserole, combine all ingredients; cover.

2. MICROWAVE on HIGH for 9 to 10 MINUTES or until mixture just begins to boil.

3. MICROWAVE on DEFROST for 60 MINUTES. Remove ham hock from broth and let cool a few minutes. Then cut meat from bone and return meat to soup.

4. MICROWAVE on HIGH for 4 to 6 MINUTES to reheat soup.

4 to 5 Servings

TIP For Ham and Split Pea Soup, substitue split peas for the lentils.

Raw vegetables MICROWAVE on HIGH.

BEEF VEGETABLE SOUP IN A HURRY

    2 cans (10½ oz. each) condensed
      beef broth
    1 cup water
    1 package (10 oz.) frozen mixed
      vegetables
    1 bay leaf
    1 teaspoon salt
    1 teaspoon celery salt
    ¼ teaspoon pepper
    1 tablespoon dry sherry, if desired

Setting: HIGH

1. Combine all ingredients in 2-quart glass casserole; cover.

2. MICROWAVE for 12 to 15 MINUTES or until vegetables are tender-crisp. Let stand, covered, 5 minutes before serving.

4 to 6 Servings

TIP Serve with toasted rounds of French bread.

SANDWICH KEY: MICROWAVE most sandwiches on HIGH. Cheese fillings MICROWAVE best on a lower setting. Choose any sandwich form: open faced, bun, whole loaf or regular sandwiches of two bread slices. Firmly textured bread works best in the oven. Toasted bread gives more body and flavor and prevents the filling from making the bread soggy. Sandwiches are placed on a paper towel or napkin in the oven to absorb any excess moisture.

Sandwich fillings are one of the best ways to utilize leftovers. Fillings can often be prepared ahead and the bread toasted; when ready to serve, just assemble the sandwiches and heat. Times do not differ between open faced and regular sandwiches because it is the filling, rather than the extra slice of bread, that determines the cooking time. Bread should be only warm when the filling is hot. If a filling is frozen, thaw first before combining with bread so the bread will not overcook in the time it takes to heat the filling. A meat sandwich such as roast beef or pastrami heats most evenly if the meat is thinly sliced. We have given cooking times for a range of individual servings with the recipes for occasions when you may need only one or a few sandwiches.

IMPORTANT: Before you begin, refer to the "Beginning to Cook" section for basic technique and these example recipes:

HOW TO GRILL CHEESE SANDWICHES ON A MICROWAVE BROWNING GRILL

• Place sliced process American cheese between 2 slices of bread.

• Butter outside of bread.

• Preheat browning grill in oven on HIGH as directed in manufacturer's instruction booklet.

• Place sandwich(es) on grill; turn over once halfway through cooking.

• Grill until cheese melts and bread is toasted.

SANDWICH	SETTING	MINUTES
1	HIGH	1 to 1½
2	HIGH	2 to 2½

Wieners and buns are cooked – just heat through.

HOT DOGS

Setting: HIGH

1. Place wieners in split hot dog buns and wrap each one loosely in paper napkin or paper towel in oven.

2. MICROWAVE until heated through;
    1 hot dog — 30 to 35 SECONDS
    2 hot dogs — 45 to 50 SECONDS
    4 hot dogs — 1 to 1½ MINUTES
    6 hot dogs — 1½ to 2 MINUTES

TIP Heat wieners without buns on glass plate. MICROWAVE until warm; 1 wiener 25 to 30 seconds; 2 wieners 35 to 40 seconds; 4 wieners 50 to 55 seconds; 6 wieners 1 to 1¼ minutes.

HAMBURGERS

Setting: HIGH

1. Prepare Ground Beef Patties as directed on page 81. Place cooked patties in split buns and wrap each one loosely in paper napkin or paper towel.

2. MICROWAVE until heated through;
    1 hamburger — 15 to 20 SECONDS
    2 hamburgers — 25 to 30 SECONDS
    4 hamburgers — 45 to 50 SECONDS
    6 hamburgers — 1 to 1½ MINUTES

Several thin slices of meat heat more quickly than one thick slice. Paper towel or napkin keeps sandwich from getting soggy.

SLICED MEAT SANDWICHES

    Butter or margarine
    Mayonnaise or salad dressing
    Buns
    Sliced cooked meat

Setting: HIGH

1. Spread butter and mayonnaise on buns. Place meat slices between split buns. Wrap loosely in paper towel or napkin.

2. MICROWAVE until heated through:
    1 sandwich   — 1 to 1½ MINUTES
    2 sandwiches — 1½ to 2 MINUTES
    4 sandwiches — 2½ to 3 MINUTES

TIP Thinly-sliced meat heats more evenly than thick meat slices.

A tasty mixture of corned beef, sauerkraut, apple and Swiss cheese, piled into pumpernickel buns and heated.

REUBEN SALAD BUNS

- 1 can (12 oz.) corned beef
- ¾ cup sauerkraut, drained
- 1 small apple, cored and shredded
- 1 cup shredded Swiss cheese
- 2 tablespoons Thousand Island Dressing
- 1 teaspoon dill weed
- 2 teaspoons prepared mustard
- 8 pumpernickel buns

Setting: HIGH

1. Break up corned beef in medium mixing bowl. Stir in remaining ingredients, except buns; mix well. Spoon ½ cup corned beef mixture between each split roll. Wrap loosely in paper towel or napkin.

2. MICROWAVE until hot through:
    1 bun — 1 to 1½ MINUTES
    2 buns — 1½ to 2 MINUTES
    4 buns — 3 to 3½ MINUTES
    8 buns — 3½ to 4 MINUTES

8 Reuben Salad Buns

TIP Substitute 8 ounces corned beef, finely cut, for canned corn beef.

Reduce calories by not frying the sandwiches.

REUBEN SANDWICHES

- 8 slices pumpernickel or other dark bread
- ½ lb. thinly sliced corned beef
- ¾ cup (8-oz. can) well drained sauerkraut
- 2 to 3 tablespoons Thousand Island Dressing
- 4 slices Swiss cheese (about 4 oz.)

Setting: HIGH

1. Toast bread and arrange 4 slices on paper towels, napkins or small paper plates.

2. Top each slice with corned beef, then drained sauerkraut, salad dressing and cheese. Top with other slices of toasted bread.

3. MICROWAVE for 3 to 3½ MINUTES or until cheese is melted in center. Serve immediately.

4 Sandwiches

TIPS For 2 sandwiches, MICROWAVE 1½ to 2 MINUTES; for 1 sandwich, MICROWAVE 1 to 1¼ MINUTES.
- Leftover sandwiches can be reheated. If they have been refrigerated, cut each sandwich in half and separate halves, leaving about an inch between for ease in heating the centers.
- For ease in placing sandwiches in oven and removing, assemble on napkins or paper towels on plastic serving tray that will fit in the oven.
- To quickly and easily drain sauerkraut, drain excess liquid and then place sauerkraut in several layers of paper towel and squeeze out excess liquid.
- MICROWAVE on MEDIUM for 3½ to 4 MINUTES.

HOT TUNA SANDWICH LOAF

- 3 hard cooked eggs, chopped
- 1 can (6½ oz.) flaked tuna fish, drained
- ¼ cup chopped onion
- 1 teaspoon salt
- ¼ teaspoon pepper
- ½ teaspoon prepared mustard
- ½ cup mayonnaise or salad dressing
- 1 loaf (1 lb.) French bread, 15 inches long
- 3 slices (¾ oz. each) process American cheese, cut in half

Setting: HIGH

1. Combine all ingredients, except bread and cheese, in medium mixing bowl; mix well; set aside. Slice off top ⅓ of bread horizontally. Hollow out bottom of loaf. Fill hollow with tuna mixture. Place cheese slices over filling. Place top crust of bread over cheese. Wrap loosely in paper towel or napkin.

2. MICROWAVE for 4 to 5 MINUTES or until hot. Slice to serve.

About 6 Servings

TIP Cut loaf of bread to fit oven if it is too long. Dry unused bread to make crumbs for dressing.

A tuna salad filling gives a new twist to hot dog buns. If the buns are toasted, they can be assembled in advance for last minute heating as needed.

TUNA SALAD BUNS

- 1 can (6½ oz.) flaked tuna, drained
- 1 cup cubed process American cheese
- 2 tablespoons chopped onion
- 2 tablespoons chopped green pepper
- 2 tablespoons pickle relish
- ¼ cup sliced pimento stuffed olives
- ⅓ cup mayonnaise or salad dressing
- 6 hot dog buns, split and toasted

Setting: HIGH

1. Combine all ingredients, except buns, in medium mixing bowl; mix well. Spread equal amounts of tuna mixture on bottom half of toasted buns. Place other half of bun on top. Wrap loosely in paper towel or napkin.

2. MICROWAVE for 2 to 3 MINUTES or until hot and cheese is melted.

6 Sandwiches

TIPS When heating one or two buns, wrap buns loosely in paper napkins and MICROWAVE 1 bun for 1 MINUTE; 2 buns for 1½ MINUTES.
- MICROWAVE on MEDIUM for 3 to 5 MINUTES.

Pictured, left to right: Sliced Meat Sandwiches, page 109, Reuben Salad Buns, this page, Fishwich in hot dog bun, page 112, and Hot Tuna Sandwich Loaf, page 110.

Frozen fish sticks are easily thawed in the oven and then popped between split hot dog buns and heated. Try some with sliced dill pickles or pickle relish for added flavor.

FISHWICHES

> 1 package (8 oz.) frozen precooked breaded fish sticks
> 4 hot dog buns, split and buttered
> Tartar sauce

Settings: DEFROST/HIGH

1. Place fish sticks on glass plate in spoke fashion.

2. MICROWAVE on DEFROST for 2 MINUTES. Spread buns with tartar sauce. Place 2 fish sticks on each bun. Arrange on paper towel in oven.

3. MICROWAVE on HIGH until heated through:
   1 fishwich — 45 to 60 SECONDS
   2 fishwiches — 1 to 1½ MINUTES
   4 fishwiches — 2½ to 3 MINUTES

TIPS A thin sliced piece of American cheese, cut the shape of the bun, can be placed on top of fish sticks in buns. Increase cooking time to 1 minute, 40 seconds or until cheese melts.
● Fishwiches are good served with coleslaw or add some to filling after heating.

Crunchy almonds make this turkey salad filling something special.

HOT TURKEY SALAD BUNS

> 2 cups chopped cooked turkey
> 1 cup shredded Cheddar cheese
> ¼ cup finely chopped celery
> ¼ cup finely chopped almonds
> ½ cup mayonnaise or salad dressing
> ¼ teaspoon salt
> 2 tablespoons pickle relish
> 6 hamburger buns, split and toasted

Setting: HIGH

1. Combine all ingredients, except buns, in medium mixing bowl; mix well. Spread turkey mixture between split toasted buns. Wrap loosely in paper towel or napkin.

2. MICROWAVE for 3 to 3½ MINUTES or until hot.

6 Sandwiches

TIPS If buns are toasted, these could be assembled ahead for last minute heating.
● Chopped peanuts or toasted sesame seeds can be used for almonds.
● MICROWAVE on MEDIUM for 3½ to 4 MINUTES.

This recipe uses the leftover small pieces of a turkey.

HOT TURKEY SANDWICHES

> 1 cup chopped cooked turkey
> ¼ cup chopped onion
> ⅓ cup mayonnaise or salad dressing
> 2 teaspoons prepared mustard
> 6 slices bread, toasted
> 6 slices (¾ oz. each) process American cheese

Setting: HIGH

1. Combine turkey, onion, mayonnaise and mustard in medium mixing bowl; mix well. Spread equal amounts of turkey mixture on each toasted bread slice. Top with cheese. Arrange on paper towel in oven.

2. MICROWAVE for about 1 MINUTE or until cheese is melted.

6 Sandwiches

TIP MICROWAVE on MEDIUM for 1½ to 2 MINUTES.

A tangy barbecue sauce turns strips of canned luncheon meat into a new sandwich taste. Keep extra prepared filling on hand for quick sandwiches. Heat sandwiches directly on serving plates because the sauce may run onto the plates.

BARBECUED LUNCHEON SANDWICHES

> 1 tablespoon butter or margarine
> ½ cup (½ pepper) chopped green pepper
> 1 can (12 oz.) luncheon meat
> ¾ cup barbecue sauce
> 6 hamburger buns, split and toasted
> 6 slices cheese

Setting: HIGH

1. In 1-quart glass casserole, combine butter and green pepper.

2. MICROWAVE for 2 MINUTES, stirring once. Cut luncheon meat into strips or cubes and add to pepper along with barbecue sauce, mixing to combine; cover.

3. MICROWAVE for 4 to 5 MINUTES or until mixture is bubbly, stirring twice. Spoon mixture onto toasted buns, topping with cheese slice and top half of bun.

4. Return to oven and MICROWAVE for about 1 MINUTE to melt cheese.

6 Sandwiches

TIPS The various seasoned luncheon meats are good used in this recipe, too.
● This idea would also be good with sliced bologna, cut into thin strips.
● To use leftover filling, spoon refrigerated filling into toasted bun; top with cheese and heat 1 bun about 1 minute or until cheese is melted.

SPOON BURGERS

- **1 lb. ground beef**
- **½ teaspoon salt**
- **⅛ teaspoon pepper**
- **¼ teaspoon chili powder**
- **Dash Tabasco sauce**
- **½ cup chopped onion or 2 tablespoons instant minced onion**
- **1 can (10½ oz.) condensed tomato-rice soup**
- **6 to 8 hamburger buns, split and toasted**

Setting: HIGH

1. In 1½-quart (8-inch round) glass baking dish, crumble ground beef.

2. MICROWAVE for 4 to 5 MINUTES, stirring once. Drain. Add seasonings, onion and soup; cover.

3. MICROWAVE for 4 to 5 MINUTES, stirring once. To serve, spoon on toasted buns.

6 to 8 Servings

DEVILISH HAMWICHES

- **1 can (2¼ oz.) deviled ham**
- **1 cup (4 oz.) shredded Swiss cheese**
- **1 tablespoon pickle relish**
- **2 teaspoons prepared mustard**
- **2 hot dog buns, split and toasted**

Setting: HIGH

1. Combine all ingredients except buns in small mixing bowl. Place buns on paper napkins or plates spread with ham mixture.

2. MICROWAVE for 1 to 1½ MINUTES or until cheese is melted.

4 Small Sandwiches

A can of chili, slices of bread and cheese combine to make a sandwich with the flavor of lasagna. Some leftover casserole with a thick consistency could be used in place of the canned chili.

OPEN-FACED LASAGNA SANDWICHES

- **4 slices bread, toasted**
- **1 can (15½ oz.) chili without beans**
- **1 cup cottage cheese**
- **4 slices American or Mozzarella cheese**
- **Parmesan cheese**

Setting: HIGH

1. Toast bread and arrange on serving plates. Top with chili, spreading to edges. Spoon cottage cheese on chili and spread evenly. Top with cheese slices; sprinkle with Parmesan cheese.

2. MICROWAVE 2 sandwiches at a time, 1½ to 2 MINUTES or until cheese is melted.

4 Sandwiches

TIP MICROWAVE on MEDIUM for 2½ to 3 MINUTES.

These burgers cook right in the teriyaki marinade, thus eliminating the need to marinate. They make good sandwiches with the tasty addition of a pineapple slice.

TERIYAKI BURGERS

- **½ cup soy sauce**
- **3 tablespoons sugar**
- **3 green onions, sliced**
- **½ teaspoon ground ginger**
- **⅛ teaspoon instant minced garlic or 1 clove garlic, minced**
- **1 lb. ground beef**
- **4 slices (8¼-oz. can) pineapple**
- **4 hamburger buns, split and toasted**

Setting: HIGH

1. In 2-quart (8 x 8) glass baking dish, combine soy sauce, sugar, onions, ginger and garlic; mix well.

2. Shape beef into 4 patties. Add to soy sauce mixture, turning over to coat.

3. MICROWAVE for 6 to 7 MINUTES or until done, turning once during last half of cooking time. Top with pineapple slice.

4. MICROWAVE for 30 SECONDS to warm pineapple. Serve on toasted buns.

4 Sandwiches

TIP If desired, make open-faced sandwiches by topping slices of French bread with meat patties and pineapple and spooning remaining teriyaki sauce over bread.

Here's a good way to use leftover cooked beef or pork. Thinly sliced meat will assure the center of the sandwich being thoroughly hot.

BARBECUE WRAP-UPS

- **4 hamburger buns, split and toasted**
- **½ lb. cooked roast beef, thinly sliced**
- **¼ cup bottled barbecue sauce**
- **4 slices (¾ oz. each) process American cheese**

Setting: HIGH

1. Place bottom half of buns on paper towel. Top each half with 1 or 2 slices of meat. Spread 1 tablespoon barbecue sauce over meat. Top with slice of cheese. Wrap loosely in paper towel or napkin.

2. MICROWAVE for 2 to 3 MINUTES or until meat is hot and cheese is melted.

4 Sandwiches

TIPS Toasting the buns gives the sandwiches more flavor and prevents the bread from becoming soggy.
- MICROWAVE on MEDIUM for 3 to 5 MINUTES.

ACCOMPANIMENTS MEAL Vegetable Charts

HOW TO MICROWAVE FRESH AND FROZEN VEGETABLES

- Microwave all fresh and frozen vegetables on HIGH setting.
- Average cooking time for a 2-lb. package of frozen vegetables is 10 to 12 minutes.
- Microwave all frozen vegetables icy side up.
- Slit all frozen vegetable pouches before cooking so steam can escape.
- Add ¼ cup water when cooking fresh vegetables except for Baked Potatoes, Squash and Eggplant.
- For softer cooked vegetables, add more water and increase total cooking time.
- Arrange spear vegetables with the stalk end which takes longest to cook toward the outside of the cooking dish.

- IMPORTANT! Pierce or prick whole fresh vegetables, such as eggplant, squash, white or sweet potatoes, before placing in the microwave.
- Microwave vegetables in a covered glass baking dish or casserole. Corn on the cob may be wrapped in wax paper.
- Rearrange or stir vegetables halfway through cooking.
- Microwave cooking continues after food is taken from the oven — especially with vegetables like squash or potatoes. This additional standing time varies from 2 to 5 minutes, depending on the amount and density of food being cooked.

VEGETABLES	AMOUNT	MINUTES	SAUCES AND SEASONINGS	
ARTICHOKES				
Fresh	1	5 to 6	Sauces:	Cream, Hollandaise,
3½ inches	2	7 to 8		Mornay
in diameter	3	9 to 10		
	4	11 to 12	Seasonings:	Butter, Lemon Juice
				Nutmeg
Frozen Hearts	10-oz. pkg.	5 to 6		
ASPARAGUS: SPEARS, CUT				
Fresh	¾ lb.	5 to 6	Sauces:	Béchamel, Cheese,
	1½ lbs.	9 to 10		Creamed Egg,
				Creamy Dill,
Frozen	9-oz. pouch	6 to 7		Hollandaise, Sour
	10-oz. pkg.	8 to 9		Cream, Creamed
			Seasonings:	Butter, Lemon Butter,
				Toasted Almonds
BEANS: GREEN AND WAX				
Fresh	1 lb.	12 to 14	Sauces:	Cream, Creamy
	2 lbs.	16 to 18		Mustard,
Frozen	10-oz. pkg.	8 to 9	Seasonings:	Butter, Cheese,
French Style	10-oz. pouch	8 to 9		Chives, Crumbled
or Cut				Bacon, Mushrooms,
				Nutmeg, Toasted
				Almonds,
				Water Chestnuts
BEANS: LIMA				
Fresh	1 lb.	10 to 12	Sauces:	Cheese,
	2 lbs.	14 to 16		Sour Cream
Frozen	10-oz. pkg.	10 to 11	Seasonings:	Butter, Chopped
	10-oz. pouch	8 to 9		Ham, Crumbled Bacon

Microwave all fresh and frozen vegetables on HIGH setting.

FRESH AND FROZEN VEGETABLE COOKING CHART

VEGETABLES	AMOUNT	MINUTES	SAUCES AND SEASONINGS	
BEETS Fresh Whole	4 medium	16 to 18	Seasonings:	Butter, Orange Juice Concentrate, Orange Marmalade
BROCCOLI Fresh	1½ lbs.	10 to 12	Sauces:	Cheese, Creamed Egg, Creamy Mustard, Hollandaise, Mornay, Sour Cream
Frozen	10-oz. pkg. 10-oz. pouch	8 to 9 8 to 9		
BRUSSELS SPROUTS Fresh	½ lb. 1 lb.	5 to 7 7 to 8	Sauces:	Cream, Cream Cheese, Creamy Mustard, Hollandaise
Frozen	8-oz. pkg. 10-oz. pouch	8 to 9 6 to 7	Seasonings:	Butter
CABBAGE Fresh Shredded	½ medium 1 medium	5 to 6 8 to 9	Sauces:	Cheese, Cream Cheese, Cream, Creamy, Mustard
			Seasonings:	Butter, Crumbled Bacon, Nutmeg
CARROTS Fresh Sliced, Diced, Slivered	2 medium 4 medium 6 medium	5 to 6 8 to 10 10 to 12	Sauces: Seasonings:	Cream Cheese, Cream Butter, Cinnamon, Cloves,
Frozen Diced or Whole	10-oz. pkg. 10-oz. pouch	8 to 10 8 to 9		Crumbled Bacon, Ginger, Glazed, Nutmeg, Parsley
CAULIFLOWER Fresh Broken into Flowerets	1 medium	7 to 8	Sauces:	Cheese, Cream, Hollandaise
Whole Whole	1 medium 1 large	8 to 9 12 to 14	Seasonings:	Butter, Chives, Nutmeg, Thousand Island Dressing
Frozen	10-oz. pkg. 10-oz. pouch	8 to 9 8 to 9		
CELERY Fresh	6 stalks	10 to 12	Sauces:	Cheese, Cream
			Seasonings:	Bouillon, Brown Gravy Mix, Butter

(Continued, next page)

Microwave all fresh and frozen vegetables on HIGH setting.

VEGETABLES	AMOUNT	MINUTES	SAUCES AND SEASONINGS	
CORN Fresh Cut from Cob Frozen	 1½ cups 3 cups 10-oz. pkg 10-oz. pouch	 6 to 7 7 to 8 6 to 7 5 to 6	Sauces: Seasonings:	Cream Cheese, Cream Butter, Chive Butter, Cream Cheese, Crumbled Bacon, Green Pepper and Pimento, Onion Dip, Parmesan Cheese
CORN ON THE COB Fresh Frozen	 2 4 6 2 4	 4 to 5 7 to 8 9 to 10 6 to 8 10 to 12	Seasonings:	Butter, Chive Butter, Onion Butter
EGGPLANT Fresh	 1 medium	 8 to 9	Sauce:	Tomato
ONIONS Fresh Quartered Frozen In Cream Sauce	 8 small or 2 large 4 large 10-oz. pkg. 10-oz. pouch	 6 to 7 8 to 9 6 to 7 6 to 7	Sauces: Seasonings:	Sour Cream, Cream, Cream Cheese Butter, Currant Jelly, Nutmeg
PARSNIPS Fresh Quartered	 4	 8 to 9	Sauces: Seasonings:	Béchamel Bacon Drippings, Brown Sugar Glaze, Butter
PEAS, GREEN Fresh Frozen Frozen Pods	 2 lbs. 3 lbs. 10-oz. pkg. 10-oz. pouch 6-oz. pouch	 8 to 9 10 to 11 6 to 7 6 to 7 3 to 4	Sauces: Seasonings:	Cream, Cream Cheese Butter, Chives Cream, Green Onions, Mint, Mushrooms, Onion Dip, Orange Marmalade
PEAS AND CARROTS Frozen	 10-oz. pkg.	 7 to 8	Sauces: Seasonings:	Cream Butter, Chives, Crumbled Bacon
PEAS, BLACK-EYED Frozen	 10-oz. pkg.	 10 to 12	Sauces: Seasonings:	Cream Bacon Drippings, Butter, Ham

Microwave all fresh and frozen vegetables on HIGH setting.

FRESH AND FROZEN VEGETABLE COOKING CHART

VEGETABLES	AMOUNT	MINUTES	SAUCES AND SEASONINGS	
POTATOES Fresh baking (Do not overcook potatoes as extreme dehydration might cause smoke or fire.)	1 medium 2 medium 4 medium 6 medium 8 medium	4 to 4½ 7 to 8 10 to 12 16 to 18 22 to 24	Seasonings:	Butter, Cheese, Chives, Crumbled Bacon, Parsley, Green Onions, Onion Soup Dip, Paprika, Sour Cream, Toasted Almonds, Whipped Cream Cheese
Fresh boiling Quartered	2 4	10 to 11 18 to 20	Sauces: Seasonings:	Cheese, Creamed Onions Bouillon, Butter, Chives, Green Onions, Onion Soup Mix, Paprika, Parsley
POTATOES, SWEET OR YAMS Fresh	1 medium 2 medium 4 medium 6 medium	4 to 4½ 6 to 7 8 to 9 10 to 11	Seasonings:	Brown Sugar Glaze, Butter, Glaze, Crumbled Bacon, Maple Syrup Glaze, Mashed, Miniature Marshmallows, Pineapple Glaze
SPINACH Fresh Frozen Leaf or Chopped	1 lb. 10-oz. pkg. 10-oz. pouch	6 to 7 7 to 8 7 to 8	Sauces: Seasonings:	Cheese, Cream Cheese, Egg, Mushroom Soup Butter, Crumbled Bacon, Lemon Juice, Nutmeg, Onion Dip, Sliced Raw Onion
SQUASH, ACORN OR BUTTERNUT Fresh Whole	1 medium 2 medium	8 to 9 14 to 16	Sauces: Seasonings:	Cranberry Brown Sugar Glaze, Honey Glaze, Butter, Cinnamon, Nutmeg, Cooked Apples or Other Fruit, Maple Syrup, Sausage
SQUASH, HUBBARD Fresh Frozen	6″ x 6″ pc. 10-oz. pkg.	8 to 9 6 to 7	Seasonings:	Brown Sugar Glaze, Butter, Maple Syrup, Mashed with Ginger or Nutmeg, Orange Marmalade, Pineapple

(Continued, next page)

MEAL ACCOMPANIMENTS Vegetables

FRESH AND FROZEN VEGETABLE COOKING CHART

VEGETABLES	AMOUNT	MINUTES	SAUCES AND SEASONINGS	
SQUASH, ZUCCHINI Fresh Sliced	2 medium or 3 cups	7 to 8	Sauces: Seasonings:	Cream, Creamed Egg Butter, Chive Sour Cream, Parmesan Cheese
TURNIPS Fresh Cut in Eighths	4 medium	12 to 14	Sauces: Seasonings:	Cream Butter, Chives Lemon Juice
TURNIP GREENS Fresh	1 lb.	6 to 8	Sauces:	Cheese, Butter
VEGETABLES, MIXED Frozen	10-oz. pkg. 10-oz. pouch	6 to 7 6 to 7	Sauces: Seasonings:	Béchamel, Cheese, Creamed, Cream Cheese Butter, Crumbled Bacon

FRESH VEGETABLE KEY: Cook all fresh vegetables on Microwave HIGH setting to capture ultimate goodness, nutrition and tender-crispness.

Remember that fresh vegetables should be eaten soon after being picked or purchased to capture flavor and vitamins.

Important! Pierce or prick whole, unpeeled vegetables, such as eggplant, squash, tiny red potatoes, white or sweet potatoes, before placing in the microwave. Piercing allows steam to escape during cooking, prevents "popping" and a messy oven. Do not be concerned if oven is steamy while vegetables-with-skin-on are cooking.

Arrange fresh spear vegetables, such as broccoli, in the cooking dish so the part that takes longer to cook (stalk) is toward the outside of the dish.

Salt brings out vegetable flavors. It is most convenient to add salt before cooking. But since salt tends to dehydrate food; it may be added at the end of the cooking period. Test and see which you prefer.

Always use a cover. A fitted glass lid or plastic wrap stretched tightly over the cooking casserole or dish helps trap steam and hasten cooking.

Pierce plastic wrap and allow steam to escape from dish before removing it from oven. Tip glass lids away from hand or arm when lifting.

Stir and rearrange vegetables halfway through the cooking period. This helps distribute moisture from the bottom of the dish and cooking is more even.

Vegetables should still be a little firm when they are removed from the oven because they will continue to cook. If you prefer vegetables with a softer texture, increase the cooking time slightly. When a recipe calls for a "standing" period, follow directions carefully.

IMPORTANT: Before you begin, refer to the "Beginning to Cook" section for basic technique and these example recipes:

Lentils cook fairly quickly for a dry pea or bean. A large casserole is used because of boiling during first cooking period.

BAKED LENTILS

    1 cup (½ lb.) dry lentils, washed and sorted
    3 cups water
    2 slices bacon, cut into pieces
    ¼ cup packed brown sugar
    ¼ cup chopped onion
    ¼ cup chili sauce
    ¼ cup molasses
    1 teaspoon salt
    1 teaspoon prepared mustard

Settings: HIGH/DEFROST

1. Combine all ingredients in 3-quart glass casserole; cover.

2. MICROWAVE on HIGH for 10 MINUTES. Stir and recover.

3. MICROWAVE on DEFROST for 50 to 55 MINUTES or until tender. Let stand, covered, 5 minutes before serving.

5 to 6 Servings

TIP Water should be added, if necessary, during cooking time.

Cauliflower has a delicious taste when cooked in the microwave oven. This idea for serving is very simple, but special looking.

TANGY MUSTARD CAULIFLOWER

    1 medium head cauliflower
    2 tablespoons water
    ½ cup mayonnaise or salad dressing
    1 teaspoon finely chopped onion
    1 teaspoon prepared mustard
    ½ cup shredded Cheddar cheese

Setting: HIGH

1. Place cauliflower in 1½-quart glass casserole. Add water; cover.

2. MICROWAVE for 8 to 9 MINUTES or until tender-crisp. Combine mayonnaise, onion and mustard in small mixing bowl. Spoon mustard sauce on top of cauliflower. Sprinkle with cheese.

3. MICROWAVE for 1½ to 2 MINUTES to heat topping and melt cheese. Let stand 2 minutes before serving.

6 to 8 Servings

TIP The topping can be spooned over cooked cauliflower floweretes. For 10-oz. package, use half the topping amounts.

Pictured, top to bottom: Tangy Mustard Cauliflower, this page, Oriental Asparagus, page 124, Corn on the Cob, page 116, (Cooked in husks rather than wax paper), Baked Lentils, this page, and Double Onion Bake, page 124.

POOR MAN'S CAVIAR

- 1 small eggplant, unpeeled and finely chopped (about 4 cups)
- 1 medium onion, chopped
- ¼ cup chopped green pepper
- 1 can (4 oz.) mushroom stems and pieces, drained
- 2 cloves garlic, finely chopped
- ⅓ cup cooking oil
- 1 teaspoon salt
- ½ teaspoon pepper
- ½ teaspoon oregano leaf
- 1 can (6 oz.) tomato paste
- ¼ cup water
- ½ cup chopped stuffed olives
- ¼ cup capers
- 2 tablespoons wine vinegar

Setting: HIGH

1. Combine eggplant, onion, green pepper, mushroom, garlic and oil in 2-quart glass casserole; mix well. Cover with glass lid.

2. MICROWAVE for 8 MINUTES. Stir in remaining ingredients. Recover.

3. MICROWAVE for 10 to 12 MINUTES or until eggplant is tender-crisp. Serve hot over fluffy white rice, green noodles, or cold as an appetizer with corn chips.

4 Servings

TIP MICROWAVE on MEDIUM for 10 MINUTES in step 2 and 15 to 18 MINUTES in step 3.

HONEY COATED CARROTS

- 4 medium carrots, sliced
- 2 tablespoons butter or margarine
- 2 tablespoons honey
- 2 tablespoons water
- ¼ teaspoon salt

Setting: HIGH

1. Combine all ingredients in 1-quart glass casserole; cover.

2. MICROWAVE for 5 MINUTES. Stir and MICROWAVE for 3 to 4 minutes or until carrots are tender-crisp. Let stand, covered 3 minutes before serving.

2 to 3 Servings

TIP If desired, add ¼ teaspoon ground ginger or 1 teaspoon chopped candied ginger with honey.

Nutmeg enhances the flavor of this recipe. Cabbage retains a fresh green color, even when cooked.

SEASONED CABBAGE CASSEROLE

- 4 cups shredded cabbage
- ½ teaspoon salt
- ¼ cup milk
- ¼ cup chopped onion
- 2 tablespoons butter or margarine
- ⅛ teaspoon ground nutmeg
- ½ cup shredded Cheddar cheese

Setting: HIGH

1. Combine cabbage, salt, milk, onion, butter and nutmeg in 2-quart glass casserole; cover.

2. MICROWAVE for 4 MINUTES. Stir and MICROWAVE for 3 to 4 MINUTES or until cabbage is tender-crisp. Stir in cheese. Let stand, covered, 2 minutes.

4 Servings

GLAZED CARROTS 'N APPLES

- 4 to 5 medium carrots, sliced
- 1 tart cooking apple, peeled, cored and chopped
- 2 tablespoons packed brown sugar
- 2 tablespoons butter or margarine
- 2 tablespoons water
- ¼ teaspoon salt

Setting: HIGH

1. Combine all ingredients in 1-quart glass casserole; cover.

2. MICROWAVE for 5 MINUTES. Stir and MICROWAVE for 3 to 4 MINUTES or until carrots are tender-crisp. Let stand, covered, 3 minutes before serving.

5 to 6 Servings

HONEYED ONIONS

- 8 medium whole onions, peeled
- 2 tablespoons butter or margarine
- ½ cup honey

Setting: HIGH

1. Place onions in 1-quart glass casserole; cover.

2. MICROWAVE for 7 to 8 MINUTES or until onions are tender-crisp. Drain. Stir in butter and honey; recover, and MICROWAVE for 2 to 3 minutes or until onions are glazed. Let stand, covered, 3 minutes before serving.

3 to 4 Servings

TIP Substitute apple jelly for honey.

Since potatoes, peas and sauce are cooked in the oven, plan to cool ... oven-dish conveniently or serve with a roast that has a long resting period before serving.

CREAMED GARDEN POTATOES AND PEAS

    1 lb. small red potatoes
 1½ cups fresh shelled peas
    2 tablespoons water
    2 tablespoons butter or margarine
    1 tablespoon chopped onion
    2 tablespoons all-purpose flour
 1¼ teaspoon salt
    1 teaspoon dill weed
  ⅛ teaspoon pepper
 1½ cups milk

Setting: HIGH

1. Prick potatoes before cooking. Place in oven.

2. MICROWAVE for 10 to 11 MINUTES or until potatoes are fork-tender. Set aside. Combine peas and water in 2-quart glass casserole; cover.

3. MICROWAVE for 6 MINUTES or until peas are tender-crisp. Set aside. Combine butter and onion in 4-cup glass measure.

4. MICROWAVE for about 1 MINUTE or until melted. Blend in flour, salt, dill and pepper. Stir in milk.

5. MICROWAVE for 4 to 5 MINUTES or until mixture thickens. Peel potatoes and add to peas in casserole. Pour hot cream sauce over vegetables; stir gently to thoroughly coat vegetables. Return to oven and MICROWAVE for 2 to 3 MINUTES or until piping hot. Let stand 3 minutes before serving.

4 to 5 Servings

Corn, green pepper and tomatoes — perfect go-togethers.

CORN FILLED TOMATOES

    6 large tomatoes
    Salt
    2 tablespoons butter or margarine
    1 tablespoon chopped onion
    2 tablespoons chopped green pepper
    1 can (16 oz.) whole kernel corn, drained
  ¼ cup potato chips, crushed
    Grated Parmesan cheese

Setting: HIGH

1. Cut tops off tomatoes; hollow out inside. Save tomato pulp for soup. Place tomatoes on glass serving platter. Sprinkle with salt. Combine butter, onion and green pepper in 4-cup glass measure.

2. MICROWAVE for 4 to 5 MINUTES or until butter is melted. Stir in corn and crushed potato chips. Spoon crumb mixture into tomatoes. Sprinkle with Parmesan cheese.

3. MICROWAVE for 6 to 7 MINUTES or until heated through. Let stand 3 minutes before serving.

6 Servings

SAVORY POTATOES

 1½ cups water
  ½ teaspoon salt
    2 tablespoons butter or margarine
  ½ cup milk
 1½ cups potato flakes
  ½ cup sour cream
  ½ teaspoon onion salt
    1 egg
    Shredded cheese

Settings: HIGH/DEFROST

1. Combine water, salt and butter in 1½-quart glass casserole; cover.

2. MICROWAVE on HIGH for 3 to 4 MINUTES or until mixture bubbles. Stir in milk and potato flakes. Blend in sour cream, onion salt and egg. Mix well. Sprinkle with cheese. Recover.

3. MICROWAVE on DEFROST for 8 to 10 MINUTES or until hot. Let stand, covered, 3 minutes before serving.

4 to 5 Servings

TIPS To make ahead, prepare as directed in steps 1 and 2. Cover with plastic wrap and refrigerate. At serving time, MICROWAVE on DEFROST for 15 to 16 MINUTES or until hot.
● MICROWAVE on MEDIUM for 6 to 8 MINUTES in step 3.

GLAZED SQUASH

    4 cups (2 lb.) 1-inch cubed Hubbard squash
  ⅓ cup butter or margarine
  ⅓ cup honey
    1 teaspoon salt
    1 tablespoon grated orange peel

Setting: HIGH

1. Combine all ingredients in 2-quart glass casserole; cover.

2. MICROWAVE for 5 MINUTES. Stir and MICROWAVE for 4 to 5 MINUTES or until fork-tender. Let stand, covered, 3 minutes before serving.

4 to 5 Servings

GLAZED SWEET POTATOES

    4 medium sweet potatoes
  ½ cup packed brown sugar
  ¼ cup butter or margarine

Setting: HIGH

1. Pierce potatoes and place in oven.

2. MICROWAVE for 8 to 9 MINUTES or until fork tender. Peel and slice into 1½-quart glass casserole. Sprinkle with brown sugar; dot with butter. Cover with glass lid or plastic wrap. MICROWAVE for 4 MINUTES. Stir and MICROWAVE for 3 to 4 MINUTES or until hot. Let stand, covered, 3 minutes before serving.

6 to 8 Servings

Apples – fresh or prepared pie filling – make a great addition to acorn squash halves.

ACORN SQUASH 'N APPLES

2 acorn or butternut squash
Salt
2 medium apples, peeled, cored and sliced
½ cup packed brown sugar
¼ cup butter or margarine
Cinnamon

Setting: HIGH

1. Pierce whole squash and place in oven.

2. MICROWAVE for 10 to 12 MINUTES, or until squash feels soft to touch. Let stand 5 MINUTES. Cut in half; remove seeds. Place, cut side up, in 2-quart (12 x 7) glass baking dish. Fill centers of squash with apples. Top each with 2 tablespoons brown sugar, 1 tablespoon butter and dash of cinnamon; cover. MICROWAVE for 6 to 7 MINUTES or until apples are tender. Let stand, covered, 2 to 3 minutes before serving.

4 Servings

TIP Substitute prepared apple pie filling mix for fresh apples and butter. Reduce final cooking time about 4 minutes.

STUFFED BAKED POTATOES

4 medium baking potatoes
2 tablespoons butter or margarine
½ cup milk
Salt and pepper
½ cup shredded process American cheese

Setting: HIGH

1. Prick potatoes and place in oven.

2. MICROWAVE for 10 to 12 MINUTES or until fork-tender. Cut potatoes in half. Carefully scoop cooked potato out of shells and into mixing bowl. Add butter, milk, salt and pepper to taste; mash until lump-free. Fill potato shells; top with cheese and place on glass serving platter. MICROWAVE for 4 to 5 MINUTES or until hot. Let stand 3 minutes before serving.

4 to 8 Servings

TIPS If made ahead and refrigerated, MICRO-WAVE for 6 to 7 MINUTES during final cooking period.
● Potatoes can be stuffed and frozen. Thaw and heat by cooking, uncovered, 15 minutes or until hot.

Pictured, top to bottom: Acorn Squash 'N Apples, this page, Harvard Beets, page 125, Stuffed Baked Potatoes, this page, and Nippy Cheese Broccoli, page 123.

FROZEN VEGETABLE KEY: Frozen vegetables are best cooked on Microwave HIGH setting. Faster cooking insures crisp, but tender eating. Frozen vegetables can be cooked in their paper carton, rearranging or stirring the contents halfway through the cooking time. Also, individual servings can be removed from the economical large plastic bags of frozen vegetables and then cooked in a serving dish.

Arrange frozen broccoli and other spear vegetables so that the stalk, which takes longest to cook, is toward the outside of the cooking dish.

Salt enhances vegetable flavor. It is more convenient to add salt before cooking. But since salt tends to dehydrate food, it may be added at the end of the cooking period.

Always cover vegetables when cooking. Use fitted, glass lids or plastic wrap stretched tightly over the cooking casserole or dish. Covers trap steam and hasten cooking. Pierce plastic wrap and allow steam to escape before removing dish from the oven.

Stir or rearrange vegetables halfway through the cooking period to help distribute moisture from the bottom of the dish and cook food more evenly.

Microwave cooking continues after food is taken from the oven. When a recipe calls for a "standing" period, follow directions carefully.

Keep stalk ends toward outside of cooking dish where they will Microwave sooner.

NIPPY CHEESE BROCCOLI

- 2 **tablespoons butter or margarine**
- 2 **tablespoons all-purpose flour**
- ½ **teaspoon salt**
- 1 **cup milk**
- 1 **cup shredded Cheddar cheese**
- 2 **packages (10 oz. each) frozen broccoli spears**
- 1 **medium tomato, sliced**

Setting: HIGH

1. Place butter in 2-cup glass measure.

2. MICROWAVE for about 1 MINUTE or until melted. Blend in flour, salt and milk.

3. MICROWAVE for 2 MINUTES. Stir and MICROWAVE for 1 to 2 MINUTES or until mixture thickens. Stir in cheese until melted. Place broccoli, icy side up, on glass serving platter; cover.

4. MICROWAVE for 6 MINUTES. Rearrange spears and MICROWAVE for 6 to 8 MINUTES or until broccoli is tender-crisp. Drain well. Top with cheese sauce and garnish with tomato slices.

5. MICROWAVE for 2 to 3 MINUTES until hot.

6 to 8 Servings

TIP Substitute fresh broccoli. See vegetable chart for cooking directions.

This company dish has a milk flavored lemon sauce poured over the broccoli. Almonds are toasted in the oven and sprinkled over the sauce.

BROCCOLI WITH LEMON SAUCE

- ½ **cup slivered almonds**
- 1 **tablespoon butter or margarine**
- 2 **packages (10 oz. each) frozen broccoli spears**
- 2 **packages (3 oz. each) cream cheese**
- ⅓ **cup milk**
- 1 **teaspoon grated lemon peel**
- 1 **tablespoon lemon juice**
- ½ **teaspoon ground ginger**
- ¼ **teaspoon salt**

Setting: HIGH

1. Combine almonds and butter in small glass bowl.

2. MICROWAVE for 2 MINUTES. Stir and MICROWAVE for 1 to 2 MINUTES or until almonds are light brown. Set aside.

3. Place frozen broccoli in 2-quart glass casserole; cover.

4. MICROWAVE for 6 MINUTES. Rearrange broccoli; cover, and MICROWAVE for 6 to 7 MINUTES or until tender-crisp. Let stand, covered.

5. Place cream cheese in 2-cup glass measure. MICROWAVE for 30 SECONDS or until softened. Cream until smooth. Stir in remaining ingredients.

6. MICROWAVE for 2 to 3 MINUTES or until hot. Place broccoli spears on serving platter and pour sauce over. Sprinkle with almonds and serve.

6 to 8 Servings

SPINACH DELISH

- 1 **package (10 oz.) frozen chopped spinach**
- ½ **cup sour cream**
- 2 **tablespoons dry onion soup mix**

Setting: HIGH

1. Place spinach, icy side up, in 1-quart glass casserole; cover.

2. MICROWAVE for 4 MINUTES. Stir and MICROWAVE for about 3 MINUTES or until tender-crisp. Stir in sour cream and onion soup mix. Recover.

3. MICROWAVE for 1 to 2 MINUTES or until hot. Let stand, covered, 2 minutes before serving.

3 to 4 Servings

TIP For 6 servings, use 1½-quart glass casserole, double ingredient amounts and use cooking periods of 8 to 10 MINUTES and 2 MINUTES.

ORIENTAL ASPARAGUS

- **2 tablespoons butter or margarine**
- **2 tablespoons slivered almonds**
- **1 package (10 oz.) frozen cut asparagus**
- **½ cup thinly sliced celery**
- **1 can (5 oz.) water chestnuts, drained and sliced**
- **1 tablespoon soy sauce**

Setting: HIGH

1. Combine butter and almonds in 1-quart glass casserole.

2. MICROWAVE for 1½ MINUTES. Stir and MICROWAVE for 2 to 3 MINUTES or until golden brown. Remove almonds. Add asparagus, celery and water chestnuts to butter; cover.

3. MICROWAVE for 5 MINUTES. Stir and MICROWAVE for 3 to 4 MINUTES or until tender-crisp. Stir in soy sauce and almonds. Let stand, covered, 3 minutes before serving.

4 Servings

PEAS WITH ONIONS AND MUSHROOMS

- **2 tablespoons butter or margarine**
- **¼ cup chopped onion or 1 tablespoon instant minced onion**
- **½ cup (4-oz. can) drained mushroom stems and pieces**
- **1½ cups (10-oz. pkg.) frozen peas**
-   **Dash pepper**
-   **Dash allspice**
- **¼ teaspoon salt**

Setting: HIGH

1. In 1-quart glass casserole, combine butter and onion; cover.

2. MICROWAVE for 2 MINUTES or until onion is tender. Add mushrooms, frozen peas, pepper and allspice.

3. MICROWAVE for 5½ to 6 MINUTES, or until peas are just about tender, stirring once; recover. Stir in salt.

4 Servings

DOUBLE ONION BAKE

- **1 teaspoon butter or margarine**
- **¼ cup slivered almonds**
- **1 package (10 oz.) frozen creamed onions**
- **¼ cup shredded Cheddar cheese**
- **1 tablespoon dried parsley flakes**
- **1 can (3½ oz.) French-fried onion rings**

Setting: HIGH

1. Combine butter and almonds in 1-quart glass casserole.

2. MICROWAVE for 1½ MINUTES. Stir and MICROWAVE for 1 to 2 MINUTES. Add onions, cheese and parsley; cover.

3. MICROWAVE for 3 MINUTES. Stir and MICROWAVE for 3 to 4 MINUTES or until onions are tender-crisp. Top with onion rings. Let stand, covered, 3 minutes before serving.

2 to 3 Servings

TIP When using frozen creamed onions in pouch, place pouch in oven. MICROWAVE for 3 to 4 MINUTES. Remove creamed onions from pouch; spoon into casserole with remaining ingredients and MICROWAVE for 2 to 3 MINUTES or until hot.

Cover keeps souffle tender.

SPINACH SOUFFLE

- **2 packages (10 oz. each) frozen, chopped spinach**
- **¼ cup butter or margarine**
- **2 cups cooked rice**
- **2 cups shredded process American cheese**
- **⅔ cup milk**
- **4 eggs**
- **½ cup finely chopped onion**
- **2 tablespoons dried parsley flakes**
- **1 teaspoon salt**
- **¼ teaspoon leaf thyme**
- **½ teaspoon nutmeg**

Settings: HIGH/DEFROST

1. Place frozen spinach, icy side up, in 2-quart glass casserole; cover.

2. MICROWAVE on HIGH for 8 to 10 MINUTES. Drain well through sieve. Stir in butter until melted. Add rice and cheese. Combine milk and eggs in 4-cup glass measure. Blend in remaining ingredients. Stir into spinach mixture until well blended. Cover with glass lid or plastic wrap.

3. MICROWAVE on DEFROST for 30 to 35 MINUTES or until knife inserted near center comes out clean. Let stand, covered, 5 minutes before serving.

6 to 8 Servings

TIP MICROWAVE on MEDIUM for 25 to 30 MINUTES.

HOW TO HEAT A CAN OF VEGETABLES

- Microwave canned vegetables either undrained or drained.
- Empty vegetables into 1-quart glass casserole and cover with glass lid or plastic wrap.
- Microwave on HIGH.
- Let stand 2 to 3 minutes to heat through.

CANNED VEGETABLE	MINUTES UNDRAINED	MINUTES DRAINED
VEGETABLES all kinds		
8-oz.	2 to 2½	1½ to 2
15-oz.	3 to 4	2½ to 3
17-oz.	4 to 5	3 to 3½

CANNED VEGETABLE KEY: Canned vegetables are already cooked — so heat them quickly on Microwave on HIGH.

Combine canned vegetables easily, too. Vegetables with similar density will heat well together — things like peas and carrots or peas and mushrooms.

See the chart, above, which tells exactly how to heat a can of vegetables.

To reheat Home Canned Vegetables, place vegetables in glass casserole. Bring to a boil on Microwave HIGH and then reduce heat to DEFROST. Simmer the recommended time of 15 minutes for all vegetables except corn and spinach which take 20 minutes.

SWEET POTATOES BRULEE

   1 **can (17 oz.) vacuum packed sweet potatoes, mashed**
   2 **tablespoons butter or margarine**
   3 **tablespoons orange juice**
     Salt
   ⅛ **teaspoon cinnamon**
   3 **tablespoons chopped nuts**
   ¼ **cup packed brown sugar**

Setting: HIGH

1. Combine potatoes, butter, orange juice, salt and cinnamon in 1-quart glass casserole. Sprinkle top with nuts and brown sugar; cover.

2. MICROWAVE for 6 to 7 MINUTES or until hot. Let stand, covered, 3 minutes before serving.

4 to 5 Servings

TIPS The amount of orange juice needed may vary with potatoes. We used a vacuum packed which does not contain liquid. If using ones with liquid, drain and add only enough orange juice to moisten.
- Try this topping with cooked squash, too.

BAKED BEANS

   1 **can (16 oz.) beans and pork in tomato sauce**
   ¼ **cup chopped onion**
   ¼ **cup catsup**
   ½ **teaspoon prepared mustard**
   2 **tablespoons packed brown sugar**
   4 **slices bacon, cut into pieces**

Setting: HIGH

1. Combine all ingredients except bacon in 1-quart glass casserole. Top with bacon pieces; cover.

2. MICROWAVE for 12 to 14 MINUTES or until mixture bubbles. Let stand, covered, 3 minutes before serving.

4 Servings

TIP MICROWAVE on MEDIUM for 16 to 18 MINUTES.

ONION TOPPED BEANS

   2 **packages (10 oz. each) frozen French-cut green beans**
   1 **can (5 oz.) water chestnuts, drained and sliced**
   2 **cans (10¾ oz. each) condensed cream of celery soup**
   1 **can (3½ oz.) French-fried onion rings**

Setting: HIGH

1. Place frozen beans in 2-quart (12 x 7) glass baking dish; cover.

2. MICROWAVE for 7 to 8 MINUTES or until beans are tender-crisp. Add water chestnuts. Spread soup over beans. Top with onion rings. MICROWAVE for about 5 MINUTES or until hot. Let stand 2 to 3 minutes before serving.

6 to 8 Servings

TIP Substitute fresh beans or other green vegetables for beans. See chart for cooking instructions.

Excellent creamy blend of flavor.

HARVARD BEETS

   ¼ **cup sugar**
   1 **tablespoon cornstarch**
   ½ **teaspoon salt**
     Dash pepper
   ¼ **cup vinegar**
   1 **can (16 oz.) diced beets**
   1 **cup beet liquid plus water**

Setting: HIGH

1. Combine sugar, cornstarch, salt and pepper in 1-quart glass casserole. Stir in vinegar and beet liquid. Add beets; cover.

2. MICROWAVE for 5 MINUTES. Stir and MICROWAVE for 4 to 5 MINUTES or until slightly thickened. Let stand, covered, 3 minutes before serving.

4 to 5 Servings

ACCOMPANIMENTS MEAL **Breads & Salads**

HOW TO WARM BREAD AND ROLLS

- Place rolls or muffins on paper plate, paper towel, cloth or paper napkin.

- Warm on HIGH since all breads are precooked.
- Do not over heat or breads will toughen — surface should be "warm" rather than "hot."

BREAD	AMOUNT	SETTING	TIME FROM ROOM TEMPERATURE	TIME FROM FREEZER
BUNS AND ROLLS Hamburger, Hot Dog, Dinner, Bagel	1 2 4 6 8	HIGH	10 to 15 sec. 15 to 20 sec. 20 to 25 sec. 25 to 30 sec. 35 to 40 sec.	15 to 20 sec. 20 to 25 sec. 25 to 30 sec. 35 to 40 sec. 50 to 55 sec.
ENGLISH MUFFINS	1 2 4 6	HIGH	20 to 25 sec. 30 to 35 sec. 55 to 60 sec. 1 to 1¼ min.	35 to 40 sec. 50 to 60 sec. 2 to 2½ min. 2¾ to 3 min.
FRENCH BREAD	1½ lb.	HIGH	30 to 45 sec.	1½ to 2 min.
DOUGHNUTS Regular, Raised, **SWEET ROLLS** **COFFEE CAKE WEDGE**	1 2 4 6	HIGH	15 to 20 sec. 25 to 30 sec. 40 to 45 sec. 50 to 60 sec.	25 to 30 sec. 35 to 40 sec. 50 to 60 sec. 1¼ to 1½ min.
MUFFINS Raisin, Fruit Date	1 2 6 6	HIGH	10 to 15 sec. 20 to 30 sec. 30 to 35 sec. 40 to 45 sec.	20 to 25 sec. 35 to 40 sec. 55 to 60 sec. 1¾ to 2 min.
NUT BREAD Canned	8 oz.	HIGH	2 to 2½ min.	
PANCAKES, FRENCH TOAST, WAFFLES	1 2 4	HIGH	20 to 30 sec. 35 to 45 sec. 1 to 1½ min.	35 to 45 sec. 1 to 1½ min. 1½ to 2 min.
POPOVERS	2 to 4	HIGH	30 to 60 sec.	

Pictured, clockwise: Creamy Wilted Lettuce, page 28 (garnished with hard-cooked eggs), Banana Bread and Corn Muffins made from mixes, page 128, English Muffin Bread, page 129, and Casserole Bread, page 130.

POPOVERS

Setting: HIGH

Popovers cannot be cooked in the microwave oven because they do not form a crust to hold their shape. The batter puffs up beautifully but they collapse as soon as the door is opened or the oven turned off. Since the conventional oven is often being used for other foods when you would like to serve popovers, it may be convenient to bake them early in the day and let them cool completely. Then just arrange them in a napkin-lined basket and MICROWAVE for about 1 MINUTE to heat to piping hot.

HOW TO MICROWAVE QUICK BREAD MIXES AND YEAST BREAD

- Prepare quick bread mix as directed on package.

- Fill glass cooking dish only half full.

- Pour extra batter into paper lined individual glass custard cups.

- MICROWAVE on DEFROST then HIGH when directed on chart; serve.

- Mix yeast bread as directed in a favorite recipe. Raise on WARM using microwave technique in English Muffin Bread, page 129.

- Bake 1 to 2 loaves of bread in well-greased glass loaf dish(es) on DEFROST as directed in chart.

- Allow bread to stand 5 minutes. Turn out on wire rack to cool before slicing.

BREADS AND QUICK BREADS	SIZE	GLASS CONTAINER	FIRST SETTING AND TIME	SECOND SETTING AND TIME
COFFEE CAKE MIX	19-oz. pkg.	9-in. round dish	DEFROST 7 min.	HIGH 4 to 5 min.
CORNBREAD MIX	16-oz. pkg.	9-in square	DEFROST 7 min.	HIGH 4 to 5 min.
DATE BREAD MIX	17-oz. pkg.	1½-qt. casserole	DEFROST 10 min.	HIGH 2 to 3 min.
BANANA BREAD MIX	15½-oz. pkg.	(8 x 4) loaf dish	DEFROST 10 min.	HIGH 2 to 3 min.
CORN MUFFIN MIX 6 Muffins	8½-oz. pkg.	Cupcake liners in individual custard cups	DEFROST 5 to 6 min.	
BLUEBERRY MUFFIN MIX 4 Muffins 6 Muffins	13½-oz. pkg.	Cupcake liners in individual custard cups	DEFROST 4 to 4½ min. 6 to 6½ min.	
HOMEMADE BREAD 1 Loaf 2 Loaves	1 lb. 1 lb. ea.	(8 x 4) loaf dish	DEFROST 10 to 11 min. 12 to 13 min.	

Extra batter makes great mini-cakes in paper lined custard cups.

YEAST BREAD KEY: Raising yeast bread is a delicate process — but fast and successful in a microwave oven on WARM. This low speed keeps yeast alive and active. Steps 3, 4 and 5 in the following English Muffin Bread recipe outline the technique for raising most any freshly mixed yeast bread dough — and the whole process takes less than one hour.

If your oven does not have a WARM setting proof bread conventionally. We have included a recipe to thaw and proof frozen bread using the automatic DEFROST setting.

Bake yeast bread dough quickly on Microwave DEFROST for even texture — and so edges stay tender while center cooks.

Always use glass bowls and dishes when raising or baking bread. Make certain dishes are well greased.

Standing time is important to finish cooking process and so breads' bottom surface will set.

Cool, then wrap baked bread tightly to preserve softness.

Bread will not brown and so does not have a hard crust. It's great for tea sandwiches — makes especially good toast and French toast.

Heat baked bread and rolls in seconds on a paper plate, paper towel, paper or cloth napkin so moisture is absorbed. Use HIGH.

Dry bread for crumbling on Microwave WARM. Then whirl it in an electric blender or crush with a rolling pin.

IMPORTANT: Before you begin, refer to the "Beginning to Cook" section for basic technique and these example recipes:

Cover dough when proofing but not while baking.

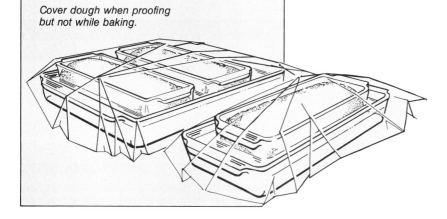

WARM setting raises bread fully; DEFROST cooks dough.

ENGLISH MUFFIN BREAD

  3 cups unsifted all-purpose flour
  2 packages active dry yeast
  1 tablespoon sugar
  ¼ teaspoon soda
  1 tablespoon salt
2½ cups milk
  2 cups unsifted all-purpose flour
  Melted butter

Settings: HIGH/WARM/DEFROST

1. Combine 3 cups flour, yeast sugar, soda and salt in large mixer bowl; set aside. Pour milk into 4-cup glass measure.

2. MICROWAVE on HIGH for 2 to 2½ MINUTES or until warm. Stir milk into flour mixture. Beat at medium speed with electric mixer until smooth. Stir in remaining 2 cups flour. Knead on floured surface until smooth and elastic, 5 to 8 minutes.

3. **Raising:** Place dough in greased large glass bowl; brush with melted butter, and cover loosely with plastic wrap or wax paper. Place bowl of dough in 3-quart (13 x 9) glass baking dish containing 3 cups warm water.

4. MICROWAVE on WARM for 40 to 45 MINUTES or until bread is doubled in size. Punch down dough; divide in half. Shape each half into a loaf. Place in 2 greased (8 x 4) glass loaf dishes. Brush tops with melted butter. Place crosswise in 3-quart (13 x 9) glass baking dish containing 3 cups warm water. Cover loosely with plastic wrap or wax paper.

5. MICROWAVE on WARM for 20 to 25 MINUTES or until loaves are light and doubled in size. Remove dish of water and uncover bread.

6. **Baking:** MICROWAVE on DEFROST for 18 to 20 MINUTES or until no longer doughy. Let stand 5 minutes. Turn out on rack to cool.

                                  2 Loaves Bread

THAWING AND PROOFING FROZEN BREAD DOUGH

Settings: HIGH/DEFROST

1. MICROWAVE on HIGH 4 cups water in 4-cup glass measure until steaming hot (8 min.). Place frozen loaf in greased (8 x 4) glass loaf dish. Place, uncovered, in oven with the water.

2. MICROWAVE on DEFROST for 2 MINUTES. Let stand 15 minutes. Repeat DEFROST and Stand sequence 3 to 4 more times or until dough is just above top of pan.

TIP If your oven has a WARM setting follow these steps:

1. Grease 1-pound loaf frozen bread dough; place in greased (8 x 4) glass loaf dish. Cover loosely with plastic wrap. Place dish of dough in 2-quart (12 x 7) glass baking dish. Pour 2 cups warm water into baking dish.

2. MICROWAVE on WARM for 30 MINUTES.

3. Let stand in oven for 15 minutes. Repeat these two steps until dough is just above top of dish, about 3 times. Remove dish of water and plastic wrap.

HOW TO BAKE BREAD DOUGH

MICROWAVE proofed and raised bread on DEFROST for 10 to 11 MINUTES or until no longer doughy. Let stand 5 minutes. Unmold. Bread will look moist when unmolded. Let stand 5 additional minutes to set.

CASSEROLE BREAD

 1½ cups cold water
 ⅓ cup yellow cornmeal
 1 teaspoon salt
 ⅓ cup molasses
 2 tablespoons butter or margarine
 ¼ cup warm water
 1 package active dry yeast
 3¼ to 3½ cups unsifted all purpose flour

Settings: HIGH/DEFROST

1. In 2 or 2½-quart glass casserole combine water, cornmeal and salt.

2. MICROWAVE on HIGH for 4 to 5 MINUTES until mixture boils, stirring occasionally. Add molasses and butter; cool to lukewarm.

3. Dissolve yeast in warm water. Stir into lukewarm cornmeal mixture. Mix in flour until well combined.

4. Arrange evenly in casserole. Rub top with oil or softened butter. Cover casserole (allowing space for bread to rise) and refrigerate overnight.

5. Next day, remove from refrigerator and MICROWAVE on DEFROST for 12 to 15 MINUTES or until no doughy spots remain. Cool 5 minutes in casserole; turn out of pan and cool completely.

             1 Loaf

GARLIC FRENCH BREAD

 1 loaf French bread
 ⅓ cup butter or margarine
 ½ teaspoon garlic salt or 1 clove garlic

Setting: HIGH

1. Cut bread into ½-inch slices, but do not slice all the way through loaf. In small cup or dish, melt butter with garlic (about 30 sec.).

2. Brush mixture on each slice of loaf. Place in oven on paper towels.

3. MICROWAVE for 45 SECONDS to 1 MINUTE or until loaf feels warm.

             1 Loaf

Bowls and baking dishes must be well greased.

WHEAT GERM BREAD

 1 cup warm water
 1 package active dry yeast
 ¼ cup packed brown sugar
 1½ teaspoons salt
 2 tablespoons cooking oil
 1 egg
 ½ cup wheat germ
 1½ cups unsifted all-purpose flour
 1 cup unsifted all-purpose flour
  Melted butter

Settings: WARM/DEFROST

1. Combine warm water and yeast in large glass mixer bowl. Stir in brown sugar, salt, oil, egg, wheat germ and 1½ cups flour. Beat about 3 minutes at medium speed with electric mixer. Stir in remaining 1 cup flour to form a stiff dough. Knead on floured surface until smooth and elastic, 5 to 8 minutes.

2. **Raising:** Place dough in greased large glass bowl; brush with melted butter and cover loosely with plastic wrap or wax paper. Place bowl of dough in 3-quart (13 x 9) glass baking dish containing 3 cups warm water.

3. MICROWAVE on WARM for 20 to 25 MINUTES or until bread is doubled in size. Punch down dough. Shape into a loaf and place in greased (8 x 4) glass loaf dish. Brush top with melted butter. Cover loosely with plastic wrap or wax paper. Return to dish with warm water.

4. MICROWAVE on WARM for 20 to 25 MINUTES or until doubled in size. Remove dish of water and uncover bread.

5. **Baking:** MICROWAVE on DEFROST for 10 to 11 MINUTES or until no longer doughy. Let stand 5 minutes. Turn out on rack to cool.

           1 Loaf Bread

QUICK BREAD KEY: Tender tasty quick breads from "scratch" or biscuit mix start cooking on DEFROST, finish up on HIGH to set the batter. It's a technique similar to cake baking.

Coffee cake from canned refrigerated biscuits cooks very quickly on HIGH because this is a "shorter" dough.

Glass cooking dishes are a must. Since batter raises higher than usual in a microwave oven, do not fill dishes more than half full.

Coffee cakes are prettiest when recipe calls for fruit toppings or brown sugar glazes because a microwave oven does not brown bread dough.

Quick breads are cooked when a toothpick inserted near center of bread comes out clean.

Popovers CANNOT be baked in a microwave oven because they do not form a crust to hold dough in shape. Leftover popovers reheat nicely. See how in the bread reheating chart.

Quick breads with toppings are prettiest.

PUMPKIN BREAD WITH PUMPKIN TOPPING

  1½ **cups unsifted all-purpose flour**
  1½ **cups sugar**
   1 **teaspoon soda**
  ¾ **teaspoon salt**
  ½ **teaspoon nutmeg**
  ½ **teaspoon cinnamon**
   1 **cup mashed cooked pumpkin**
  ½ **cup cooking oil**
  ⅓ **cup water**
   2 **eggs**
  ½ **cup chopped walnuts**
  ½ **cup chopped pitted dates**

Pumpkin Topping
   1 **cup whipping cream**
  ¼ **cup powdered sugar**
  ¼ **teaspoon nutmeg**
  ¼ **teaspoon cinnamon**
  ¾ **cup mashed cooked pumpkin**

Settings: DEFROST/HIGH

1. Combine all bread ingredients, except walnuts and dates, in large mixer bowl. Beat at medium speed about 1 minute. Fold in walnuts and dates. Pour batter into 2-quart (9 x 5) glass loaf dish.

2. MICROWAVE on DEFROST for 20 MINUTES.

3. MICROWAVE on HIGH for 5 to 6 MINUTES or until toothpick inserted near center comes out clean. Let stand 2 minutes; unmold. Serve with Pumpkin Topping.

4. Pumpkin Topping: Whip cream with powdered sugar and spices. Fold in pumpkin.

                                1 Loaf Bread

TIP 1 can (16 oz.) pumpkin is enough for both bread and topping.

Quick bread microwave technique is similar to the one for baking cake.

BISCUIT MIX COFFEE CAKE

   2 **cups biscuit mix**
   2 **tablespoons sugar**
  ⅔ **cup water**
   1 **egg**

Topping
  ⅓ **cup biscuit mix**
  ⅓ **cup packed brown sugar**
  ½ **teaspoon cinnamon**
  ¼ **cup butter or margarine**

Settings: DEFROST/HIGH

1. Combine 2 cups biscuit mix, sugar, water and egg in medium mixing bowl; mix well. Spread in 9-inch round glass baking dish. Sprinkle with Topping.

2. MICROWAVE on DEFROST for 7 MINUTES.

3. MICROWAVE on HIGH for 4 to 4½ MINUTES or until toothpick inserted near center comes out clean.

4. Topping: Combine ⅓ cup biscuit mix, brown sugar and cinnamon; cut in butter.

                                About 6 Servings

Super-fast no-think coffee cake will delight the family at breakfast.

CARAMEL BISCUIT RING-A-ROUND

  ⅓ **cup packed brown sugar**
   3 **tablespoons butter or margarine**
   1 **tablespoon water**
  ⅓ **cup chopped nuts**
   1 **can (8 oz.) refrigerated biscuits**

Setting: HIGH

1. Combine brown sugar, butter and water in 1-quart glass casserole.

2. MICROWAVE for about 1 MINUTE or until butter is melted. Stir in nuts. Separate biscuits; cut each one into quarters. Add biscuits to sugar mixture; stir to coat each piece. Push biscuits and coating away from center of casserole and set a custard cup or glass, open end up, in center.

3. MICROWAVE for 3 to 3½ MINUTES or until biscuits are no longer doughy. Let stand 2 minutes; twist out custard cup and invert biscuit ring on serving plate. Serve warm with forks to pull sections apart into individual servings.

                                About 6 Servings

TIPS Use dark brown sugar instead of light brown for a richer, darker color.

● Use a sharp pointed knife to loosen custard cup if it sticks to caramel and will not twist out easily.

● MICROWAVE on MEDIUM for 2 MINUTES in step 2 and 5 to 5½ MINUTES in step 3.

SALADS AND SALAD DRESSING KEY: You can use your oven for a variety of tasks to make salad preparation easier and simpler. Use it to cook bacon or potatoes for a salad, to dissolve gelatin a mold or to soften cream cheese that has been removed from the foil wrapper. If you wish, the oven can bring refrigerated fruits and vegetables to room temperature before they are combined in a salad.

Salad dressings can be cooked in the same bowl in which the salad is served. Most hot salads can be made ahead and then reheated which allows your meal preparation to be even more relaxed.

IMPORTANT: Before you begin, refer to the "Beginning to Cook" section for basic technique and these example recipes:

OLD-FASHIONED POTATO SALAD

    3 to 4 medium potatoes
    3 hard-cooked eggs, chopped
    1 small onion, chopped
    2 stalks celery, chopped
    ¼ cup chopped pickle
Dressing
    2 tablespoons all-purpose flour
    2 tablespoons sugar
    1 teaspoon salt
    1 teaspoon dry mustard
    ¾ cup milk
    1 egg, slightly beaten
    1 tablespoon butter or margarine
    ¼ cup vinegar

Setting: HIGH

1. MICROWAVE potatoes as directed in cooking chart, page 117. Set aside to cool. While potatoes cook, cook eggs conventionally.

2. Prepare Dressing in large mixing bowl (can be dish you'll store or serve salad in) by combining flour, sugar, salt and mustard. Stir in milk and egg, mixing until smooth.

3. MICROWAVE for 2½ to 3 MINUTES or until mixture boils, stirring occasionally. Stir to make smooth. Blend in butter and vinegar. Cool slightly.

4. Peel potatoes and slice into warm dressing. Add cooked eggs, onion, celery and pickle; mix well. Refrigerate until served.

4 to 6 Servings

TIPS If you prefer to use mayonnaise or salad dressing, allow the potatoes to cool before mixing with about 1 cup of dressing.
• When you need just a little more dressing, add mayonnaise or salad dressing.
• MICROWAVE on MEDIUM for 4½ to 6 MINUTES in step 3.

PEACHY CHICKEN-RICE SALAD

    1 package (12 oz.) frozen rice pilaf
    ¼ cup mayonnaise or salad dressing
    1 tablespoon chopped onion or
    1 teaspoon instant minced onion
    ½ teaspoon curry powder
    1½ cups (1-lb. can) cubed, drained sliced
       peaches
    2 cups cubed cooked chicken
    ½ cup chopped celery
    ¼ cup chopped green pepper

Setting: HIGH

1. Place frozen pouch of rice in oven.

2. MICROWAVE for 3½ to 4 MINUTES, or until thawed.

3. Empty into serving bowl and cool. Stir in mayonnaise, onion, curry, peaches and chicken. Chill thoroughly.

4. Just before serving, stir in celery and green pepper. If desired, garnish with toasted almonds.

4 Servings

TIP Pineapple chunks can be used for part or all of peaches.

MAKE AHEAD FRUIT SALAD

    1 egg, beaten
    2 tablespoons sugar
    ½ cup fruit syrup (from pineapple or other
       fruit)
    2 tablespoons lemon juice
    5 cups fresh fruit (blueberries, melon
       balls, banana chunks, apple pieces,
       grapes, pear cubes or orange segments)
    1 cup drained pineapple (crushed, chunk
       or tidbits)
    2 cups miniature or cut up large
       marshmallows
    ½ cup whipping cream, whipped, or 1 cup
       frozen whipped topping, thawed

Setting: HIGH

In large glass bowl, combine egg, sugar, fruit syrup and lemon juice. MICROWAVE for 1 to 1½ MINUTES or until mixture is slightly thickened, stirring occasionally. Cool. Add fruit, pineapple, marshmallows and whipped cream. Fold together just until well mixed. Cover and refrigerate at least 3 hours before serving.

6 to 8 Servings

TIP The salad can be made a day ahead, but apples are best if stirred in a few hours before serving; they may turn a little brown when added a day ahead.

ACCOMPANIMENTS MEAL **Rice & Pasta**

HOW TO COOK RICE AND PASTA

● Choose a glass cooking dish two to three times as large as the amount of dry rice or pasta cooked — they expand during cooking.

● Add 1 teaspoon salt and 1 tablespoon butter to water.

● Bring water and seasonings to a full rolling boil on MICROWAVE HIGH.

● Stir in raw rice and MICROWAVE on DEFROST.

● Always cook rice and pasta covered. Use a fitted glass lid or tautly-stretched plastic wrap.

● Let cooked rice and pasta stand, covered, 5 minutes after being removed from the oven.

● Cook quick-cooking rice in a glass or pottery serving casserole without silver, gold or other metal trim. Boil water on MICROWAVE HIGH. Stir in quick-cooking rice; cover, and let stand as directed on package.

● Wild rice is most tender if washed, drained, covered with tap water and soaked 2 to 3 hours.

RICE/PASTA	COVERED GLASS CASSEROLE	WATER	FIRST SETTING AND TIME	RICE/PASTA	SECOND SETTING AND TIME
SHORT GRAIN WHITE	2-qt.	2 cups	HIGH 4 to 5 min.	1 cup	DEFROST 15 to 16 min.
LONG GRAIN WHITE	2-qt.	2 cups	HIGH 4 to 5 min.	1 cup	DEFROST 15 to 18 min.
WHITE AND WILD MIX	2-qt.	2½ cups	HIGH 5 to 6 min.	6-oz. pkg.	DEFROST 30 to 35 min.
BROWN	3-qt.	3 cups	HIGH 6 to 7 min.	1 cup	DEFROST 25 to 30 min.
WILD RICE soaked in water 3 hours	3-qt.	3 cups	HIGH 6 to 7 min.	1 cup raw or 2 cups soaked	DEFROST 50 to 60 min.
QUICK-COOKING	1-qt.	1 cup	HIGH 3 to 4 min.	1 cup	Rest, covered, 5 min. or until all water absorbs
SPAGHETTI	3-qt. casserole	4 cups	HIGH 8 to 10 min.	7-oz. pkg.	DEFROST 10 to 12 min.
MACARONI	3-qt. casserole	3 cups	HIGH 6 to 8 min.	2 cups	DEFROST 10 to 12 min.
EGG NOODLES	3-qt. casserole	6 cups	HIGH 10 to 12 min.	4 cups	DEFROST 12 to 14 min.
LASAGNA NOODLES	3-qt. (13 x 9) baking dish	6 cups	HIGH 10 to 12 min.	8-oz. pkg.	DEFROST 12 to 14 min.

ACCOMPANIMENTS MEAL **Sweet & Savory Sauces**

SAUCE KEY: MICROWAVE all sauces on HIGH setting. Most of these sauces are easy to make ahead before serving with a main course or to keep on hand in the refrigerator for quick reheating. Sauces are exceptionally failproof in a microwave oven, without danger of scorching or burning. You may want to adapt one of your own sauce recipes, using a similar recipe in this chapter as a guide to the timing and method. Sauces that you buy already prepared can also be heated if first transferred to a container that can be used in the oven.

IMPORTANT: Before you begin refer to the "Beginning to Cook" section for basic technique and this example recipe:

SPICY RAISIN SAUCE

- ½ cup firmly packed brown sugar
- 1 tablespoon cornstarch
- 1½ teaspoons dry mustard
- ⅛ teaspoon ground cloves
- 1 cup water
- ¼ cup raisins
- 2 tablespoons lemon juice
- 1 tablespoon butter or margarine

Setting: HIGH

1. In 4-cup glass measure, combine all ingredients.

2. MICROWAVE for 4 to 4½ MINUTES or until mixture boils and raisins are plump, stirring occasionally during last half of cooking time.

1½ Cups Sauce

TIP If desired, prepare sauce ahead and MICROWAVE from room temperature, 2½ to 3 MINUTES, or until hot.

CRANBERRY SAUCE

- 1½ cups fresh or frozen cranberries
- ½ cup sugar
- ¼ cup water

Setting: HIGH

1. In 1-quart glass casserole, combine cranberries, sugar and water; cover.

2. MICROWAVE for 4 to 5 MINUTES or until cranberries have popped, stirring once. Let stand, covered, several minutes to finish cooking. Serve warm or cold.

2 Cups Sauce

TIP For orange flavor, use orange juice for water and add 1 tablespoon grated orange peel.

CHERRIES JUBILEE

- 1 can (21 oz.) cherry pie filling
- ¼ cup currant jelly
- 1 teaspoon grated orange rind
- ¼ cup rum
- ¼ cup brandy
- Vanilla ice cream

Setting: HIGH

1. Combine cherry pie filling with jelly, orange rind and rum in medium glass bowl; stir to blend.

2. MICROWAVE for 5 to 6 MINUTES or until heated in center; stir.

3. Measure brandy into 1-cup glass measure.

4. MICROWAVE for 15 to 20 SECONDS until warm. Pour brandy over cherry sauce and ignite. Immediately spoon over ice cream.

About 4 Cups Sauce

FUDGE SAUCE

- 1 cup light cream
- 2 cups sugar
- 4 squares unsweetened chocolate
- 2 tablespoons butter or margarine
- ½ teaspoon salt
- 1 teaspoon vanilla

Setting: DEFROST

1. Combine all ingredients, except vanilla, in 4-cup glass measure.

2. MICROWAVE for 7 MINUTES. Stir and MICROWAVE for 7 to 8 MINUTES or until thickened. Stir in vanilla. Beat sauce light and smooth by hand or for 10 seconds at "low" speed in a blender.

About 2 Cups Sauce

TIP MICROWAVE on MEDIUM for 5 MINUTES and then 5 to 6 MINUTES in step 2.

APPLESAUCE

- 8 medium cooking apples, peeled, cored and quartered
- ½ cup water
- 1 cup sugar

Setting: HIGH

1. Combine apples and water in 2-quart glass casserole. Cover with glass lid or plastic wrap.

2. MICROWAVE for 10 to 12 MINUTES or until apples are tender. Stir in sugar; let stand, covered, 2 to 3 minutes to dissolve sugar. Stir before serving.

About 6 Servings

A good sauce for fondue, ice cream or spice cakes and puddings. Keeps well in the refrigerator for quick reheating in the jar.

Butterscotch Fondue Sauce

BUTTERSCOTCH FONDUE SAUCE

   ½ **cup evaporated milk or light cream**
1½ **cups packed brown sugar**
   3 **tablespoons butter or margarine**
   1 **teaspoon vanilla or 2 tablespoons rum**

Setting: HIGH

1. In 4-cup glass measure, combine evaporated milk, brown sugar and butter.

2. MICROWAVE for 4 to 5 MINUTES, stirring occasionally. Stir in vanilla; cool slightly. Serve in fondue pot or warmer dish at the table with fruits, cake or cookies to dip into the sauce.

1 ⅓ Cups Sauce

TIP For more sauce, use 2-quart casserole, double the ingredients and MICROWAVE for 6 to 8 MINUTES.

A good dessert idea for company. Any leftover sauce can be stored in the refrigerator for serving on ice cream.

HEAVENLY CHOCOLATE FONDUE

   1 **can (14 oz.) sweetened condensed milk**
   1 **jar (10 oz.) marshmallow creme**
   ½ **cup milk**
   1 **teaspoon vanilla**
   1 **package (12 oz.) semi-sweet chocolate pieces**

Setting: HIGH

1. Combine all ingredients in medium glass mixing bowl.

2. MICROWAVE for 3 to 4 MINUTES. Beat until well blended and creamy.

About 4 Cups Fondue

TIPS Pineapple chunks, fresh apple slices, orange sections, banana chunks, marshmallows, angel food and other cake squares are good fondue dunkers.
• Keep fondue sauce warm while serving in a chafing dish over hot water or in a heavy pottery crock over very low heat.
• MICROWAVE on MEDIUM for 4 to 6 MINUTES.

NUTMEG SAUCE

   ½ **cup sugar**
   1 **tablespoon cornstarch**
   ½ **teaspoon nutmeg**
   1 **cup water**
   ¼ **cup butter or margarine**
   2 **tablespoons rum or brandy;
      or 1 teaspoon vanilla**

Setting: HIGH

1. In 2-cup glass measure, combine sugar, cornstarch and nutmeg; stir in water and butter.

2. MICROWAVE for 3 to 4 MINUTES or until mixture boils and thickens, stirring occasionally. Stir in flavoring. Serve warm.

1½ Cups Sauce

White Sauce is easy to reheat if made ahead or leftover.

WHITE SAUCE

    1 cup milk
    2 tablespoons all-purpose flour
    ¼ teaspoon salt
    ⅛ teaspoon pepper
    2 tablespoons butter or margarine

Setting: HIGH

1. Combine all ingredients in 2-cup glass measure; mix well.

2. MICROWAVE for 2 MINUTES. Stir and MICROWAVE for 1 to 1½ MINUTES or until thickened.

About 1 Cup Sauce

TIPS Make EGG WHITE SAUCE by stirring 2 to 3 hard cooked eggs, finely chopped, into Basic White Sauce when sauce is stirred during step 2.
• Make CHEESE SAUCE by stirring ¼ teaspoon dry mustard and ½ cup shredded American process cheese into Basic White Sauce when sauce is stirred in step 2.

Hollandaise sauce is easy to make or reheat in the oven for serving with vegetables or fish.

HOLLANDAISE SAUCE

    ¼ cup butter or margarine
    ¼ cup light cream
    2 egg yolks, beaten
    1 tablespoon lemon juice or vinegar
    ¼ teaspoon salt
    ½ teaspoon dry mustard

Setting: HIGH

1. In 2-cup glass measure, MICROWAVE for 30 SECONDS. Add remaining ingredients; mix well.

2. MICROWAVE for 1 to 1½ MINUTES or until thickened, stirring every 15 SECONDS. Remove and beat until light.

⅔ Cup Sauce

TIPS If sauce curdles, it is overcooked.
• For half a recipe, use half the ingredient amounts, MICROWAVE in 1-cup measure for 30 SECONDS.
• MICROWAVE on MEDIUM for 1½ to 2 MINUTES.

GRAVY

    ⅓ cup meat or poultry drippings
    ⅓ cup unsifted all-purpose flour
    2 cups warm broth or water
    Salt
    Pepper

Setting: HIGH

1. Combine drippings and flour in 4-cup glass measure. Stir in broth. Season to taste.

2. MICROWAVE for 2 MINUTES. Stir and MICROWAVE for 1 to 2 MINUTES or until thickened.

About 2 Cups Gravy

TIP Make gravy for beef, veal, pork roasts and turkey using this recipe.

This mild flavored cheese sauce complements flavors of veal, pork and lamb, and vegetables such as broccoli or artichokes.

MORNAY SAUCE

    2 tablespoons butter or margarine
    2 tablespoons flour
    ⅓ cup milk or cream
    1 cup water
    1 cube or teaspoon chicken bouillon
    ¼ cup grated Parmesan cheese
    ¼ cup shredded Swiss cheese

Setting: HIGH

1. In 2-cup glass measure, MICROWAVE for 30 SECONDS. Stir in flour. Add milk, water and bouillon; mix well.

2. MICROWAVE for 2½ to 3 MINUTES, or until mixture boils, stirring occasionally during last half of cooking time. Stir in cheeses and let stand, covered, until cheeses melt.

1⅔ Cups Sauce

Try this mushroom sauce over your next barbecued or broiled steak or hamburger.

MUSHROOM SAUCE

    ¼ cup butter or margarine
    1 cup (8 oz. or ½ pt.) sliced fresh mushrooms
    4 teaspoons cornstarch
    1 teaspoon salt
    1 teaspoon Worcestershire sauce
    1 cup water

Setting: HIGH

1. In 1-quart glass casserole, combine butter and mushrooms; cover.

2. MICROWAVE for 2 MINUTES, stirring occasionally. Stir in remaining ingredients.

3. MICROWAVE for 3½ to 4 MINUTES, or until mixture boils, stirring occasionally during last half of cooking time.

2 Cups Sauce

TIPS Sauce can be prepared ahead; MICROWAVE from room temperature, uncovered, 1½ to 2 MINUTES or until hot.
• If desired, ½ cup (4-oz. can) drained mushroom stems and pieces can be substituted for fresh mushrooms.
• MICROWAVE on MEDIUM for 3 MINUTES in step 2 and 4 to 5 MINUTES in step 3.

FOR DESSERT **Fruit, Puddings & Custards**

Serve this hot over ice cream. Easy to make if pears are on hand; no other special ingredients are necessary.

PEARS A LA CREME

  2 tablespoons butter or margarine
  ⅓ cup packed brown sugar
  ½ teaspoon cinnamon
  ¼ teaspoon nutmeg
  ¼ teaspoon ginger
  2½ cups (1 lb. 13-oz. can) drained pear halves
    Vanilla ice cream

Setting: HIGH

1. In 2-quart glass casserole or shallow glass baking dish, combine butter, brown sugar and spices.

2. MICROWAVE for 1½ to 2 MINUTES, stirring once. Add pears; cover.

3. MICROWAVE for 4 to 5 MINUTES. Serve a hot pear half, cut-side down, over a scoop of ice cream, spooning the glaze over pears.

                        6 to 8 Servings

Wine flavored bananas are good served plain or as topping for ice cream or cake.

GOING BANANAS

  3 tablespoons butter or margarine
  3 tablespoons packed brown sugar
  ⅛ teaspoon ground cloves
    Pinch salt
  ¼ cup lemon juice
  ½ cup muscatel wine or cream sherry
  5 bananas

Setting: HIGH

1. In shallow baking dish, MICROWAVE butter for 1 MINUTE. Stir in remaining ingredients except bananas. Slice bananas once lengthwise and once crosswise and add to sauce, turning to coat.

2. MICROWAVE for 3 to 3½ MINUTES or until fruit is softened and hot, rearranging bananas once.

                        4 to 6 Servings

A quick, flaming sauce to serve over ice cream. Serve any leftovers cold because reheating would overcook bananas.

BANANAS ROYALE

  6 tablespoons butter or margarine
  6 tablespoons packed brown sugar
  ¼ teaspoon cinnamon
  ¼ teaspoon nutmeg
  ¼ cup light cream
  4 medium bananas, peeled
  ¼ cup brandy, rum or flavored liqueur
    Vanilla

Setting: HIGH

1. Place butter in 9-inch round glass baking dish.

2. MICROWAVE for 1 MINUTE or until melted. Stir in brown sugar, cinnamon, nutmeg and cream. Slice bananas once lengthwise, then once crosswise, into butter mixture. Stir to coat.

3. MICROWAVE for about 3 MINUTES or until bubbly. Measure ¼ to ½ cup brandy into 1-cup glass measure.

4. MICROWAVE for 15 to 20 SECONDS or until warm. Pour over dessert and ignite. Serve immediately over ice cream.

                        4 to 8 servings

TIP When serving as dessert immediately following a meal, you can prepare it in advance through the step of coating the bananas and have ice cream spooned into serving dishes in freezer. Then, while clearing dishes, cook mixture and flame brandy, if desired.

EASY PEACH MELBA

1¼ cups (10-oz. pkg.) frozen sweetened
   raspberries
1¼ cups (10-oz. pkg.) frozen sweetened
   peaches
 1 tablespoon cornstarch
 ½ cup currant jelly
   Vanilla ice cream

Settings: DEFROST/HIGH

1. In 1-quart glass casserole place frozen raspberries and peaches.

2. MICROWAVE on DEFROST for 2½ to 3 MINUTES or until thawed.

3. Strain juices into 2-cup glass measure. Add cornstarch and currant jelly. MICROWAVE on HIGH for 4 to 5 MINUTES, stirring twice during last half of cooking time. Pour over fruit in bowl and mix. (This will bring the sauce to a warm temperature for serving.) Spoon sauce over vanilla ice cream.

6 Servings

TIP To use 1-lb. can sliced peaches in place of frozen peaches, drain peaches adding ¼ cup of syrup, and increase cornstarch to 2 tablespoons. MICROWAVE frozen raspberries on DEFROST for 1½ to 2 MINUTES.

BERRIES AND DUMPLINGS

4 cups (20 oz.) fresh or frozen
  blackberries, boysenberries or
  blueberries
¾ cup sugar
¼ cup water

Dumplings

1 cup unsifted all-purpose flour
2 tablespoons sugar
1 teaspoon baking powder
½ teaspoon salt
2 tablespoons cooking oil
½ cup milk

Setting: HIGH

1. In 2-quart glass casserole, combine berries, ¾ cup sugar and water; cover.

2. MICROWAVE for 5 MINUTES or until mixture just begins to bubble. (If berries are frozen, time will be about 7 to 8 MINUTES.)

3. Meanwhile, prepare **Dumplings** in mixing bowl by combining flour, sugar, baking powder and salt. Add oil and milk; mix just until moistened. Drop by spoonfuls onto hot fruit mixture; cover.

4. MICROWAVE for 5 to 6 MINUTES or until dumplings are no longer doughy underneath. Serve warm.

5 to 6 Servings

TIP To prepare with biscuit mix, use 1 cup mix, 2 tablespoons sugar and ½ cup milk.

A spicy mincemeat sauce to serve over ice cream. Try it for a fall or early winter dinner party.

MINCED ORANGE DESSERT

1 can (11 oz.) mandarin oranges,
  undrained
1 can (21 oz.) mincemeat pie filling
1 can (1 lb. 4 oz.) pear halves, drained
  Ice cream

Setting: HIGH

1. In medium glass bowl, combine oranges and pie filling.

2. MICROWAVE for 2 to 3 MINUTES or until hot, stirring once. Spoon mixture over pear halves filled with ice cream.

6 to 8 Servings

TIPS If desired, add 2 tablespoons brandy to sauce before serving or warm brandy about 15 seconds, add to sauce, and flame.
• The sauce is also good served over ice cream without the pears.

FRUIT CRUNCH

 2 cups (21-oz. can) favorite prepared pie
   filling
 ¼ cup butter or margarine
 ⅓ cup rolled oats
12 gingersnaps or 10 graham cracker
   squares, crushed (1 cup)
 ¼ cup sugar
 ½ teaspoon cinnamon

Setting: HIGH

1. Spread pie filling in 2-quart (8 x8) or 1½-quart (8-inch round) glass baking dish.

2. In a small glass bowl, MICROWAVE for 30 SECONDS. Stir in remaining ingredients. Sprinkle crumb mixture over pie filling.

3. MICROWAVE for 6 to 8 MINUTES or until hot and bubbly. Serve warm.

4 to 6 Servings

MIXED FRUIT AMBROSIA

½ cup flaked coconut
2 tablespoons graham cracker crumbs
1 can (20 oz.) pineapple chunks, drained
1 can (16 oz.) sliced peaches, drained
1 can (11 oz.) mandarin oranges, drained
6 maraschino cherries, halved

Setting: HIGH

1. Combine all ingredients in 2-quart glass casserole; mix well.

2. MICROWAVE for 6 to 7 MINUTES or until hot.

6 to 8 Servings

A good last minute dessert for a busy fall evening.

APPLE PUDDING CAKE

    3 eggs
    3 cups (3 med.) chopped peeled cooking
      apples
    ½ cup unsifted all-purpose flour
    1 cup rolled oats
    1 cup packed brown sugar
    1½ teaspoons baking powder
    ½ teaspoon salt
    1 teaspoon cinnamon
    ¼ teaspoon nutmeg
    1 teaspoon vanilla
    ½ cup chopped nuts

Setting: HIGH

1. In 2-quart glass casserole, beat eggs. Stir in remaining ingredients except nuts, mixing until well combined. Sprinkle nuts over top.

2. MICROWAVE for 10 to 12 MINUTES or until toothpick comes out clean and apples are tender. Serve spooned into dishes and topped with ice cream, whipped cream or Nutmeg Sauce, page 135.

6 to 8 Servings

TIPS If desired, use 1¼ teaspoons apple pie spice for cinnamon and nutmeg.

• Substitute chopped fresh peaches for apples.

Refrigerated biscuits make easy dumplings cooked in a caramel sauce under apple slices. The wax paper cover holds in the heat to cook apples quickly.

APPLES 'N DUMPLINGS

    1 can (8 oz.) refrigerated biscuits
    4 medium cooking apples, peeled and
      sliced
    ½ cup raisins, if desired
    ½ cup chopped nuts, if desired
    ½ cup water
    ½ cup dark corn syrup
    ½ cup packed brown sugar
    ¼ cup butter or margarine

Setting: HIGH

1. Separate biscuits and cut each in half. Arrange in 2-quart (12 x 7) glass baking dish. Top with apples, raisins and nuts.

2. In 2-cup glass measure, combine water, corn syrup, brown sugar and butter.

3. MICROWAVE for 2 to 3 MINUTES, or until mixture boils. Pour over apples, coating most of apples. Cover with wax paper.

4. MICROWAVE for 8 to 9 MINUTES or until apples are tender. Serve warm with cream or ice cream.

6 to 8 Servings

TIP This dish freezes well. Thaw and reheat to serve.

APPLE CRISP

    6 cups cooking apples, peeled, cored and
      sliced
    ½ cup unsifted all-purpose flour
    ½ cup quick-cooking rolled oats
    ¾ cup packed brown sugar
    1 teaspoon cinnamon
    ¼ cup butter or margarine

Setting: HIGH

1. Place apple slices in 2-quart (8 x 8) glass baking dish. Combine flour, oats, sugar and cinnamon in medium mixing bowl. Cut in butter until crumbly. Sprinkle evenly over apples.

2. MICROWAVE for 14 to 16 MINUTES or until apples are tender.

5 to 6 Servings

TIP In late winter, apples tend to be less juicy so you may want to add 1 to 2 tablespoons water to apples before adding topping.

This homemade type biscuit shortcake cooks right in the serving dishes.

LAST MINUTE SHORTCAKE

    1 cup unsifted all-purpose flour
    3 tablespoons sugar
    1 teaspoon baking powder
    ¼ teaspoon salt
    ¼ cup butter or margarine
    ⅓ cup milk
    1 egg
    Sweetened fruit
    Whipped cream

Settings: DEFROST/HIGH

1. Combine flour, sugar, baking powder and salt in large mixing bowl. Cut in butter until crumbly. Measure milk in small bowl and beat in egg. Blend into flour mixture. Spoon into 4 or 5 individual glass custard cups.

2. MICROWAVE on DEFROST for 3 MINUTES.

3. MICROWAVE on HIGH for 2 to 3 MINUTES or until cake is no longer doughy.

4. Serve warm topped with sweetened fruit and whipped cream.

4 to 5 Servings

TIP If desired, use 1½ cups biscuit mix adding sugar, milk and egg.

PUDDING AND CUSTARD KEY: DEFROST is the key microwave setting for custards and desserts with baked custard bases.

A microwave oven eliminates the possibility of scorched puddings and custards because the cooking occurs from all sides, rather than only the bottom. And, for real convenience, you can measure, mix and cook puddings right in a 4-cup glass measure. A glass pitcher is also handy for preparing puddings.

Custards can be cooked in individual custard cups and are great make aheads for dessert or a busy morning's breakfast.

IMPORTANT: Before you begin, refer to the "Beginning to Cook" section for basic technique and these example recipes:

This delicate molded dessert should be made at least 4 hours before serving to have time to chill. Serve with sweetened fresh fruit.

CUSTARD BAVARIAN CREME

    1 tablespoon (1 envelope) unflavored
      gelatin
    ⅓ cup sugar
    ⅛ teaspoon salt
    2 cups milk
    4 eggs
    2 teaspoons vanilla or 2 tablespoons
      orange flavored liqueur
    2 cups whipping cream, whipped, or,
      4 cups (9-oz. pkg.) frozen whipped
      topping, thawed

Setting: DEFROST

1. In 2-quart glass casserole, combine gelatin, sugar, salt, milk and eggs; beat until well mixed.

2. MICROWAVE for 12 to 14 MINUTES or until mixture bubbles around edges, stirring occasionally during last half of cooking time. Cool until mixture thickens.

3. Add vanilla and fold in whipped cream. Pour into 8-cup mold or 8 individual molds. Refrigerate 4 hours or until set. Unmold and serve.

8 Servings

TIPS Overcooking will result in separation of milk and egg mixture; cook only until mixture bubbles. If it does separate, beat with rotary beater to make smooth.

• The mold should be no more than 2 to 3 inches high. If you are using a high mold like a Turk's head mold, add ½ tablespoon (½ envelope) more gelatin to assure it holding its shape when unmolded.

COCONUT PUDDING IN ORANGE CUPS

    ¼ cup sugar
    3 tablespoons cornstarch
    ⅛ teaspoon salt
    2 cups milk
    1 cinnamon stick
    1 egg, beaten
    1 can (3½ oz.) flaked coconut (1-⅓ cups)
    1 teaspoon vanilla
    4 large oranges, hollowed-out

Settings: HIGH/DEFROST

1. Combine sugar, cornstarch and salt in 4-cup glass measure. Gradually, stir in milk, add cinnamon stick.

2. MICROWAVE on HIGH for 3 MINUTES. Stir well.

3. MICROWAVE on DEFROST for 5 MINUTES, stirring twice during cooking. Cover with plastic wrap and MICROWAVE on DEFROST for 2 to 3 MINUTES or until thickened. Remove cinnamon stick. Stir about ½ cup thickened mixture into beaten egg. Return to milk mixture along with coconut, mix well.

4. MICROWAVE on DEFROST for 2 MINUTES to blend flavors. Stir in vanilla. Cool slightly.

5. Fill orange shells with pudding. Chill.

4 Servings

TIP Top with whipped cream or topping; garnish with a curl of orange peel.

Egg whites are beaten and folded into this easy pudding to give it a light, airy texture.

TAPIOCA PUDDING

    2 cups milk
    ¼ cup sugar
    2½ tablespoons quick-cooking tapioca
    ¼ teaspoon salt
    2 eggs, separated
    2 tablespoons sugar
    1 teaspoon vanilla

Setting: DEFROST

1. Combine milk, ¼ cup sugar, tapioca, salt and egg yolks in 4-cup glass measure; mix well.

2. MICROWAVE for 8 MINUTES. Stir and MICROWAVE for 6 to 7 MINUTES or until mixture boils.

3. Beat egg whites in small mixer bowl until frothy. Gradually add 2 tablespoons sugar, beating until mixture forms soft peaks. Beat in vanilla. Fold egg white mixture into pudding. Serve warm or cold.

4 to 6 Servings

TIP If desired, fold in ½ cup finely chopped dates, peaches, apricots, strawberries, raspberries or other desired fruit.

A delightfully tasty and pretty combination: fresh strawberries (or other fresh fruit), creamy custard sauce and a topping of fluffy meringue. The meringues can be briefly cooked just before serving because glass or crystal dishes can be used in the oven.

SNOW-CAPPED CUSTARD

  2 eggs, separated
  ¼ cup sugar
  1 teaspoon cornstarch
  1½ cups milk
  ½ teaspoon vanilla
  3 tablespoons sugar
  ½ teaspoon vanilla
  2 cups (1 pt.) fresh whole strawberries
     or other fruit

Setting: DEFROST

1. Separate eggs, placing whites in small mixer bowl and yolks in 4-cup measure. To yolks, add ¼ cup sugar and cornstarch, mixing well. Stir in milk.

2. MICROWAVE for 7 to 8 MINUTES or until mixture just about boils, stirring occasionally during last half of cooking time (mixture will be thin). Stir in ½ teaspoon vanilla; cool until ready to serve.

3. Just before serving, beat egg whites until frothy. Gradually beat in 3 tablespoons sugar, beating until mixture forms soft peaks. Beat in ½ teaspoon vanilla.

4. Divide strawberries among 4 or 5 dessert dishes.

5. Pour cooked custard over berries; top each with mound of beaten egg white. Place desserts in oven.

6. MICROWAVE for 1 to 1½ MINUTES to set meringue. Serve within a few hours.

4 to 5 Servings

TIP The desserts can stand longer than a few hours, but there will be some wateriness from the juice in the fruit and meringue.

GLORIFIED ORANGE RICE

  1 can (8¾ oz.) crushed pineapple
  1 can (11 oz.) mandarin oranges
  1 cup quick-cooking rice
  ¼ cup sugar
  ½ cup flaked coconut
  ½ cup whipping cream, whipped, or 1 cup
     frozen whipped topping, thawed

Setting: HIGH

1. Drain pineapple and oranges, reserving syrup. Add enough water to syrup to make 1¼ cups liquid.

2. Pour into 1½-quart casserole and MICROWAVE, covered, for 2 to 3 MINUTES or until mixture boils.

3. Stir in rice and sugar. Let stand, covered, to cool to room temperature.

4. Fold in pineapple, mandarin oranges and coconut. Chill thoroughly. Before serving, whip cream until stiff and fold into rice mixture.

6 Servings

SWEDISH RICE PUDDING

  2 cups milk
  2 eggs, slightly beaten
  ½ cup sugar
  1 teaspoon vanilla
  ¼ teaspoon cinnamon
  ½ cup quick-cooking rice
  ½ cup raisins

Settings: HIGH/DEFROST

1. Measure milk into 4-cup glass measure.

2. MICROWAVE on HIGH for 3 to 3½ MINUTES or until hot.

3. In 1½-quart glass casserole, combine eggs, sugar, vanilla and cinnamon, mixing well. Mix in rice, raisins and hot milk. Set in baking dish with about 1 inch hot water.

4. MICROWAVE on HIGH for 2 MINUTES.

5. MICROWAVE on DEFROST for 8 MINUTES. Stir to move cooked portion to center and MICROWAVE on DEFROST for 8 to 10 MINUTES, or until knife inserted near center comes out clean.

5 to 6 Servings

Microwave the custard for most any cooked custard ice cream recipe – use this one as a guide.

VANILLA CUSTARD ICE CREAM

  2 cups milk
  2 eggs
  ¾ cup sugar
  ⅛ teaspoon salt
  1 tablespoon vanilla
  2 cups light cream

Setting: DEFROST

1. Combine milk, eggs, sugar and salt in 4-cup glass measure. Beat well with rotary beater.

2. MICROWAVE for 8 MINUTES. Stir and MICROWAVE for 7 to 8 MINUTES or until mixture comes to a boil and thickens; stir well. Cool completely. Stir in vanilla.

3. Prepare ice cream freezer according to manufacturer's directions. Pour prepared custard into freezer along with cream. Freeze as directed by manufacturer.

2 Quarts Ice Cream

TIPS Make Chocolate Custard Ice Cream. Increase sugar to 1 cup. Add 2 envelopes premelted chocolate to custard sauce before cooking.
● Make Strawberry Ice Cream. Wash, hull and crush 2 cups (1 pt.) fresh strawberries. Stir in ¼ cup sugar. Omit vanilla from custard sauce. Add sugared berries to custard sauce with cream.

CHOCOLATE MOUSSE

    2 **squares (1 oz. each) semi-sweet chocolate**
    ⅓ **cup sugar**
    1 **envelope unflavored gelatin**
    ⅛ **teaspoon salt**
    3 **eggs, separated**
    1 **cup milk**
    1 **teaspoon vanilla**
    ⅓ **cup sugar**
    1 **cup whipping cream, whipped**

Settings: HIGH/DEFROST

1. Place chocolate in large glass mixing bowl.

2. MICROWAVE on HIGH for 2 to 3 MINUTES or until melted. Stir in ⅓ cup sugar, gelatin, salt, egg yolks and milk.

3. MICROWAVE on DEFROST for 5 MINUTES. Stir and MICROWAVE on DEFROST for 2 to 3 MINUTES or until slightly thickened. Add vanilla; mix well. Refrigerate until cool.

4. Beat egg whites in small mixer bowl until soft peaks form. Gradually beat in ⅓ cup sugar until stiff peaks form, fold egg whites and whipped cream into chocolate mixture. Spoon mixture into individual dishes or 9 to 10-inch chocolate cookie crumb crust. Chill about 3 hours or until set.

                            6 to 8 Servings

These cups are made conveniently one at a time; while you are forming one cup, the next one can be cooking.

CHOCOLATE CUPS

Setting: HIGH

1. Place paper cupcake liner in 5 or 6 oz. custard cup. Add one heaping tablespoon of semi-sweet chocolate pieces.

2. MICROWAVE for 1 MINUTE or until chocolate is soft. With a table knife, spread chocolate evenly in liner.

3. Chill and fill with Chocolate Mousse, ice cream or other chilled dessert fillings. Peel off paper liner for serving.

CHOCOLATE PUDDING CAKE

    2 **cups water**
    1 **cup unsifted all-purpose flour**
    ¾ **cup sugar**
    ½ **cup chopped nuts**
    2 **tablespoons unsweetened cocoa**
    1 **teaspoon baking powder**
    ½ **teaspoon salt**
    1 **teaspoon vanilla**
    2 **tablespoons oil**
    ½ **cup milk**
    ¾ **cup sugar**
    ¼ **cup unsweetened cocoa**

Setting: HIGH

1. Measure water in 4-cup glass measure and MICROWAVE for about 4 MINUTES or until boiling.

2. In 2½-quart glass casserole, combine flour, sugar, nuts, cocoa, baking powder and salt. Add vanilla, oil and milk; mix until well combined. Spread evenly in dish.

3. Combine sugar and cocoa; sprinkle over top of cake. Pour boiling water over all.

4. MICROWAVE for 9 to 10 MINUTES or until cake is no longer doughy. Serve with ice cream or whipped cream.

                          5 to 6 Servings

TIP MICROWAVE on MEDIUM for 12 to 15 MINUTES.

Chilled Lemon Soufflé

The gelatin custard is easily cooked in the oven.

CHILLED LEMON SOUFFLE

  ½ cup sugar
  1 tablespoon (1 envelope) unflavored gelatin
  ¼ teaspoon salt
  1 cup water
  3 eggs, separated
  1 tablespoon grated lemon peel
  3 to 4 tablespoons lemon juice
  ⅓ cup sugar
  1 cup whipping cream, whipped, or 2 cups (4½-oz. pkg.) frozen whipped topping, thawed

Setting: DEFROST

1. Prepare a 3 to 4-cup soufflé dish by forming a collar of wax paper around top of dish that extends about 3 inches above dish. (Greasing inside upper edge of dish holds paper in place.)

2. In 4-cup glass measure, combine ½ cup sugar, gelatin, salt and water. Separate eggs, placing whites in small mixer bowl and adding yolks to gelatin mixture. Beat in yolks until well mixed.

3. MICROWAVE for 5 to 6 MINUTES, or until mixture just begins to boil, stirring occasionally during last half of cooking time. Stir in lemon peel and juice. Cool until mixture is thickened, but not set.

4. Beat egg whites until frothy. Beat in ⅓ cup sugar until mixture forms stiff peaks. Fold in lemon mixture and whipped cream.

5. Pour into prepared dish. Refrigerate 6 hours or until served. Remove wax paper before serving from soufflé dish. Spoon into individual serving dishes and if desired, top with whipped cream.

                             5 to 6 Servings

TIP For a large group, double recipe and use a 7 to 8-cup soufflé dish. MICROWAVE about 8 MINUTES.

EASY BREAD PUDDING

  1 package (3¼ oz.) vanilla pudding and pie filling mix
  2 cups milk
  ½ cup raisins
  1 cup cubed white bread (2 slices)

Setting: HIGH

1. In 4-cup glass measure or 1-quart glass casserole, combine all ingredients.

2. MICROWAVE for 6 to 8 MINUTES or until mixture boils, stirring occasionally during last half of cooking. Serve warm or cool.

                             4 to 6 Servings

BREAD PUDDING

  2 cups soft bread cubes
  2 cups milk
  2 eggs, slightly beaten
  ⅓ cup sugar
  ½ cup raisins
  1 teaspoon vanilla
  ⅛ teaspoon salt
  Cinnamon

Settings: HIGH/DEFROST

1. Place bread in 1-quart shallow glass casserole.

2. MICROWAVE on HIGH for 2 MINUTES to dry bread. Measure milk into 4-cup glass measure.

3. MICROWAVE for 3 to 3½ MINUTES, or until hot. Combine remaining ingredients except cinnamon. Mix in hot milk. Add to bread in casserole, mixing well. Sprinkle with cinnamon.

4. Set in baking dish with about 1 inch hot water.

5. MICROWAVE on HIGH for 2 MINUTES.

6. MICROWAVE on DEFROST for 8 MINUTES. Stir and MICROWAVE on DEFROST for 8 to 10 MINUTES, or until knife inserted near center comes out clean.

                             5 to 6 Servings

CRUNCHY PUDDING SQUARES

  2 cups milk
  1 package (4-serving size) butterscotch or vanilla pudding and pie filling mix
  3 tablespoons butter or margarine
  1¼ cups (20 squares) graham cracker crumbs or pre-packaged crumbs
  ¼ cup sugar
  ¼ cup peanut butter

Setting: HIGH

1. In 4-cup glass measure, combine milk and pudding mix.

2. MICROWAVE for 5 to 6 MINUTES or until mixture boils, stirring occasionally during last half of cooking time. Set aside.

3. In mixing bowl, MICROWAVE butter for 10 SECONDS. Stir in cracker crumbs, sugar and peanut butter, mixing until crumbly. Press ¾ of mixture on bottom of 1½-quart (10 x 6) or 2-quart (8 x 8) glass baking dish. Top with pudding, spreading evenly. Sprinkle remaining crumbs over top. Refrigerate several hours or until chilled. To serve, cut into squares and top with whipped cream.

                             5 to 6 Servings

TIP Try with other pudding flavors and cookie crumbs such as gingersnaps, vanilla wafers or chocolate creme-filled cookies.

FOR DESSERT **Cookies & Candies**

COOKIE KEY: Microwave most cookies on DEFROST setting. Bar cookies will normally save the greatest amount of time when you are preparing cookies in your microwave oven. When cooking a large number of individual cookies, you may use your conventional oven more frequently to save time and also because the texture of individual cookies is often different when cooked with microwaves. The next time you bake individual cookies conventionally, test a couple of them in your microwave oven to see how well that particular recipe works. Use the Sugar Cookie recipe as a guide to timing on individual cookies.

It is usually easiest to obtain a thoroughly cooked center of bars if you use an oblong dish. The cookies that have been found to be successful in a square dish have been noted in the recipes. If cookies are overbaked, brown spots will appear in the interior. You may grease the pan or not as you wish. However, do not add flour because it will combine with the grease to form a layer on the bottom of the cookies.

To recapture that "just baked" flavor of a cookie, reheat it on a napkin (about 15 seconds if room temperature, 30 seconds if frozen) and taste the amazing freshness.

BROWNIES

  2 **squares or envelopes unsweetened chocolate**
  ⅓ **cup butter or margarine**
  1 **cup sugar**
  2 **eggs**
  1 **cup unsifted all-purpose flour**
  ¼ **teaspoon baking powder**
  ¼ **teaspoon salt**
  ½ **teaspoon vanilla**
  ½ **cup chopped nuts**

Settings: HIGH/DEFROST

1. Combine chocolate and butter in medium glass mixing bowl.

2. MICROWAVE on HIGH for 1½ MINUTES or until melted. Stir in sugar; beat in eggs. Stir in remaining ingredients. Spread batter into 2-quart (8 x 8) glass baking dish.

3. MICROWAVE on DEFROST for 7 MINUTES.

4. MICROWAVE on HIGH for 3 to 4 MINUTES or until puffed and dry on top. Cool until set; cut into bars.

                                         24 Bars

TIP If nuts are omitted, reduce baking time by 1 minute.

SURPRISE TEACAKES

  1 **cup butter or margarine**
  1 **egg**
  1 **teaspoon vanilla**
  ½ **cup powdered sugar**
  2⅓ **cups unsifted all-purpose flour**
  1 **cup finely chopped nuts**
  1 **package (5¾ oz.) milk chocolate kisses**
  Powdered sugar

Setting: DEFROST

1. Place butter in small glass mixing bowl.

2. MICROWAVE for about 1½ MINUTES or until softened. Beat in egg, vanilla and powdered sugar until light and fluffy. Blend in flour and nuts. Make teacakes by shaping 1 tablespoon dough around 1 unwrapped chocolate kiss. Arrange 12 teacakes on wax paper in oven, 1 inch apart.

3. MICROWAVE for 5 to 6 MINUTES or until no longer doughy. Roll in powdered sugar and cool.

                                  About 36 Cookies

TIPS Candied cherries can be substituted for chocolate kisses.
• If dough has been refrigerated, increase cooking time about 1 minute.

Pictured: Brownies from mix, page 145, with chocolate frosting, Sugar Cookies, page 146, Surprise Teacakes, above, and No Fail Fudge, page 147.

HOW TO MICROWAVE COOKIES AND BARS

- Prepare mix as directed on package.
- Grease baking dish, if desired, but do not flour as it will layer on bottom of bar.
- Microwave bars, uncovered, in a glass baking dish.
- Cool and cut bars as directed on package.
- Frost or glaze before cutting. Bars have a slightly irregular top.

- Mix cookies according to package or recipe directions.
- Microwave cookies on wax or parchment paper placed on oven floor.
- Allow enough space between cookies because they spread during cooking.
- Allow cookies to cool on wax paper; remove, and store.

COOKIE OR BAR	PACKAGE SIZE	CONTAINER	FIRST SETTING	MINUTES	SECOND SETTING	MINUTES
BROWNIE MIX	16 oz. 22.5-oz.	glass (8 x 8) glass (12 x 7)	DEFROST	7	HIGH	3 to 4 4 to 5
DATE BAR MIX Filling Bars	14 oz.	2-cup glass measure glass (8 x 8)	HIGH DEFROST	2 12	HIGH	2 to 3
PEANUT BUTTER CHOCOLATE CHIP BAR MIX	21-oz.	glass (12 x 7)	DEFROST	8	HIGH	4 to 5
CHOCOLATE COOKIE MIX 4 Cookies 6 Cookies 12 Cookies	10-oz.	parchment or wax paper	DEFROST	2 to 2½ 3 to 3½ 5 to 5½		
HOMEMADE COOKIES 4 Cookies 6 Cookies 12 Cookies		parchment or wax paper	DEFROST	2 to 3 3 to 4 5 to 6		

TOFFEE PIECES

   10 graham cracker squares
   ½ cup butter or margarine
   ¾ cup packed brown sugar
   ¼ cup chopped nuts
   1 package (6 oz.) semi-sweet chocolate pieces

Settings: HIGH/DEFROST

1. Place crackers on bottom of buttered 2-quart (12 x 7) glass baking dish; set aside. Combine butter and brown sugar in 4-cup glass measure.

2. MICROWAVE on HIGH for about 2 MINUTES or until butter is melted. Stir in nuts. Pour syrup over crackers.

3. MICROWAVE on DEFROST for 5 to 6 MINUTES or until bubbly. Top with chocolate pieces and MICROWAVE on DEFROST for 2 to 2½ MINUTES or until chocolate is softened. Spread chocolate evenly over top. Chill for about 30 MINUTES or until cool; cut into bars.

                    About 24 Bars

These popular treats can be quickly prepared in the oven without fear of scorching the marshmallows.

KRISPIE MARSHMALLOW TREATS

   ¼ cup butter or margarine
   5 cups miniature or 40 large marshmallows
   5 cups crispy rice cereal

Setting: HIGH

1. Place butter in 1½-quart (10 x 6) glass baking dish.

2. MICROWAVE for about 1 MINUTE or until melted. Stir in marshmallows.

3. MICROWAVE for 1 MINUTE. Stir and MICROWAVE for about 1 MINUTE or until marshmallows are softened. Stir until smooth. Mix in cereal. Press into baking dish. Cool until set; cut into squares.

                    24 to 30 Krispie Squares.

Many cookie recipes spread and flatten when cooked in the microwave oven but we found that this recipe holds its shape nicely during cooking.

SUGAR COOKIES

- **1 cup butter or margarine**
- **1 cup sugar**
- **2 eggs**
- **3 cups unsifted all-purpose flour**
- **1 teaspoon cream of tartar**
- **½ teaspoon soda**
- **½ teaspoon salt**
- **1 teaspoon almond extract**

Setting: DEFROST

1. Cream butter in large mixer bowl until fluffy. Beat in sugar and eggs until well blended. Stir in remaining ingredients and chill. Shape into 1-inch balls; place on wax paper, 1 inch apart; flatten with glass dipped in water, then sugar. Place cookies on wax paper in the oven.

2. MICROWAVE until tops have set appearance:
    4 cookies — 2 to 3 MINUTES
    6 cookies — 3 to 4 MINUTES
    12 cookies — 5 to 6 MINUTES
Cool on wax paper; remove, and store in tightly covered container.

About 48 Cookies

TIPS Substitute 2 teaspoons anise seed or 1 teaspoon anise extract for almond extract.
• Form dough into 2 rolls, 2 inches in diameter, and freeze. Slice ¼ inch thick and place on wax paper. MICROWAVE — 9 cookies about 4 to 5 MINUTES.

SIX LAYER BARS

- **½ cup butter or margarine**
- **1½ cups (18 squares) graham cracker crumbs**
- **1 cup chopped nuts**
- **1 cup (6-oz. pkg.) semi-sweet chocolate pieces**
- **1⅓ cups (3½-oz. can) flaked coconut**
- **1⅓ cups (15-oz. can) sweetened condensed milk**

Setting: DEFROST

1. In 2-quart (12 x 7) glass baking dish, MICROWAVE butter for 45 SECONDS. Add the next five ingredients, layer by layer.

2. MICROWAVE for 10 to 15 MINUTES or until mixture just begins to show brown areas. Cool. Cut into bars.

48 to 54 Bars

CANDY KEY: Microwave candy on DEFROST. Making candy in your microwave oven takes the worry out of scorching because the cooking occurs on all sides, rather than only the bottom. The stirring in candy recipes equalizes the heat that is beginning from all sides of the dish. As with conventional candy making, the cooking dish should be two to three times as large as the volume of the candy mixture to allow sufficient boiling space.

If you are using a candy thermometer, be certain to *carefully* remove the cooking container from the oven before testing the temperature. Never use a thermometer while the oven is on because microwave energy will ruin the thermometer by causing the mercury in it to separate. You may find it more convenient to use the soft ball test: dip a clean spoon into the boiling syrup and then let a small amount of the syrup drip into a cup of very cold water. Test with your fingers if it has reached the right consistency.

If you have stored candy in the refrigerator or freezer, you can use the oven to bring it to room temperature before serving.

PRALINES

- **2 cups sugar**
- **1 cup packed brown sugar**
- **½ cup milk**
- **1 can (6 oz.) evaporated milk**
- **¼ cup butter or margarine**
- **¼ teaspoon salt**
- **3 cups coarsely chopped pecans**

Setting: DEFROST

1. Combine all ingredients except nuts in buttered large glass mixing bowl; cover.

2. MICROWAVE for 20 MINUTES. Stir and MICROWAVE for 15 to 20 MINUTES or until a soft ball forms in cold water. Beat with mixer at medium speed until creamy. Stir in nuts.

3. Pour into a 3-quart (13 x 9) glass baking dish. Cool until firm. Cut into pieces.

60-72 Pieces

TIP MICROWAVE on MEDIUM for 15 MINUTES and then 13 to 15 in step 2.

NO FAIL FUDGE

- **3 cups sugar**
- **¾ cup butter or margarine**
- **1 can (5 oz.) evaporated milk**
- **1 package (12 oz.) semi-sweet chocolate pieces**
- **1 jar (10 oz.) marshmallow creme**
- **1 cup chopped nuts**
- **1 teaspoon vanilla**

Setting: DEFROST

1. Combine sugar, butter and milk in buttered large glass mixing bowl; cover.

2. MICROWAVE on DEFROST for 15 MINUTES. Stir and MICROWAVE for 8 to 10 MINUTES or until mixture forms a soft ball in the cold water. Stir in chocolate pieces until melted. Fold in marshmallow creme, nuts and vanilla.

3. Pour into buttered 3-quart (13 x 9) pan. Chill until firm; cut into squares.

72 Fudge Squares

TIP MICROWAVE on MEDIUM for 10 MINUTES and then 5 to 6 MINUTES in step 2.

Six Layer Bars, page 146, Krispie Marshmallow Treats, page 145.

POPCORN BALLS

- **⅓ cup light corn syrup**
- **⅓ cup water**
- **1 cup sugar**
- **1 teaspoon salt**
- **¼ cup butter or margarine**
- **1 teaspoon vanilla**
- **7 cups popped corn**

Setting: DEFROST

1. Combine syrup, water, sugar, salt and butter in buttered 4-cup glass measure; cover.

2. MICROWAVE for 10 MINUTES. Stir and MICROWAVE for 5 MINUTES. Stir and MICROWAVE for 5 to 5½ MINUTES or until candy forms a hard ball (250°F.) in cold water. Stir in vanilla. Pour in thin stream over popped corn in large buttered bowl; mix well. Butter hands and shape into balls.

10 to 12 Balls

TIPS MICROWAVE on MEDIUM for 8 MINUTES, then 4 MINUTES and 4 to 4½ MINUTES in step 2.

Make popcorn using a conventional method.

POPCORN: Cooking popcorn in a microwave oven is not recommended. There are too many variables — things such as time, temperature and age of popcorn.

Regardless of popcorn age, microwaves pop too few kernels to make the technique successful. Prolonged cooking does not yield more popped corn, but can cause fire or make the cooking dish too hot to handle and even break.

Never attempt to pop corn in a paper bag. Oil plus extended cooking can cause smoking and, eventually, fire.

GLAZED ALMONDS

- **1 cup almonds, blanched**
- **½ cup water**
- **½ cup sugar**

Settings: HIGH/DEFROST

1. Combine water and sugar in a 4-cup glass measure.

2. MICROWAVE on HIGH 4 MINUTES.

3. Add almonds. MICROWAVE on DEFROST for 3 to 3½ MINUTES or until almonds are tender. Remove with slotted spoon to drain on paper toweling.

4. Sprinkle more sugar over nuts, coating all sides. Let dry. Store in covered container.

1 cup almonds

TIP MICROWAVE on MEDIUM for 2½ to 3 MINUTES in step 3.

FOR DESSERT Cakes, Frostings & Fillings

CAKE KEY: Cakes microwave on DEFROST to raise, then on HIGH to set the batter. Cupcakes bake on DEFROST throughout cooking because of the small amount of batter in each one.

Cakes raise higher than usual in a microwave oven, so fill baking dishes no more than half full. Use extra batter for cupcakes. See chart on page 149.

Use glass dishes for cakes. Round shapes work especially well — try layer cake dishes and large mixing bowls.

Push a glass down in the center of the batter, open end up, when cake is baked in a bowl. This creates a tube-type baking dish that allows cake center to cook evenly and completely.

Line the bottom of any flat cake dish with wax paper if the cake is to be unmolded.

Bake layers one at a time. Use the same dish for the second layer, but replace the wax paper. If the dish is still warm, cake may cook about 30 seconds faster.

Cakes can be cooked in rectangular dishes when recipe specifies but surface will be slightly uneven.

Do not grease or flour cake dishes; the mixture forms a layer on the bottom of the cake.

Cakes are done when a toothpick inserted near the center comes out clean.

Frosting spreads most easily and evenly if a cake has been standing long enough to dry the surface slightly or if it has been cooled in the refrigerator.

Cakes do not brown in a microwave oven, so white cakes are really white — and there are no dark crumbs in the frosting.

Moist-top cakes absorb toppings quickly and well.

Cake batter made from a mix may be refrigerated up to a week in a covered dish.

Want to adapt a favorite cake recipe to the microwave oven? Reduce leavening ¼ to ⅓ (experiment) and bake as outlined above.

IMPORTANT: Before you begin, refer to the "Beginning to Cook" section for basic technique and this example recipe:

Pineapple Upside Down Cake **31**

Pictured: Birthday Cake Cones, page 151, topped with ice cream, Cupcakes from mix, page 149, frosted with Five-Minute Snowy White Frosting, page 153, Party Cake in a Bowl, page 152, frosted with confectioner's sugar icing.

HOW TO BAKE CAKE

- Prepare batter as directed in recipe or on cake mix package.
- Use glass dish specified in chart. It will not always be the same as suggested on the recipe or package.
- Do not fill dish more than half full.
- Use extra batter to make cupcakes as directed in chart.
- Line bottom of flat dishes with wax paper if cake is to be unmolded.

- Bake layers one at a time. Second layer may be baked in the same dish but replace wax paper. If dish is warm, decrease cooking time about 30 seconds.
- When cake batter is cooked in a large bowl, press a glass into the center of the batter, open end up.
- Cake is done when a toothpick inserted near center comes out clean.
- Let cake stand 5 minutes to set.
- Turn out on serving plate to cool or cool in dish on wire rack.

CAKE	GLASS CONTAINER	FIRST SETTING AND TIME	SECOND SETTING AND TIME
CAKE MIX 17 to 18½-oz. pkg.	9-in. round dish	DEFROST 7 min.	HIGH 3 to 4 min.
	3-qt. (13 x 9) baking dish	DEFROST 9 min.	HIGH 6 to 7 min.
SNACKING CAKE MIX 14.5-oz. pkg.	9-in. round dish	DEFROST 7 min.	HIGH 3 to 4 min.
CUPCAKES FROM MIX 2 4 6	Paper cupcake liners in individual custard cups	DEFROST 2 to 2½ min. 3 to 3½ min. 4½ to 5 min.	
POUND CAKE MIX 14-oz. pkg.	1½-qt. casserole	DEFROST 10 min.	HIGH 2 to 3 min.
GINGERBREAD MIX 15-oz. pkg.	2-qt. (8 x 8) baking dish	DEFROST 7 min.	HIGH 3 to 4 min.
HOMEMADE CAKE	9-in. round dish	DEFROST 7 min.	HIGH 3 to 4 min.

EASY COMPANY CAKE

- ¼ **cup butter or margarine**
- ¾ **cup sugar**
- 2 **eggs**
- ¼ **teaspoon vanilla**
- ¾ **cup unsifted all-purpose flour**
- ½ **teaspoon baking powder**
- ½ **teaspoon salt**
- ¼ **cup milk**

Topping
- ¼ **cup butter or margarine**
- ¼ **cup sugar**
- 1 **tablespoon milk**
- 1 **tablespoon all-purpose flour**
- ⅓ **cup slivered almonds**

Settings: HIGH/DEFROST

1. Place butter in large mixing bowl.

2. MICROWAVE on HIGH for about 30 SECONDS or until softened. Beat in sugar, eggs and vanilla until light and fluffy. Stir in dry ingredients alternately with milk; mix well after each addition. Beat until smooth. Pour into 9-inch round glass baking dish.

3. MICROWAVE on DEFROST for 7 MINUTES.

4. MICROWAVE on HIGH for 3 to 4 MINUTES or until toothpick inserted near center comes out clean. Pour Topping over warm cake. Serve warm or cold.

5. **Topping**: combine butter, sugar and milk in 2-cup glass measure; stir until blended. Blend in flour. Stir in almonds.

6. MICROWAVE on HIGH for ½ to 1 MINUTE or until slightly thickened; stir to blend.

6 to 8 Servings

Frosting cooks along with the cake in this recipe.

ONE-STEP GERMAN CHOCOLATE CAKE

- ½ **cup butter or margarine**
- ⅔ **cup milk**
- 1 **package (9.9 oz.) coconut almond or pecan frosting mix**
- 1 **package (17.5 oz.) German chocolate cake mix**
- 2 **eggs**
- 1½ **cups water**

Settings: DEFROST/HIGH

1. MICROWAVE on HIGH ¼ cup butter in each of two 1½-quart (8-inch round) glass baking dishes. Stir ⅓ cup milk and half of frosting mix (1 cup) into each. Set aside.

2. Prepare and beat cake mix with eggs and water as directed on package. Remove 1 cup of batter for cupcakes. Pour half of remaining batter into each prepared pan.

3. MICROWAVE on DEFROST one layer at a time for 7 MINUTES.

4. MICROWAVE on HIGH for 3 to 4 MINUTES or until toothpick comes out clean. Cool 5 minutes.

5. Loosen edges and invert to cool. If some of frosting sticks in pan, just remove with spatula and spread on cake. When cool enough to handle, stack layers.

8-inch Layer Cake

TIP MICROWAVE 4 cupcakes on DEFROST for 3 to 3½ MINUTES or until toothpick comes out clean.

CHERRY CHEESECAKE

Crust
- ¼ **cup butter or margarine**
- 12 **graham cracker squares, crushed (⅔ cup crumbs)**
- 2 **tablespoons flour**
- 2 **tablespoons sugar**
- ¼ **teaspoon cinnamon**

Filling
- 1 **package (8 oz.) cream cheese**
- ⅓ **cup sugar**
- 1 **egg**
- 1 **tablespoon lemon juice**

Topping
- 1 **cup sour cream**
- 3 **tablespoons sugar**
- ½ **teaspoon almond or vanilla extract**
- 1 **can (21 oz.) prepared cherry pie filling**

Setting: DEFROST

1. **Crust**: MICROWAVE butter in 1½-quart (8-inch round) glass baking dish for 1 MINUTE. Mix in remaining Crust ingredients and press mixture on bottom and halfway up sides of dish.

2. **Filling**: MICROWAVE cream cheese for 1 MINUTE or until soft. Beat with remaining Filling ingredients. Pour into Crust.

3. MICROWAVE for 6 to 7 MINUTES.

4. **Topping**: combine Topping ingredients. Spread over partially-cooked filling.

5. MICROWAVE for 4 to 5 MINUTES, or until set. Chill several hours or overnight. Spoon cherry pie filling on top.

6 to 8 Servings

STREUSEL RHUBARB CAKE

      2 cups unsifted all-purpose flour
    ½ cup sugar
   1½ teaspoons baking powder
      1 teaspoon salt
      1 cup milk
    ¼ cup cooking oil
      1 egg
      4 cups cut-up rhubarb
      3 tablespoons (half of 3-oz. pkg.) strawberry or raspberry-flavored gelatin

Topping
    ½ cup unsifted all-purpose flour
    ¾ cup sugar
    ½ cup rolled oats
    ½ teaspoon cinnamon
    ¼ cup butter or margarine

Settings: DEFROST/HIGH

1. In mixing bowl, combine flour, sugar, baking powder, salt, milk, oil and egg. Mix until smooth. Pour into unlined 2-quart (12 x 7) glass baking dish. Top with rhubarb; sprinkle evenly with gelatin.

2. **Topping**: combine ingredients and cut in butter. Sprinkle over gelatin.

3. MICROWAVE on DEFROST for 15 MINUTES .

4. MICROWAVE on HIGH for 5 to 6 MINUTES or until cake is no longer doughy under rhubarb. Serve warm or cool.

12 x 7-inch Cake

Flat bottom ice cream cones become holders for cooking cake batter. Frost the cooked cones or top with whipped cream, ice cream or frozen pudding for a quick children's snack.

BIRTHDAY CAKE CONES

      1 package (9 oz.) cake mix
      8 flat bottom ice cream cones

1. Prepare cake mix as directed on package. Spoon about 2 tablespoons batter into each ice cream cone. Place in oven; allow about 1-inch space between each one.

2. MICROWAVE on DEFROST:
     1 cone — 45 SECONDS to 1 MINUTE
     2 cones — 1½ to 2 MINUTES
     4 cones — 3 to 3½ MINUTES
     6 cones — 4½ to 4¾ MINUTES
     8 cones — 5 to 5½ MINUTES
Cake Cones are done when toothpick inserted near center of each cake comes out clean. Cake will be slightly soft around edges when cones come from oven. Cool on wire rack. Frost.

8 Cake Cones

TIP Top each Cake Cone with a scoop of ice cream and use colored gum drops to make a face on ice cream "head".

Pictured, clockwise: Streusel Rhubarb Cake, this page, Angel Squares, this page, (topped with fresh peaches), Cherry Cheesecake, page 150, and One-Step German Chocolate Cake, page 150.

ANGEL SQUARES

      4 egg whites (⅔ cup)
    ¼ teaspoon cream of tartar
    ½ cup sugar
      1 cup unsifted all-purpose flour
    ½ cup sugar
      1 teaspoon baking powder
    ½ teaspoon salt
    ½ cup milk
    ½ teaspoon vanilla

Settings: DEFROST/HIGH

1. In mixer bowl, beat egg whites with cream of tartar until soft mounds form. Gradually add ½ cup sugar, beating until stiff peaks form; set aside.

2. In another mixing bowl, combine flour, ½ cup sugar, baking powder and salt. Measure milk in 1-cup glass measure.

3. MICROWAVE on HIGH for 45 SECONDS or until hot. Add milk and vanilla to flour mixture. Beat until smooth. Pour over egg white mixture and by hand, fold in until well combined. Pour into 2-quart (8 x 8) glass baking dish.

4. MICROWAVE on DEFROST for 7 MINUTES.

5. MICROWAVE on HIGH for 3 to 4 MINUTES or until mixture has pulled away from sides of dish. Cool. If desired, frost with favorite butter frosting. Top with chopped cashew nuts and shaved chocolate.

9 Servings

CHOCO-DATE CAKE

    ¾ cup butter or margarine
      1 cup sugar
      2 eggs
   1¾ cups unsifted all-purpose flour
      1 tablespoon unsweetened cocoa
    ¾ teaspoon soda
    ½ teaspoon salt
      1 teaspoon vanilla
    ¾ cup water
      1 cup chopped dates
      1 cup (6-oz. pkg.) semi-sweet chocolate pieces
    ½ cup chopped nuts

Settings: HIGH/DEFROST

1. In large mixing bowl, MICROWAVE on HIGH butter for 30 SECONDS. Beat in sugar and eggs. Add flour, cocoa, soda, salt, vanilla, water and dates. Stir until combined. Spread in ungreased 2-quart (12 x 7) glass baking dish. Sprinkle with chocolate pieces and nuts.

2. MICROWAVE on DEFROST for 8 MINUTES.

3. MICROWAVE on HIGH for 7 MINUTES, or until toothpick inserted in center comes out clean.

HONEY 'N SPICE CARROT CAKE

- **2 eggs**
- **2 medium carrots, cut into pieces**
- **½ cup butter or margarine softened**
- **½ cup honey**
- **½ teaspoon vanilla**
- **1 cup unsifted all-purpose flour**
- **½ teaspoon soda**
- **½ teaspoon salt**
- **½ teaspoon cinnamon**
- **½ teaspoon nutmeg**
- **½ cup chopped nuts**

Sauce
- **¼ cup orange juice**
- **¼ cup honey**
- **¼ cup butter or margarine**
- **1 to 2 tablespoons orange liqueur, if desired**

Settings: DEFROST/HIGH

1. In blender, process eggs and carrots at medium speed until carrots are in fine pieces.

2. In glass bowl, MICROWAVE on HIGH butter for 20 SECONDS. Blend in honey and vanilla.

3. Beat in with mixer carrot-mixture. Stir in flour, soda, salt, cinnamon, nutmeg and nuts. Spread evenly in ungreased 1½-quart (10 x 6) glass baking dish.

4. MICROWAVE on DEFROST for 7 MINUTES.

5. MICROWAVE on HIGH for 3 to 4 MINUTES, or until toothpick inserted in center comes out clean.

6. Pierce cake at ½ inch intervals with toothpick or long-tined fork.

7. **Sauce**: combine orange juice, honey and butter in 2-cup glass measure.

8. MICROWAVE on HIGH, uncovered, for 1½ to 2 MINUTES, or until mixture boils. Stir in liqueur. Pour warm sauce over cake. Cool. If desired, serve with whipped cream.

10 x 6-inch Cake

TIP If you don't have a blender, grate the carrot before adding to the butter-egg mixture.

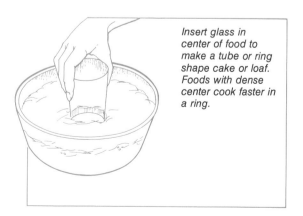

Insert glass in center of food to make a tube or ring shape cake or loaf. Foods with dense center cook faster in a ring.

FINNISH CHRISTMAS CAKE

Filling
- **1 package (12 oz.) pitted dried prunes, chopped**
- **1 package (12 oz.) pitted dried apricots, chopped**
- **1 cup sugar**
- **1 cup cold water**
- **2 teaspoons vanilla**

Cake
- **1 package active dry yeast**
- **1⅓ cups lukewarm water**
- **2 egg whites**
- **1 package (18½ oz.) white cake mix**

Frosting
- **½ box (3 oz.) whipped topping mix (1 envelope)**

Settings: HIGH/DEFROST

1. **Filling**: combine ingredients in 4-cup glass measure . Mix.

2. MICROWAVE on HIGH for 5 MINUTES. Stir and MICROWAVE on HIGH for 2 to 3 MINUTES or until fruit is tender. Cool.

3. **Cake**: dissolve yeast in water. Combine egg whites, cake mix, and yeast mixture in large mixing bowl. Beat as directed on package. Let batter stand 10 minutes if time permits.

4. Line bottom of two 9-inch round glass baking dishes with wax paper. Pour half cake batter into each dish. Bake layers, one at a time.

5. MICROWAVE on SIMMER for 7 MINUTES.

6. MICROWAVE on HIGH for 2 to 3 MINUTES or until toothpick inserted near center comes out clean. Let stand in dishes 5 minutes. Turn out on rack to cool.

7. To Assemble: Place 1 layer cake on serving plate. Top with half filling. Put second layer over filling and spread remaining filling on top.

8. **Frosting**: prepare whipped topping as directed on package. Frost sides of cake.

TIP Dried fruits may be chopped easily with scissors or kitchen shears.

PARTY CAKE IN A BOWL

Settings: DEFROST/HIGH

1. Prepare 1 package (18½ oz.) cake mix as directed on package using a large glass mixer bowl; beat well. Push a water glass, open end up, into center of batter.

2. MICROWAVE on DEFROST for 7 MINUTES.

3. MICROWAVE on HIGH for 6 to 7 MINUTES or until toothpick inserted near center comes out clean. Let cool 1 minute. Remove glass with a twisting motion and invert cake on serving platter. Frost or sprinkle with powdered sugar.

About 12 Servings

FROSTINGS AND FILLINGS KEY: We have given some recipes that can be used as a guide to most frostings and fillings and sauces that have a cooking preparation step.

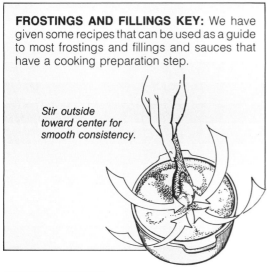

Stir outside toward center for smooth consistency.

FUDGE FROSTING

⅔ **cup milk**
2 **cups sugar**
½ **cup butter or margarine**
3 **squares (1 oz. each) unsweetened chocolate**
½ **teaspoon salt**
2 **teaspoons vanilla**

Setting: DEFROST

1. Combine all ingredients, except vanilla, in small glass mixer bowl.

2. MICROWAVE for 8 MINUTES. Stir and MICROWAVE for about 4 MINUTES or until mixture reaches a full rolling boil. Stir in vanilla. Cool.

3. Beat with electric mixer at high speed until frosting is spreading consistency.

Frosts 13 x 9-Inch or Two 9-Inch Layers

TIP MICROWAVE on MEDIUM for 6 MINUTES and then about 3 MINUTES in step 2.

COCONUT PECAN FROSTING

1 **cup evaporated milk**
3 **eggs**
1 **cup sugar**
½ **cup butter or margarine**
1 **teaspoon vanilla**
1⅓ **cups flaked coconut**
1 **cup chopped nuts**

Setting: HIGH

1. Combine milk, eggs, sugar and butter in 4-cup glass measure. Beat well with rotary beater.

2. MICROWAVE for 3 MINUTES. Beat with rotary beater and MICROWAVE for 2 to 3 MINUTES or until mixture boils. Stir in remaining ingredients; beat well.

Frost 13 x 9-Inch or Two 9-Inch Layers

TIP MICROWAVE on MEDIUM for 5 MINUTES and then 2 to 3 MINUTES in step 2.

FIVE-MINUTE SNOWY WHITE FROSTING

1 **cup sugar**
½ **cup water**
¼ **teaspoon cream of tartar**
Dash salt
2 **egg whites**
1 **teaspoon vanilla**

Setting: DEFROST

1. Combine sugar, water, cream of tartar and salt in 2-cup glass measure.

2. MICROWAVE for 6 to 7 MINUTES or until mixture boils.

3. Beat egg whites in small mixer bowl until soft peaks form. Gradually pour in hot syrup; beat about 5 minutes or until thick and fluffy. Blend in vanilla.

Frosts 13 x 9-Inch or Two 9-Inch Layers

TIP MICROWAVE on MEDIUM for 4 to 5 MINUTES.

Eggs need gentle cooking – stirring keeps filling smooth.

VANILLA CREAM FILLING

1½ **cups milk**
⅓ **cup sugar**
2 **tablespoons cornstarch**
¼ **teaspoon salt**
2 **egg yolks**
2 **teaspoons vanilla**

Setting: HIGH

1. Combine all ingredients, except vanilla, in 2-cup glass measure. Beat well with rotary beater.

2. MICROWAVE for 3 MINUTES. Stir and MICROWAVE for 2 to 2½ MINUTES or until thickened. Stir in vanilla; beat until smooth. Cool and spread on cake.

2 Cups Filling

TIP MICROWAVE on MEDIUM for 4 MINUTES, and then 3 to 3½ MINUTES in step 2.

LEMON FILLING

½ **cup sugar**
2 **tablespoons cornstarch**
⅛ **teaspoon salt**
⅔ **cup water**
1½ **teaspoons grated lemon peel**
2 **tablespoons lemon juice**
1 **tablespoon butter or margarine**

Setting: HIGH

1. Combine all ingredients in 2-cup glass measure; mix well.

2. MICROWAVE for 2 MINUTES. Stir and MICROWAVE for 2 to 2½ MINUTES or until thickened; beat well. Cool and spread on cake.

1 Cup Filling

TIP Yellow food coloring may be added, if desired.

FOR DESSERT Pies

Lemon Cloud Pie, page 156, (pastry shell as cooked in oven).

PIE KEY: Microwave pie crust in a 9-inch glass pie plate on DEFROST heat that cooks and sets a pastry mixture without burning it. Favorite pastry (mixed with water), pie crust mixes and crumb crust mixtures all microwave well. Prick pastry shells before cooking. Cool crusts before filling.

Custard pies cook in 9-inch baked shells on DEFROST. Custards are critical mixtures that need low heat to prevent curdling or separation. Cook these pies in glass pie plates.

Gelatin-base pie fillings heat and melt together quickly on HIGH. Fill 9-inch baked pie shells. Chill before serving.

Fruit pies call for a microwave-conventional oven technique that's an outstanding success and bakes a 2-crust, 9-inch fruit pie made "from scratch" in less than 25 minutes. Assemble pie in a 9-inch glass pie plate. Microwave on HIGH to quickly heat and start cooking. Transfer pie to preheated conventional 450°F. oven to finish cooking and brown crust.

Freezer to Table chapter outlines techniques for baking and heating frozen uncooked and cooked pies.

IMPORTANT: Before you begin, refer to the "Beginning to Cook" section for basic technique and this example recipe:

Fresh Apple Pie **33**

MARGARITA PIE

CRUMB CRUST
- ¾ **cup pretzel crumbs**
- ⅓ **cup butter or margarine, melted**
- 3 **tablespoons sugar**

Filling
- ½ **cup lemon juice**
- 1 **envelope unflavored gelatin**
- 4 **eggs, separated**
- 1 **cup sugar**
- ¼ **teaspoon salt**
- 1 **tablespoon grated lemon rind**
- ⅓ **cup Tequilla**
- 3 **tablespoons Triple Sec**

Settings: HIGH/DEFROST

1. Combine all crust ingredients in 9-inch glass pie plate. Press mixture over bottom and up sides of pie plate. Chill.

2. Sprinkle lemon juice with unflavored gelatin. Let stand until softened. Combine egg yolks with ½ cup sugar, salt, and lemon rind in medium glass mixing bowl.

3. MICROWAVE on HIGH for 30 SECONDS. Stir in softened gelatin.

4. MICROWAVE on DEFROST for about 4 to 5 MINUTES until slightly thickened, stirring once during cooking. Blend in Tequilla and Triple Sec. Chill until mixture is cold, but not thickened.

5. Beat egg whites until foamy. Gradually beat in remaining ½ cup sugar until soft peaks form. Gently fold whites into cooked mixture. Swirl into a pie shell. Chill until set.

1 (9-inch) Pie

TIP Garnish with whipped cream and sliced almonds.

The pie crust sticks and mix have a yellow color that cooks nicely in the oven. You don't get as much browning as in the conventional oven, but the crust is exceptionally flaky. Making the pastry shell in the microwave oven is especially convenient on a warm summer day.

BAKED PASTRY SHELL

Settings: DEFROST/HIGH

1. Prepare pie crust stick or enough mix for one crust pie as directed on package. Roll out and fit into 9-inch glass pie plate. Flute edge and prick bottom and sides with fork.

2. MICROWAVE on DEFROST for 4 MINUTES.

3. MICROWAVE on HIGH for 2 to 3 MINUTES, or until crust is bubbly and brown spots begin to appear.

9-inch Baked Pastry Shell

TIP We also had good results with home recipe pastry when about 4 drops of yellow food color were added to the water.

Cookie crumb crusts hold their shape and have a crunchier texture if cooked a few minutes before adding a filling.

COOKIE CRUMB CRUST

⅓ **cup butter or margarine**
¼ **cup sugar**
1½ **cups crushed cookies**

Setting: DEFROST

1. Place butter in 9-inch glass pie plate.

2. MICROWAVE for 2 to 2½ MINUTES or until melted. Stir in sugar and cookie crumbs; mix well. Press in bottom and sides of 9-inch glass pie plate.

3. MICROWAVE for 3½ to 4½ MINUTES or until set. Cool before filling.

9-inch Crumb Crust

TIPS Make 1½ cups crumbs from about 18 graham crackers, 36 vanilla wafers, 30 gingersnaps or 24 chocolate wafers.
● MICROWAVE on MEDIUM for 1½ to 2 MINUTES in step 2 and 2½ to 3½ MINUTES in step 3.

Grasshopper Pie: (example of plate with metal trim not to be used in the oven).

GRASSHOPPER PIE

3 **cups miniature marshmallows**
½ **cup milk**
2 **tablespoons crème de cocoa**
2 **tablespoons green crème de menthe**
1 **cup whipping cream, whipped**
1 **(9-inch) chocolate Cookie Crumb Crust**

Setting: HIGH

1. Combine marshmallows and milk in large glass mixing bowl.

2. MICROWAVE for about 2 MINUTES or until marshmallows begin to puff; stir to blend. Stir in crème de cocoa and crème de menthe; mix well. Cool about 30 minutes or until consistency of unbeaten egg white.

3. Fold whipped cream into cream mixture. Pour into crust. Refrigerate at least 4 hours or until ready to serve.

9-Inch Pie

TIPS Garnish with whipped cream and chocolate curls.
● Substitute 1 package (4½ oz.) frozen whipped topping for whipped cream.
● Stir 4 to 5 drops green food coloring in with liqueurs for a richer green color.

Fresh Fruit Pie, with rhubarb-strawberry filling (combination of microwave and conventional cooking).

Two crust fruit pies do well when started in a microwave oven and finished in a conventional oven to gain a golden brown color.

FRESH FRUIT PIE

Setting: HIGH

1. Preheat conventional oven to 450°F. Prepare favorite recipe for 2-crust 9-inch fresh fruit pie. Assemble in 9-inch glass pie plate.

2. MICROWAVE for 7 to 8 MINUTES or until juices start bubbling through slits in pie crust. Transfer to preheated conventional oven and bake 10 to 15 minutes or until golden brown.

9-Inch Pie

TIP MICROWAVE an 8-inch 2-crust fruit pie for 6 or 7 MINUTES; MICROWAVE a 10-inch pie for 8 to 9 MINUTES.

PECAN PIE

   3 tablespoons butter or margarine
   3 eggs, slightly beaten
   1 cup dark corn syrup
  ¼ cup packed brown sugar
1½ teaspoons all-purpose flour
   1 teaspoon vanilla
1½ cups pecan halves
   1 (9-inch) Baked Pastry Shell in glass pie plate

Setting: DEFROST

1. Place butter in medium glass mixing bowl.

2. MICROWAVE for about 2 MINUTES or until melted. Stir in remaining ingredients, except Baked Pastry Shell; mix well; pour filling in shell.

3. MICROWAVE for 20 to 25 MINUTES or until knife inserted near center comes out clean. Cool.

9-Inch Pie

Here is a way to cook lemon meringue pie in the microwave oven. Since meringue on top of a pie does not cook well in the oven, fold it into the filling to make a light, creamy texture.

LEMON CLOUD PIE

   9-inch Baked Pastry Shell
  ¾ cup sugar
   3 tablespoons cornstarch
   1 cup water
   1 teaspoon grated lemon peel
  ¼ to ⅓ cup lemon juice
   2 eggs, separated
   1 package (3 oz.) cream cheese
  ¼ cup sugar

Setting: HIGH

1. In mixing bowl, combine ¾ cup sugar with cornstarch. Stir in water, lemon peel and juice.

2. Separate eggs, placing whites in small mixer bowl and yolks in measuring cup or small bowl. Beat egg yolks slightly and add to lemon mixture, stirring to combine.

3. MICROWAVE for 4 to 5 MINUTES or until mixture starts to bubble, stirring occasionally during last half of cooking time.

4. Add cream cheese and allow to soften; mix well. Cool mixture until it begins to thicken. Beat egg whites until foamy.

5. Gradually beat in ¼ cup sugar, beating until mixture forms stiff peaks. Fold into lemon mixture. Pour into pastry shell.

6. Refrigerate at least 2 hours or until served.

9-inch Pie

Pumpkin pie filling cooks before it has a chance to soak into the crust, which sometimes happens in conventional cooking. Stirring after partial cooking allows the filling to cook evenly. Since the crust is already cooked and some shrinking may have taken place, there will be leftover filling to make into pumpkin custards.

PUMPKIN PIE

2 eggs
½ cup sugar
½ cup packed brown sugar
1 tablespoon all-purpose flour
½ teaspoon salt
2 teaspoons pumpkin pie spice
1 can (16 oz.) mashed cooked pumpkin
1 can (13 oz.) evaporated milk
1 (9-inch) Baked Pastry Shell in glass pie plate

Setting: DEFROST

1. Combine all ingredients, except Baked Pastry Shell; beat until smooth; pour in shell.

2. MICROWAVE for 35 to 40 MINUTES or until knife inserted near center comes out clean. Cool.

9-Inch Pie

TIPS Extra filling can be cooked separately in individual custard cups.

● Individual spices can be used for pumpkin pie spice. Use 1 teaspoon cinnamon and ¼ teaspoon each nutmeg, ginger and allspice.

A refreshing pie for a summer day. By using the oven for both the crust and filling, you can keep your kitchen cool.

KEY LIME PIE

2 eggs, separated
½ cup water
⅓ cup lime juice
¾ cup sugar
1 envelope unflavored gelatin
4 to 5 drops green food coloring
1 teaspoon grated lime peel
2 tablespoons sugar
1 cup whipping cream, whipped
1 (9-inch) Baked Pastry Shell

Setting: HIGH

1. Beat egg yolks in large glass mixing bowl. Add water, lime juice, ¾ cup sugar and gelatin; mix well.

2. MICROWAVE for 2 MINUTES. Beat mixture smooth with spoon and MICROWAVE for 1½ to 2 MINUTES or until mixture begins to bubble. Stir in food coloring and lime peel. Cool until consistency of unbeaten egg whites. Beat egg whites in small mixer bowl until frothy. Gradually beat in 2 tablespoons sugar, beating until mixture holds stiff peaks. Fold egg whites and whipped cream into gelatin. Pour into Baked Pastry Shell. Refrigerate at least 4 hours before serving.

9-Inch Pie

TIPS If gelatin-egg mixture should curdle, beat well with rotary beater until smooth.

● Substitute 1 package (4½ oz.) frozen whipped topping for whipping cream.

● A crumb crust or coconut crust can also be used for pie.

● If you need a little extra lime juice, just use the bottled juice or add lemon juice.

Pumpkin Pie (pastry shell as cooked in oven).

MICROWAVE TIME SAVERS **Freezer to Table**

PRECOOKED FROZEN FOOD KEY: Precooked frozen foods in this section range from commercially blanched vegetables, with or without instant-mix sauces, through homemade cooked main dishes and fried chicken.

As with conventional food preparation, ingredients are a guide for freezer to table microwave cooking. So are the volume or amount of food to be thawed and heated, the density or compactness and whether the mixture includes a sauce.

All precooked foods without critical ingredients thaw and heat quickly on HIGH.

Precooked individual foods and main dish mixtures with mushrooms, cheese, sour cream and/or eggs thaw and heat on DEFROST to prevent "popping," overcooking or separation.

Foods such as pizza and egg rolls which have crusts will retain a soft texture when cooked in the microwave oven.

Large volumes and/or quite dense precooked foods thaw on DEFROST until icy in the center, then usually heat on a higher setting for fastest to-table service. For example, gentle defrosting of large casserole dishes prevents overcooking at edges. Stirring is often called for to distribute heat evenly.

Note that volume, density and sauces may make similar foods vary in thawing and heating time as much as 5 to 10 minutes — even when these foods microwave at the same setting.

Use package labels on commercially frozen food to decide what microwave technique to follow. Packages instruct the user to "heat" precooked food and "cook" uncooked food. Check ingredient lists for "critical" ingredients before deciding on the thaw-heat setting to use.

Some frozen meals include a bread roll. Remove roll from tray before cooking meal. Return to oven during last 20 seconds of cooking.

Most commercially frozen food can be heated in its aluminum foil or plastic tray. Foil trays must be no more than ¾ inch high. Remove cover from tray; then slip food back into its carton or cover it with plastic wrap.

If food is placed in a cooking or serving dish, use glass or pottery without silver or other metal trim. Use a dish about the same size as the tray so sauces do not dehydrate.

Follow standing time directions to assure complete heating — a process that continues after food comes from oven. Stir when called for to distribute heat.

Different brands of frozen foods vary in size so heating times may vary slightly. Check food at lowest time given.

APPETIZER GUIDE

Egg Roll Appetizers

Remove 6 ounces frozen Egg Rolls from carton. Place on 8-inch glass pie plate or serving dish (without metal trim). MICROWAVE on DEFROST for 3 to 3½ MINUTES or until hot. Let stand 1 minute.

FISH AND SEAFOOD GUIDE

Arrange frozen Fish Sticks on glass or pottery dinner or serving plate (without metal trim). MICROWAVE on HIGH until fish is hot and flakes easily when lifted with a fork near center — 4 Fish Sticks, 2 to 3 MINUTES; 6 Fish Sticks, 3 to 4 MINUTES; 8 Fish Sticks, 4 to 5 MINUTES; 12 Fish Sticks, 5 to 6 MINUTES.

Breaded Fish Patties or Fillets

Arrange patties or fillets on glass dinner or serving plate (without metal trim). MICROWAVE on HIGH until fish is hot and flakes easily when lifted near center with a fork — 1 patty or fillet, 1½ to 2 MINUTES; 2 patties or fillets, 2½ to 3 MINUTES; 4 patties or fillets, 3½ to 4 MINUTES; 6 patties or fillets, 4 to 4½ MINUTES.

Shrimp Newburg

Remove 6½ ounces frozen Shrimp Newburg from plastic pouch. Place in 1-quart glass casserole. Cover with glass lid or plastic wrap. MICROWAVE on DEFROST for 6 MINUTES; stir. Recover, and MICROWAVE on DEFROST for 3 to 4 MINUTES or until hot. Let stand, covered 3, minutes.

POULTRY AND MEAT GUIDE

Fried Chicken

Heat either a frozen home-cooked 2½ to 3 pound cut-up fryer or a 32-ounce commercially frozen package of cooked chicken pieces. Place chicken pieces in 2-quart (12 x 7) glass baking dish. MICROWAVE on HIGH for 10 to 12 MINUTES or until hot. Let stand 3 minutes.

Cooked Meat Slices

Place frozen meat slices on glass dinner plate or platter (without metal trim). Cover with plastic wrap. MICROWAVE on HIGH until hot — 1 slice, 30 to 40 SECONDS; 4 slices, 2 to 2½ MINUTES; 8 slices, 3 to 3½ MINUTES. Let stand, covered, 2 to 3 minutes. Note that thickness of meat slice and kind of meat make heating time vary. Use these times as guides.

Corn Dogs

Remove frozen Corn Dogs from plastic wrap. Place in glass baking dish, and MICROWAVE on DEFROST until hot — 2 Corn Dogs, 2 to 2½ MINUTES; 4 Corn Dogs, 3 to 4 MINUTES.

Wieners

Remove frozen wieners from package. Place on glass plate. MICROWAVE on HIGH until hot — 2 wieners, 1 to 1½ MINUTES; 4 wieners, 2 to 2½ MINUTES; 6 wieners, 2½ to 3 MINUTES.

Ham TV Dinner

Remove cover from 10½-ounce dinner. Leave food in foil tray if it is no more than ¾ inch high; slip back in carton or cover with plastic wrap. MICROWAVE on HIGH for 7 to 8 MINUTES or until hot. Let stand, covered, 2 to 3 minutes.

Swiss Steak TV Dinner

Remove foil cover from 10-ounce dinner. Leave food in foil tray if no more than ¾ inch high; slip back in carton or cover with plastic wrap. MICROWAVE on HIGH for 8 to 10 MINUTES. Let stand, covered, 2 to 3 minutes.

Turkey TV Dinner

Remove foil cover from 19-ounce dinner. Leave food in foil tray if no more than ¾ inch high; slip back in carton or cover with plastic wrap. Cover cranberry sauce portion with piece of foil. MICROWAVE on HIGH for 10 to 12 MINUTES. Let stand, covered, 2 to 3 minutes.

MAIN DISHES GUIDE

Homemade Main Dishes

Unwrap frozen main dish mixture and place in glass casserole or baking dish. Cover with glass lid or plastic wrap.

MICROWAVE 2 individual (4 oz.) dishes on HIGH for 7 to 10 MINUTES; let stand, covered, 3 minutes. MICROWAVE 1-quart casserole on DEFROST for 7 MINUTES; then HIGH for 12 to 14 MINUTES. Let stand, covered, 5 minutes.

MICROWAVE 1½-quart casserole on DEFROST for 8 MINUTES; then HIGH for 15 to 18 MINUTES. Let stand, covered, 5 minutes.

MICROWAVE 2-quart casserole on DEFROST for 10 MINUTES; then HIGH for 23 to 28 MINUTES; let stand, covered, 5 minutes. Stir in 1 to 2-quart main dishes halfway through final cooking period.

Beef Enchiladas

Remove frozen Beef Enchiladas with Chili Gravy from plastic pouch. Place in 2-quart (8 x 8) glass baking dish. Cover with plastic wrap. MICROWAVE on DEFROST until hot — 12 ounces, 9 to 10 MINUTES; 22 ounces, 20 to 22 MINUTES. Let stand, covered, 3 minutes.

Salisbury Steak

Remove 32 ounces frozen Salisbury Steak with gravy from carton and metal container. Place in 2-quart (12 x 7) glass baking dish. Cover with plastic wrap. MICROWAVE on DEFROST for 18 MINUTES; turn over and rearrange. Recover and MICROWAVE on DEFROST for 15 to 16 MINUTES or until hot. Let stand, covered, 3 minutes.

Beef Stew

Remove 10 ounces frozen Beef Stew from plastic pouch. Place in 1-quart glass casserole. Cover with glass lid or plastic wrap. MICROWAVE on HIGH for 7 to 8 MINUTES or until hot. Let stand, covered, 3 minutes.

Spaghetti Sauce

Remove 15 ounces frozen Spaghetti Sauce from plastic pouch. Place in 1-quart glass casserole. Cover with glass lid or plastic wrap. MICROWAVE on HIGH for 5 MINUTES; stir. Recover, and MICROWAVE on DEFROST for 4 to 6 MINUTES or until hot. Let stand, covered, 3 minutes before serving.

Stuffed Cabbage Rolls

Remove 14 ounces frozen Stuffed Cabbage Rolls from foil container. Place in 1-quart glass casserole. Cover with glass lid or plastic wrap. MICROWAVE on HIGH for 11 to 12 MINUTES or until hot. Let stand, covered, 3 minutes.

Turkey Tetrazzini

Remove 12 ounces frozen turkey Tetrazzini from plastic pouch. Place in 1-quart glass casserole. Cover with glass lid or plastic wrap. MICROWAVE on DEFROST for 8 MINUTES; stir. Recover, and MICROWAVE on DEFROST for 6 to 8 MINUTES or until hot. Let stand, covered, 3 minutes.

Welsh Rarebit

Remove 10 ounces frozen Welsh Rarebit from plastic pouch. Place in 1-quart glass casserole. Cover with glass lid or plastic wrap. MICROWAVE on DEFROST for 4 MINUTES. Stir; recover, and MICROWAVE on DEFROST for 3 to 4 MINUTES or until hot. Let stand, covered, 3 minutes.

RICE AND PASTA GUIDE

Rice or Pasta Dishes

Place pouch of frozen rice or pasta mixture in glass casserole or baking dish. Slit top of pouch. MICROWAVE mixtures with cheese, sour cream, eggs or cream on DEFROST; others on HIGH — 8 ounces Macaroni and Cheese, DEFROST for 8 to 10 MINUTES; 22 ounces Lasagna, DEFROST for 16 to 18 MINUTES; 14 ounces Spaghetti and Meat Sauce, HIGH for 8 to 10 MINUTES; 12 ounces brown or white rice, HIGH for 9 to 10 MINUTES. Let stand, covered, 2 to 5 minutes, depending on amount of food.

SOUPS AND SANDWICHES GUIDE

Soups

Remove 8 ounces frozen soup from plastic pouch. Place in 1-quart glass casserole. Cover with glass lid or plastic wrap. MICROWAVE on HIGH for 4 to 6 MINUTES or until hot. Let stand, covered, 3 minutes.

Frozen Chuck Wagon Sandwich

Remove 2 (9 oz.) frozen Chuck Wagon sandwiches from carton and foil wrap. Place on paper towel or napkin. MICROWAVE on DEFROST for 4 to 5 MINUTES or until warm.

VEGETABLE GUIDE

Au Gratin Potatoes

Remove 11½ ounces frozen Au Gratin Potatoes from plastic pouch. Place in 1-quart glass casserole. Cover with glass lid or plastic wrap. MICROWAVE on DEFROST for 10 MINUTES. Stir; recover, and MICROWAVE on DEFROST for 6 to 8 MINUTES or until potatoes are cooked. Let stand, covered, 3 minutes.

Baked Potatoes

Remove 12 ounces frozen Baked Potatoes from carton. Place in 1-quart glass casserole. MICROWAVE on HIGH for 10 to 11 MINUTES or until hot.

Cauliflower Au Gratin

Remove 10 ounces frozen Cauliflower Au Gratin from foil container. Place in 1-quart glass casserole. Cover with glass lid or plastic wrap. MICROWAVE on DEFROST for 8 MINUTES; stir. Recover, and MICROWAVE on DEFROST for 6 to 8 MINUTES or until hot and tender. Let stand, covered, 3 minutes.

Scalloped Corn

Remove 12 ounces frozen Scalloped Corn from foil container. Place in 1-quart glass casserole. Cover with glass lid or plastic wrap. MICROWAVE on DEFROST for 8 to 10 MINUTES or until hot and tender. Let stand, covered, 2 to 3 minutes.

Tater Tots

Remove potatoes from plastic bag. Place in glass casserole or baking dish. MICROWAVE on HIGH until hot — 16 ounces, 8 to 10 MINUTES; 32 ounces, 12 to 14 MINUTES.

UNCOOKED FROZEN FOOD KEY: Uncooked frozen foods are handled in much the same manner as precooked. However times will be longer. See Precooked Frozen Food Key on page 158.

Note that uncooked frozen vegetables are cooked on HIGH. See How to Microwave Fresh and Frozen Vegetables, page 114.

Small pieces of frozen uncooked fish, as found in TV dinners, will cook on HIGH.

FISH AND SEA FOOD GUIDE

Frozen Sole Diet TV Dinner

Remove cover from 18-ounce dinner. Place fish only in 1½-quart (10 x 6) glass baking dish or glass plate. Cover with plastic wrap. MICROWAVE on HIGH for 5 MINUTES. Turn sole over; add vegetables. Recover and MICROWAVE on HIGH for 10 to 12 MINUTES or until fish flakes when lifted with fork.

MEAT AND POULTRY GUIDE

Frozen Pork Chops

Place 4 frozen pork chops (up to ½ inch thick) in 2-quart (12 x 7) glass baking dish. Season to taste. Cover with plastic wrap. MICROWAVE on DEFROST for 12 MINUTES. Turn chops over and MICROWAVE on DEFROST for 8 to 10 MINUTES or until no longer pink. Let stand, covered, 3 minutes before serving.

Frozen Ground Beef Patties

Place 4-ounce frozen pattie(s) in glass baking dish or plate in a single layer. MICROWAVE on DEFROST — 1 pattie, 3 MINUTES, turn over, drain, MICROWAVE for 2 to 4 MINUTES: 2 patties, 5 MINUTES, turn over, drain, MICROWAVE for 3 to 4 MINUTES; 4 patties, 6 MINUTES, turn over, drain, MICROWAVE for 4 to 5 MINUTES. Extra-thick patties take 1 to 2 MINUTES longer. Patties will continue to cook after being taken from oven.

Frozen Turkey Roast

Remove 2-pound frozen turkey roast from aluminum foil pan. Place in (8 x 4) glass loaf dish. Cover with plastic wrap. MICROWAVE on DEFROST for 30 MINUTES. Turn meat over and MICROWAVE on DEFROST for 15 to 18 MINUTES or until microwave meat thermometer registers 175°F. Let stand, covered, 5 minutes. If roast is packaged with gravy mix, follow package directions for preparing gravy.

Frozen Meatballs

Place 18 to 20 (1-inch) frozen meatballs in 2-quart (8 x 8) glass baking dish. Cover with plastic wrap. MICROWAVE on DEFROST for 8 MINUTES. Turn meat over and rearrange. MICROWAVE on DEFROST for 6 to 8 MINUTES or until no longer pink. Let stand, covered, 5 minutes before serving. If cooked with sauce, cooking time will be longer.

Frozen Scrambled Eggs And Sausage

Remove foil cover from 6¼-ounce package of scrambled eggs and sausage. Leave food in foil tray if no more than ¾ inch high. Cover with plastic wrap or return to carton. MICROWAVE on DEFROST for 6 to 8 MINUTES.

Frozen Breakfast Links

Remove 8 ounces links from plastic pouch. Place in 9-inch glass pie plate. Cover with plastic wrap. MICROWAVE on HIGH for 4 to 5 MINUTES or until hot. Turn links over halfway through cooking period. Let stand, covered, 2 minutes before serving.

PIE GUIDE

Frozen Fruit Pie

Preheat conventional oven to 425°F. Remove 33-ounce frozen fruit pie from carton and aluminum pan. Place in glass pie plate. MICROWAVE on HIGH for 15 MINUTES. Transfer pie to preheated conventional oven. Bake for 10 to 12 minutes or until crust is brown.

Frozen Pie Shell

Place 1 frozen (9-inch) commercial or homemade pie shell in glass pie plate; prick bottom and sides of dough. MICROWAVE on DEFROST for 8 to 10 MINUTES or just until brown spots begin to appear in crust.

THAWING FROZEN FOOD KEY: Microwave thawing on DEFROST takes the fuss and waiting out of defrosting food which stays freshest when stored in a freezer. Thawing times are short. Low heat allows defrosting without cooking.

Remove lids from jars and paper containers.

Open cartons before putting these in the oven.

Place cookies, bars, cake squares and sandwiches on paper towel or napkin to absorb moisture.

Food may be thawed in a foil tray that is no more than ¾ inch high. Otherwise, remove food to a glass or pottery plate (without silver or other metal trim).

Thaw moist and liquid foods only until icy in the center. "Dry" foods like baked goods defrost until center is no longer icy. If food thaws completely in a microwave oven, edges will begin to dry and overcook.

Shake or stir liquids after taking them from the oven to distribute heat and finish thawing center.

Let foods stand a few minutes to complete thawing process.

Different brands of frozen foods vary in size so thawing times may vary slightly. Check food at lowest time given.

Frozen Egg Substitute

Thaw opened 8-ounce carton on MICROWAVE DEFROST for 4 to 6 MINUTES. Let stand 3 minutes. Shake well before pouring into glass cooking dish.

Frozen Orange Juice

Remove lid and place container in oven. MICROWAVE on DEFROST until icy in center only — 6-ounce can 3½ to 4 MINUTES; 12-ounce can, 6 to 7 MINUTES. Let stand 2 to 3 minutes. Pour in pitcher; dilute and stir to blend as directed on container.

Frozen Non-Dairy Creamer Or Topping (Liquid)

Place opened ½-pint carton in oven. MICROWAVE on DEFROST — 8-ounce, 4 to 5 MINUTES; 16-ounce, 9 to 10 MINUTES. Shake or stir to complete thawing. Let stand 2 to 3 minutes before using.

Frozen Pudding

Loosen lid on 17½-ounce container. MICROWAVE on DEFROST for 8 to 10 MINUTES. Stir to blend. Let stand 2 minutes before serving.

Frozen Fruit

Remove lid or top from carton or jar. Remove fruit from a plastic package and place in 1-quart glass casserole; cover with glass lid or plastic wrap. MICROWAVE on DEFROST until fruit is icy in center only — 10-ounce carton or package, 4 to 6 MINUTES; 16-ounce jar, 8 to 10 MINUTES. Stir to loosen fruit before serving.

Frozen Home-Baked Fruit-Filled Cookies

Place cookie(s) on paper napkin or towel. MICROWAVE on DEFROST until warm — 2 cookies, 40 to 45 SECONDS; 4 cookies, 50 to 55 SECONDS; 6 cookies, 60 to 65 SECONDS.

Frozen Chocolate Frosted Brownies

Remove foil cover from 13-ounce package. Place uncut baked brownies in oven on glass plate. MICROWAVE on DEFROST for 3 to 4 MINUTES or until just warm on top and edges. Center will be cool. Let stand 5 minutes before serving.

Frozen Cake

Remove cake from carton. Place on glass or pottery serving plate (without metal trim). MICROWAVE on DEFROST until cake is icy in center only. — 17-ounce Frosted Chocolate Fudge Layer Cake, 3 to 4½ MINUTES; 14-ounce Frosted Banana Cake, 2½ to 3 MINUTES. Let stand 5 minutes before serving.

Index